Fisons
Guide to Gardens

With 14 maps
drawn by Vicky Fisher
showing over
300 gardens
open to the public

Specially for Teen

*in memory of John Tradescant II
and for all 'the Virginians
whose delight is in planting'.*

Fisons
Guide to Gardens

*in England, Scotland,
Ireland and Wales*

Mea Allan

LESLIE FREWIN : LONDON

By the same author:

The Tradescants
The Hookers of Kew
Etc

First published in 1970 by
Leslie Frewin Publishers Limited,
One New Quebec Street, Marble Arch,
London W1

Set in Imprint
Printed by Anchor Press
and bound by William Brendon
both of Tiptree, Essex
WORLD RIGHTS RESERVED

09 101551 0 *(Paperback)*
09 101550 2 *(Casebound)*

Contents

Introduction

THIS GUIDE IS intended for visitors from overseas and for Britons themselves who wish to know at a glance where they can see the great and interesting gardens of England, Scotland, Ireland and Wales which are open to the public.

It tells the motorist how to get there and where he will find a good hotel. For the benefit of those travelling by train or bus, the existence of public transport is indicated in the special index dealing with opening times and restaurant facilities.

The Guide is divided into thirteen Zones, so that a district, irrespective of county boundaries, can be explored from a convenient centre. It will also be easy for the long-distance traveller to pick out gardens en route and so make his journey the more interesting.

The gardens are described and their history given. Where they are laid out by a famous landscapist, such as Repton or 'Capability' Brown, this fact is mentioned. Where applicable, the history of the plants themselves is given together with the names of the plant-hunters who first brought them to this country. I believe that by the time you have toured even half a Zone, a garden will mean much more than a mere collection of plants, however beautiful.

Napoleon's derisive comment about the British, that they

are 'a nation of shopkeepers', has long ago ceased to have any meaning, for Britain is much more passionately a nation of gardeners. Nowhere in the world are there to be found such gardens, great and small, and tended with such loving care. The temperate climate we enjoy, our contact with the friendly Gulf Stream, and the irregular rainfall which garden-loving Virginians envy, all make it possible to grow most of the world's exotics. So out of doors here you will find such plants as the hibiscus, yucca and tree fern, Himalayan rhododendrons and Chinese roses, as well as the native primrose and violet.

Seeing the gardens of Britain is an experience everybody can enjoy, whether gardener or non-gardener. For gardening is an art that needs no explanation. The pictures it paints are of living Nature and please all five senses. It is a delight to look at a garden, to hear the birds that sing in it, to smell the varied perfumes of flower and leaf, to touch a fallen petal, to taste the goodness of home-grown vegetables.

Too many gardeners stay at home and see none but their own gardens. I urge them to buy this book and go and see others, so that they may come home inspired. To those who think they do not care about gardens, or think they are only for the garden-minded, I say the same thing. Never to have seen an English garden in all its beauty, never to have seen at least some of the great gardens of England, Scotland, Ireland and Wales, is to have lived life by only half.

For those who are planning a holiday that is different, this Guide supplies a perfect answer. Zone Centres have been selected where possible not only as convenient points from which to visit gardens, but with an eye to historical and architectural interest, and – when garden-viewing is over for the day – where a theatre or concert can be enjoyed or a meal in an ancient inn.

So why not this spring, this summer or this autumn, make your holiday a Gardens Tour and enjoy an unforgettable experience?

The four beautiful pictures of gardens shown on the cover – The Canal at Bodnant, Wales; the Herbaceous Borders at Ilnacullin, Ireland; the Parterre at Pitmedden, Scotland, and the rose and topiary lawn at Compton Wynyates, England – were taken by Grace Woodbridge who accompanied me on my 13,000-mile tour of the gardens (more than 300 of them) described in this Guide. She logged the roads travelled and the locations of the gardens on them, and finally co-ordinated the information gathered on our pilgrimage.

M E A

Walberswick
December 1969

How to Use this Guide

ON THE MAP of Britain provided, select the route you intend to follow.

I have divided Britain into thirteen Zones – eight in England, three in Scotland, one to cover Welsh gardens, and one to cover Ireland. There is a Zone Map for each, with suggested Centres where you will find good hotel accommodation. The routes from each Centre to the groups of gardens are detailed. Gardens which are open frequently and are a 'must' are marked *. Smaller interesting gardens or those not open so often are marked ■. Gardens which may still be great gardens but which are open only occasionally are marked ▲.

It is possible, therefore, to start at any Centre and radiate from it, to select one or more Zones, or indeed to tour the whole of Britain garden-wise from Centre to Centre.

There are useful supplementary indices, such as those listing gardens of special interest, Zone Centres, hotels, times of opening, and so on. With the help of one index or another you can plan your holiday – be it a weekend, fortnight or just a day out – to get the best out of it.

It is perhaps superfluous to add that preferably the Guide should be read through before you decide your tour. You will then be sure when you set out that, in the time you have allotted, your itinerary includes the gardens you most wish to see.

The information in this Guide was correct at the time the author visited the gardens. Plantings, however, can be varied, gardens evolve and even change ownership. To keep the Guide up to date the publishers hope to issue a revised edition every alternate year.

ZONE 1   In and around London.

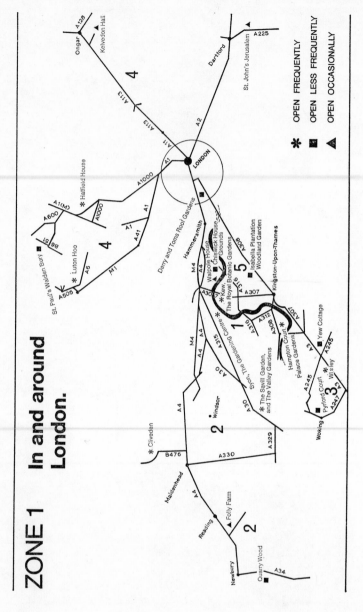

OPEN FREQUENTLY

OPEN LESS FREQUENTLY

OPEN OCCASIONALLY

Ongar
A128
Kelvedon Hall
A113
4
A11
Dartford
A225
St. John's Jerusalem
A2
LONDON
A1
A1000
Hatfield House
A1(M)
A600
A6000
A1
A41
A1
St. Paul's Walden Bury
5198
Luton Hoo
A6
M1
A505
4
Derry and Toms Roof Gardens
Hammersmith
M4
Walpole House
Chiswick House
Kew, The Royal Botanic Gardens
A205
Isabella Plantation Woodland Garden
Kingston-Upon-Thames
A316
A307
5
A30
A315
Syon, The Gardening Centre
A4
A4
A312
A318
A308
1
Hampton Court Palace Gardens
A307
M4
A4
A30
The Savill Garden, and The Valley Gardens
A309
Yew Cottage
A243
A3
Wisley
Cliveden
A4
Windsor
2
A245
A247
Pyrford Court
3
A30
B476
A330
A329
Woking
Maidenhead
A4
Folly Farm
Reading
2
Newbury
Quarry Wood
A34

ZONE 1

In and around London

WITH LONDON AS the Centre for this Zone it is natural that some of its gardens should have historical associations with the Court, and this is true of Hampton Court Palace, a royal garden since Henry VIII's time, and of Hatfield, built by the First Earl of Salisbury, who was Secretary of State. It is also natural that close to the capital should be the Royal Botanic Gardens and the garden of the Royal Horticultural Society. Both demonstrate that although basically scientific establishments they can be beautiful as well as useful to horticulture and botany. There are two magnificent royal gardens of modern times in Windsor Great Park open to the public, both laid out by Sir Eric Savill, who is Director of Gardens for the Crown Estate. One holds the country's finest rhododendron collection, those great flowering plants which swept away the drab Victorian shrubbery. A new garden has appeared on the scene, the national Gardening Centre at Syon House on the opposite side of the river from Kew, where gardeners, especially the enthusiastic amateur, can see and buy plants and all kinds of gardening equipment, get ideas from demonstration gardens and information on all gardening problems.

The gardens in this Zone are in Bedfordshire, Berkshire, Essex, Hertfordshire and Surrey, in a circle around the capital, with some in Greater London itself. The countryside is attractive, each county having its own character. Often the soil differs sharply from one garden to the other. I once knew a Covent Garden porter who could tell exactly where vegetables had come from by the colour of the soil clinging to their roots. The winding Thames Valley is full of woods and glimpses of the river. Surrey, with its sandy pine-clad heaths, is famous for its gardens, and Berkshire – 'the wood of Berroc where the box-tree grows' – is rich pastoral land. Hertfordshire, more hilly country, is mainly agricultural and grows quantities of fruit and vegetables for the London market.

Chiswick House Grounds

Zone Centre: London, Route 5

Owner: The Borough of Hounslow

The grounds were laid out in 1728 by William Kent, England's first true landscapist. A painter and architect, he worked with the idea that a house should be set in surroundings as romantic as a landscape painted by Claude or Poussin. His first garden was for this Palladian villa which his friend and patron, Lord Burlington, had designed. In fact, between them Kent and Burlington had invented the Palladian school of architecture. Kent laid out the garden in keeping, with avenues of statuary (procured from Hadrian's

Villa at Tivoli). He planted cedars and picturesque woodlands, created vistas, and constructed a cascade which ended in an islanded pool and a classic bridge by Wyatt. A century later another young man, Joseph Paxton, was taken on as a pot-boy at Chiswick. Later, grown famous as head gardener and friend of the Duke of Devonshire, to whom Chiswick now belonged, he eyed the avenue of statues and decided they would look better in the Italian Garden. During the last war forty-two bombs fell in the gardens, and then the Army moved in. Now it is all being restored to what it was in Kent's time. Some people are disappointed that the plantings are not being kept in period, but the myrtles Kent used refuse to prosper in London's polluted atmosphere: the Superintendent is substituting rhododendrons. There is a fantastic collection of camellias (280 different cultivars) to be seen, first introduced into England in 1739, a year before William Kent died. The indoor ones at Chiswick are in a glasshouse 130 yards long.

Cliveden

Zone Centre: London, Route 2

Owner: The National Trust

The great house of Cliveden can be seen from the Thames,
nestling in wooded heights and dominating the landscape.
The view from Cliveden to the Thames is equally spectacular,
especially as you look from the great terrace over the vast
parterre set in a majestic lawn headed by the balustrade
which came from the Villa Borghese at Rome. It was brought
to Cliveden by Lord Astor who also acquired the bronze
statue of Pluto and Proserpine (after Giovanni di Bologna
1524–1608) beyond the parterre. No flowers grow in this
garden: the twin avenues of sixteen box-edged triangles are
filled with silver-leaved santolina. But on the walls of the
staircase descending to it are magnolias and wistaria and a
very fine pomegranate. Close to the east wing you will find
the Duel Sword commemorating the fatal fight between the
Duke of Buckingham and Lord Shrewsbury. The prize was
Shrewsbury's Countess. Buckingham carried her off to
Cliveden, and tiny flower beds picked out in purple candytuft
mark the date 1668. Away from the house to the north, and
not far from the entrance, is a delightful water garden in the
Japanese manner. Its two-tiered pagoda came from the Great
Exhibition of 1851. You reach it by stepping-stones across the
water, a little lake which reflects charming groups of trees
and shrubs, in spring a blaze of azaleas, cherries underplanted

6

with snowdrops and narcissus, and the airy grace of a weeping birch beneath which autumn crocuses appear in the late days of August to herald the flaming colours of the acers, the gold coins of a cercidiphyllum and the burning leaves of a liquidambar. Round a second pool are rhododendrons, viburnums and other good shrubs, dogwoods, roses and a weeping willow. The hugely decorative rhubarb leaves of *Gunnera manicata* strike a dramatic note. The site was the old private golf course. Bunkers make ideal contours! There is plenty more to explore: the magnificent woodlands and the view from the Canning Oak; the Blenheim Pavilion, the rhododendron valley and the rustic theatre. The promise of Cliveden's magnificence is apparent whenever you enter the place. There, at the start of the broad formal avenue, is set a group of figures upon a gigantic cockleshell of Siena marble. It stands in a large stone pond and was the work of an American sculptor, Thomas Waldo Story, made for William Waldorf Astor, the first American to be created a British viscount.

Derry and Toms Roof Gardens

Zone Centre: London, Route 5

Owner: Derry and Toms

It seems something of a miracle to wander about a garden perched one hundred feet above the streets of London, a garden not only full of flowers but of trees, lawns, and ponds where ducks paddle happily. The water is pumped up from three artesian wells four hundred feet below this busy London store. They feed the wandering stream, the waterfall and fountains. In an acre and a half you will find an Old English Garden, Tudor Courts, and a Spanish Garden with Moorish pergolas and a Court of Fountains. Over carved stone arches grow vines. Against walls grow peaches and figs. In spring, cherries and laburnums burst into flower and hawthorns scent the air. In summer, the borders riot with colour. It is no mere bedding-out effort either, though the Court of Fountains is all bright with red geraniums. The Spanish Garden has big herbaceous borders and Fan Palms live there all the year round. It is the size of the trees that astounds you, most of them planted in 1935 when the garden was made. It was opened to the public three years later and in the first twenty years hospitals and charities benefited by over £120,000 from the modest shilling entrance fee.

Hampton Court Palace Gardens

Zone Centre: London, Route 5

Owner: HM the Queen

It is a queenly garden of fifty-four acres, first laid out by
Cardinal Wolsey but principally now the work of William
and Mary between 1696 and 1700. There is of course the
Great Vine whose colossal trunk (7 ft 1 in at ground level)
sends out branches bearing 650 bunches of grapes, each
weighing between one and two pounds. It was planted in
1769 in the reign of George III. There is the celebrated
Maze in which to lose yourself. But first we must delve back
into history. The gardens were begun in 1514 when Wolsey
rented the manor from the Knights Hospitallers of St John
of Jerusalem, a prize which, after his opposition to Henry
VIII's marriage with Anne Boleyn, he tried to barter
for the King's favour. He did not regain it and he lost his
beloved Hampton Court. Thus the great domain came into
royal possession. Henry scrapped the Cardinal's gardens,
made new pleasure grounds, bowling greens, archery butts
and 'tennis plays'. He also made a rose garden for his 'Awne
Darling' and planted an orchard and herb garden. These
filled what is now the Privy or South Garden, and you can
still see there, up a little flight of steps, the ancient pleached
alley today known as Queen Mary's Bower but then called
Queen Anne's Bower, and you can gaze at the curious
Kinges Beastes, the series of heraldic animals with which

Henry decorated his garden. With the Restoration, grandeur was added to Hampton Court. In exile Charles II had seen and admired the great gardens Le Nôtre was making in France. At Hampton Court he tried to create an English Versailles. With the help of his gardener, John Rose, who was one of Le Nôtre's pupils, the Long Canal was soon in being and fashionably lined with lime trees brought from Holland. When William of Orange came to the throne he made more changes. He planted the Maze and constructed the Great Fountain Garden, while Mary with her passion for 'exoticks' spent endless money in procuring all the new plants. Whatever gardens you 'do' from London, Hampton Court must be one of them. To see its vast borders, which include one of the best herbaceous borders in the country, to peep into the two peaceful little gardens facing the Lower Orangery, to sense the shades of kings and queens who have walked there before you, is something you must not miss. So much of the history of England, and indeed of all Britain, was made and lived here. It is all about you, at every step, in the splendour of great vistas – the Broad Walk with its noble alleys of trees radiating out and embracing in their midst the Great Fountain, and in the relics of small loved gardens made for a tragic queen hundreds of years ago.

Hatfield House

Zone Centre: London, Route 4

Owner: The Marquess of Salisbury

Hatfield is something unique in the annals of garden history. Preserved in its archives are almost complete records of the plants that grew in it from its very first days, when John Tradescant was despatched abroad by his master, Robert Cecil, First Earl of Salisbury, to buy trees, shrubs, bulbs and all other plants for the great new garden of the great new house. Tradescant set forth on 25th September 1611 with six pounds in his pocket 'towards bearing of his Chardges into Flanders & other partes beyonnd the seas to buy plants for your honor', as he afterwards headed his expenses bill. The bill for plants amounted to £3,500 in our money, and we know exactly what plants he bought and where he bought them. What is even more interesting is the list of new plants 'Strang and Rare' he introduced. One was his 'Larus Serus', our *Laurus cerasus*, the cherry bay, which he bought for '2s the peece'. There were dozens of others and vastly superior Dutch varieties of fruits including two new quinces, six hundred lime trees to make great avenues, and the novel bulb – the tulip – which he procured from Haarlem. Though known in England the tulip was still classed by Parkinson in 1629 as 'an outlandish flower'. At Hatfield John Tradescant grew them by the thousand. Five years later the garden was complete, and on the Grand Staircase of the house a carved newel post shows Tradescant with some of the fruits and flowers he brought from Europe, among them the 'Martygon Pompony'. Today little remains of his work. Changing fashions have obliterated most of it, but the garden on the west side was restored in 1900 to its original Tradescant lay-out. The Maze in the East Garden was made at the end of the eighteenth century. But still at the four corners of the West Garden remain the mulberry trees planted in the reign of James I, perhaps the very ones Tradescant procured at Delft three hundred and fifty years ago.

The Isabella Plantation Woodland Garden

Zone Centre: London, Route 5

Owner: The Ministry of Public Buildings and Works

To walk through the Isabella Plantation in azalea time is like finding yourself in a kaleidoscope. From a well-worn path in Richmond Park you open a small wooden gate to see sheets of colour – pink to brightest scarlet, yellow to deepest orange – in every direction. There are mounds of them, carpets of them, under the trees and banks above the stream, those lining it being the rose-pink Hinomayo and the bright scarlet Hinodegiri, the latter one of the famous Japanese Kurumes introduced into America by Dr E H

Wilson at the end of the First World War. The plantation was started in 1951 and in 1966 extended by a further twenty-two acres. The whole garden now covers forty-two acres. There are three ponds with connecting streams, and these provide natural homes for the moisture-loving plants which fringe them: primulas and mimulus, ferns, irises and calthas – golden kingcups of enormous size. There are also camellias, heathers and some of the better rhododendrons, species and hybrid. The trees are mainly oaks, and even when all the flowers are over a visit to the Isabella Plantation is worth while to see them in golden leaf.

The Royal Botanic Gardens, Kew

Zone Centre: London, Route 1

Owner: The Ministry of Agriculture, Fisheries and Food

Here is surely the best-known and best-loved garden in the world. Through its entrance gates every year a million people pass. To its herbarium and library every year come hundreds of botanists, mostly from overseas, to read about plants, to study them as dried specimens and to see them growing outside and in the huge glasshouses, where temperatures range from cool to tropical. The notion of Kew as a national botanic garden was conceived by the great Sir Joseph Banks and was brought into being by his protégé

William Jackson Hooker who, even before becoming Kew's first Director in 1841, was knighted for his services to botany. He it was who extended the eleven acres of royal pleasure ground to their present three hundred acres and, with his son Joseph, laid out the gardens as we know them today. Every kind of garden is there, a beautiful rock garden (Sir Joseph Hooker installed the original one) with alpine plants that grow in every mountainous region of the globe; the Rhododendron Dell made by Sir William to receive the great new *falconeri* and other species rhododendrons Joseph sent home from his expeditions in the Himalaya; the Chalk Garden constructed in 1944 to meet the needs of lime-loving plants; the Herbaceous Ground, laid out in a series of parallel beds to show the families of plants and their species; the Aquatic Garden with its water lilies and marsh plants; the Pinetum that Joseph Hooker dreamed of during his Antarctic expedition with Ross; the Rose Garden and the others, including the new seventeenth-century garden with period plantings. Many of Kew's visitors come solely to enjoy the displays of flowers at every season. A board near the entrance gates tells you what to look for. Who, visiting the gardens in spring, can forget the showers of cherry blossom greeting you as you enter, the haze of bluebells by the Queen's Cottage, the Mound with its thousands of snowdrops, crocuses and daffodils, and the magnolias, laburnums and lilacs? Who, coming from the roar of London's traffic on a hot summer's day, cannot find peace in the green stretches where there are no KEEP OFF THE GRASS notices, relaxing in the shade of a tree whose parent came from some distant part of the world, or by the lake where you might be miles away in the country? Who, coming here in the autumn, cannot fail to rejoice at the sight of even one liquidambar tree, a pyramid of fire, to say nothing of the thousands of other trees and shrubs, golds and scarlets in bewildering beauty. In winter there is refuge among flowers still. You can wander down tropical alleys among palms and tree ferns to admire exotic blooms few people ever see in their native hot countries; discover cacti in flower, and the astounding Giant Water Lily which caused a sensation in Victoria's reign, one leaf of which is kept upturned to show the marvellous network of ribs and veining which was Paxton's design for the Crystal Palace, the world's largest glass house, made for the 1851 Exhibition (it was erected in Hyde Park and covered twenty acres). Kew is a world of its own, a world of science, a world of beauty.

Luton Hoo

Zone Centre: London, Route 4

Owner: Major-General Sir Harold Wernher, Bt, GCVO

Here is a lovely garden. Its ten acres begin on a formal terrace with herbaceous borders and walls topped by square-cut yew. Standard roses in a border at the bottom are an introduction to the rose garden proper which is really the heart of Luton Hoo. The staircase down to it is ingenious, the concave top half coming down to a circular paved setting for a sundial, the lower half convex, completing the series of circles. You are now in the rose garden, a yew-hedge enclosure of box-edged beds and box topiary, in the centre of which is a wonderful fountain. People who design these

15

things must sometimes scratch their heads to find a suitable motif. Here the choice is admirable, two splendid mermen holding a basin in which sits a boy clasping a dolphin. It is one of the finest fountains in England and scatters its waters into a round pond jewelled with water lilies. At each far corner of the garden is a domed temple. The yew hedges with their ball finials, and the box birds, spirals and pyramids are clipped to exquisite perfection. The roses, which fill the place, are some of the most beautiful hybrid teas, one named after Lady Zia Wernher, who devotes herself to their care. And it is not only in this delightful part of the garden one finds roses. There is a little avenue of standard roses leading to a Venetian well-head grown over with clematis and past it to crescent rose beds framing the entrance to the tennis court where more standard roses are used as a screen. Nearby a grass path takes you to a figure of Venus. She stands in a circle of roses, and on the way you have passed more rose beds. From the end of June onwards the scent from their thousands of blooms fills the air. In autumn a huge dahlia border outside the formal garden is sensational. For springtime flowers you cross a stretch of grass to find, hidden among trees, the very beautiful rock garden spanned by a charming bridge. The garden is built into rising ground with acers stepping up to a leaning pine tree and with paths up and paths down, one leading to a grotto and a cave under the brows of huge slabs of rock. The house overlooks a park of nearly fifteen hundred acres laid out by 'Capability' Brown. There are two lakes, which he achieved by damming the River Lea, and many fine trees, a long lime avenue, and a beech avenue planted in the eighteenth century.

Pyrford Court

Zone Centre: London, Route 3

Owner: Burnhill Estates

A wonderfully planned and planted garden, part of it designed by the famous Miss Gertrude Jekyll who gave it
colour-borders of red-gold-and-blue, all gold and all silver.
The whole place is crammed with unusual things, all beautifully displayed: the pergola, for instance, which forms an
angled end-piece to the large lawn. Pyrford is notable for
wistarias, and here they grow, single and double, blue and
white – one with racemes measuring up to 4 ft 7 in long.
What a sight and what a scent in early summer! Among them
twine ornamental vines for autumn colouring, a *Vitis
coignetiae* bowering the apex with scarlet flames. It forms the
background for the Italian fountain on the lawn, and
behind it is a charming yew-hedged parterre called the
Jester Garden in honour of the lead figure there with his
cap and bells. In spring golden Siberian wallflowers surround him and in summer bright petunias. If you are interested in tender shrubs and climbers, a high brick wall
nearby displays them to advantage: the Japanese Loquat with
its yellow fruits, *Akebia quinata* from China whose small
chocolate-purple flowers are fragrant in April, a pomegranate which fruits here, and the lovely yellow flowers of
Sophora tetraptera like large golden fuchsias. Each square
yard of the wall has its own treasure, and each part of the

garden its own delightful feature. It is a large garden which with the woodlands, where grow azaleas and rhododendrons, covers three hundred acres. Gorgeous autumn foliage is provided by such beautiful things as the Cockspur Thorn (*Crataegus crus-galli*), amelanchiers and fothergillas. It was the home of the late Earl and Countess of Iveagh, the latter a dedicated gardener and both close friends of Gertrude Jekyll who lived not far away.

Quarry Wood

Zone Centre: London, Route 2

Owners: Mr and Mrs Martyn Simmons

The late and famous Walter Bentley, VMH, laid out this garden in 1934. It is mainly woodland, with grass paths wandering through glades where rhododendrons and azaleas grow with magnolias, camellias and mecbanopsis. I have not mentioned the lilies. When Mr and Mrs Simmons took over the garden some lilies were there, an inspiration to Mrs Simmons who practically lives for them: October lilies, Martagon lilies and their crosses, Nerines, *Lilium japonicum* with its gorgeous pink trumpets, Kaffir lilies and almost every lily there is. She also has a big collection of alpines, one thousand different kinds, and down in the woodland she grows drifts of the beautiful mecanopsis, the Blue Poppy of the Himalaya and its lovely cousins. Trilliums are another favourite and all sorts of primulas and species geraniums. The original garden was about a dozen acres. Mr and Mrs Simmons have added fourteen more. I found them sheer enchantment.

Saint Paul's Walden Bury Gardens

Zone Centre: London, Route 4

Owner: Lady Bowes-Lyon

In Saxon times the Bury was a royal manor belonging to the kings of Mercia. Much more recently it was the childhood home of HM Queen Elizabeth the Queen Mother, and what a garden it must have been for her to explore! It has three dramatic beech alleys (maintained at 12 ft) fanning out from the lawn into woodland. Truly magnificent they are – almost Le Nôtre: laid end to end they would measure five miles; yet there is something friendly about them, perhaps the freshness of their English green in spring and the golden brown of them in autumn. The centre walk frames a figure of Hercules in the distance. Cross-walks have eye-catchers at each end, one on the right leading to a charming little white Georgian temple by Sir William Chambers, which is reflected in the lake that was the medieval fish pond. Here under the trees daffodils and narcissi make white and gold drifts in April, and in June *Lilium monadelphum* with

B

golden-capped heads grows side by side with rosy lupins.
At the top of the left-hand ride is a Mount with a classic
rotunda guarded by two sphinxes, with a long stone pool
below surrounded by yew hedging with plinths in the angles.
In an informal garden by the house a ruined orangery
makes an attractive support for clouds of clematis and
climbing roses.

The Savill Garden and the Valley Gardens

Zone Centre: London, Route 2

Owner: HM the Queen. Managed by the Crown Estate Commissioners

The Savill Garden is a small part of Windsor Great Park,
twenty-five of the total 4,500 acres, but it is enough to keep
any garden-lover busy for hours. The approach is spectacular. You come through the turnstile to see the lovely place
spread below you, with a little stream at the bottom of the
valley and to the right, most unexpectedly, a carpet of
bright green moss which is quite unique. Coming down to
the stream another beauty will strike you, the spire of the
Yugoslavian *Picea omorika* whose lower branches flare out
like the skirts of a dancer. Seen from the bridge it is reflected
in a pool which also catches the colours of a large group of
Whitethroat azaleas, brilliant-leaved in autumn. Up the

hill to the right is the Temperate House where tender rhododendrons and camellias are grown, seen at their best in March when, under the trees, the little yellow bulbocodiums are in bloom with *Narcissus cyclamineus* and thousands of wild daffodils. April sees the glory of the bigger daffodils and the flowers of the Alpine Meadow, outdoor camellias and rhododendrons, dog's-tooth violets and bell-like trilliums. May is the month for the rock garden plants and June for the start of the lilies. In the Savill Garden lilies are considered of first importance, the woodland conditions being ideal and their flowering period going on through September. Both species and hybrids are grown. In July and August the borders of roses and herbaceous plants are at their best, and in September and October the colours of leaf and berry make a new spectacle. And still linger the flowers, the pink Nerine lilies and the amaryllis, the pink and white patches of little cyclamen under the trees. Sir Eric Savill who created this lovely garden emphasises the importance of light in the appreciation of a landscape and indeed of a plant. Just as when taking a photograph you should stand with your back to the sun, so, he advises, to enjoy the garden at its best in the morning you should do the same thing: turn left after crossing the stream and continue clockwise, and in the afternoon turn right after entering the garden and walk anti-clockwise. If after crossing the stream you keep left along the Main Ride you will come to three rhododendron gardens, one with lilies, one with camellias and the third with magnolias. There is also the Rhododendron Ride round the eastern perimeter, and if you are particularly interested in these wonderful shrubs it is to the nearby Valley Gardens you must go. There is no charge for admission to the **Valley Gardens**, but you will need a good strong pair of legs to explore their three hundred acres thoroughly. They lie south of the Savill Garden and forty acres are devoted to the famous Windsor collection of species rhododendrons which is now the best in Britain.

People (that is, the uninitiated) are inclined to think that when rhododendrons have finished flowering their beauty is over. Try, then, visiting the species rhododendrons when they are throwing up their new shoots – in coppery, green and silver torches almost as beautiful as their blooms. Camellias here form another vast collection, of both the *japonica* and the *williamsii* crosses, and there is almost every known tree magnolia. A large area is devoted to azaleas and there all sorts of primulas, hydrangeas and, in a large heath garden, summer and winter flowering ericas. There is a collection of conifers, North American and Eastern Asiatic trees and nothofagus. On the south side the gardens are bounded by Virginia Water, one and a half miles long. Strange, every Scot will muse, when he hears that this lovely lake was made by their old hated enemy 'Butcher' Cumberland who slaughtered their forefathers on the field of Culloden. Perhaps its beauty will soften that obstinate memory, if indeed such thoughts could compete with the glories of the Valley Gardens.

Syon Park Gardening Centre

Zone Centre: London, Route 1

Owner: The Gardening Centre Ltd

One after another small Garden Centres have been springing up all over the country, each attached to an individual nursery, but it was a brilliant idea to have a national one where every leading grower could exhibit his plants and every leading manufacturer of garden tools and products his wares, a Centre where the public could come and see plants growing as they would in their own gardens; which does not happen at Chelsea where plants are often forced into bloom or retarded to meet the deadline, and coddled and cosseted into super-perfection. The Syon Gardening Centre was opened on 1st May 1968, and throughout the wet summer four hundred thousand people came to see it. The whole thing is beautifully laid out among woodlands, with a Perimeter Path you can follow round and among the fifty-five acres of gardens and exhibits, where literally tons of bulbs have been planted under the trees. The Woodland Garden is a superb example of informal plantings of modern flowering and foliage trees blending with the grand old trees already there. The herbaceous borders are good for plenty of note-taking, and the six-acre rose garden is breathtaking, with four hundred varieties of roses, and twelve thousand actual rose plants from all the main rose growers. Most of them are in a huge formal garden where you can see many of the varieties growing both as bush and standard. Others nearby mingle happily with shrubs, and a great mass of them are reflected in the Water Hazard against the golden background of Syon House. It is a gardener's paradise, for here you can see it all. Each plant is clearly labelled, and if you fall in love with any of them you can go to the Selling Centre in the huge building that was Syon's old Riding School, to buy it there and then, or order it to be sent. How to grow the perfect lawn? Flora's Lawn demonstrates what can be achieved with a piece of old grass full of weeds on poor soil, a most attractive lawn, too, with its curved shrub borders. What about garden pests, insecticides and garden problems in general? There are seven information kiosks where you can ask questions and have your problems solved. Special help is given to the small gardener who owns anything from a courtyard space of a hundred square feet to an acre, with demonstration gardens planned and planted to give you ideas. And besides its Gardening Products Pavilion, its Machinery Hall, its Ornamental Walk (where paving, garden statuary, gates and so on are shown), its Garden Buildings exhibition area and all the other exhibits, Syon is worth visiting for its delightful setting alone. There is a stretch of water contrived by 'Capability' Brown where fine specimen trees follow its bank, and there is the Great Conservatory built between 1820 and 1830, designed by Charles Fowler for the Third Duke of Northumberland. An enchanting piece of work of Bath stone, delicate tracery in gun metal, and sparkling glass, it is the oldest of its type and size in the world and in it is what to me is the most exciting exhibit of all, a display of what today are called house plants, products of tropical countries whose leaves, flowers, birds and butterflies make our colours seem as drab as sparrows. I can only call this perfect arrangement of house plants a living mosaic. Fitting that Syon, the great new experiment in the gardening world, should once have been looked after by William Turner, the 'Father of English

Botany', who there created England's first botanical gardens
and thus started Syon's horticultural history.

Wisley

Zone Centre: London, Route 3

Owner: The Royal Horticultural Society

People who go to Wisley generally make a habit of it. They
go in the different seasons to follow the sequence of plants
and, if they can, they even pop in to see how a particular
plant is getting on, just as they would do in their own
garden. Plenty of people who go there are not members of
the RHS. You can just pay and go in. And soon you will
find the places you want to visit and visit again: the Alpine
Meadow with its conifers and outcrops of rock, gay as a
lark in April with hundreds of thousands of little yellow
Hoop Petticoat daffodils; the Rock Garden where you can
climb about to examine small flowery treasures tucked away
in corners; the broad grass slope of Battleston Hill where
there is a garden of Kurume azaleas, the famous 'Wilson
Fifty', originating from the town of that name eight hundred
miles south-west of Tokyo. They are small-leaved, dwarf-
growing and evergreen, and when they bloom their flowers
smother the leaves in masses of colour from pure white
through all the pinks to deep rose, from pale lavender to
rosy mauve, to red and even scarlet. And what names they

25

have! Kureno Yuki with her white flowers hose-in-hose, Ima Shojo, Omoine and Kirin. They were discovered by the late Dr E H Wilson, who was sent to the Orient by America's Arnold Arboretum to look for new plants. His first Kurume azaleas came to America in 1917. There are very few complete collections of the 'Wilson Fifty', but Wisley has them all, though it was wondered at the time of planting how many would survive, especially early on when a piercing nor' easter blew hard for a week. This is true Wisley, not just a well-planted and beautiful garden but a place of plant trials where new introductions and new varieties of flowers, fruits and vegetables are tested for staying power and excellence. The Floral Trial Ground is a succession of colour from March to October. The Model Fruit Garden is not only useful to the amateur but a joy in blossom, and the area known as Seven Acres is devoted to a wide range of trees and shrubs. The pinetum, the herbaceous borders, the rose beds and the Award of Garden Merit Collection are other features to be learnt from and enjoyed. Wisley undertakes the training of student gardeners, turning them into skilled horticulturalists. The seal of being a 'Wisley man' is proof of that.

Yew Cottage

Zone Centre: London, Route 3

Owner: Ronald Parrett, Esq

The owner of this garden is one of the happiest fanatics I know. In his three-quarters of an acre garden he grows nothing but delphiniums. Well, a few other things, but delphiniums are his passion. Not ones that will soar up ten feet tall. Ronald Parrett is a practical man who sees a big future for delphiniums of a maximum height of four to five feet, ideal for the small garden. In June and July his garden is a wonderful sight with one hundred named and unnamed delphiniums throwing up their handsome spires. He breeds all his own varieties – Theodora, a lilac blush-pink, Prussia Cove and the twice-flowering Coral, the white King Penguin with a sepia bee and a fabulous creamy unnamed one with a yellow bee. He has won RHS awards for his delphiniums and written a book about them which the RHS published in conjunction with a paperback firm.

Open occasionally are:

FOLLY FARM **(Zone Centre: London, Route 2. Owner: The Hon Hugh Astor)** is a skilful combination of

27

yew hedges and informal borders planted by Gertrude Jekyll and planned by her partner Sir Edwin Lutyens, with a lime walk and a sunken rose garden. The present owner has added an azalea and rhododendron garden.

KELVEDON HALL (Zone Centre: London, Route 4. Owner: Paul Channon, MP) is one of England's most interesting gardens, open, alas, only two or three times a year, so catch it if you can. It is an early example of the 'outdoor room' type of garden, and was the home of the aeronaut Wright Brothers' ancestors.

ST JOHN'S JERUSALEM (Zone Centre: London, Route opt. Owner: The National Trust) is a four-acre garden east of London, worth visiting en route for Canterbury for its associations with the Knights Hospitallers, its double half-moat lined with cricket-bat willows, its lovely herbaceous borders and collection of lilacs.

WALPOLE HOUSE (Zone Centre: London, Route 5. Owners: Mr and Mrs Jeremy Benson) is a half-acre of magnolias, camellias, azaleas and rhododendrons, with special collections of species paeonies, irises, and hellebores.

ZONE 2   The Kentish Weald and The South Downs.

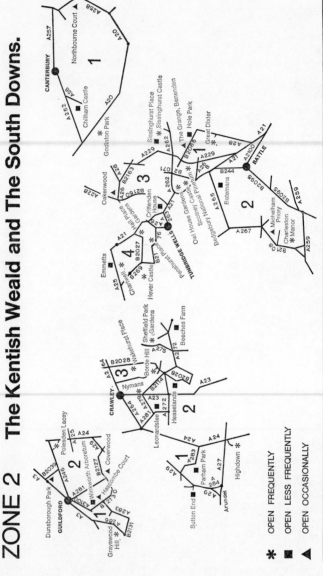

OPEN FREQUENTLY

OPEN LESS FREQUENTLY

OPEN OCCASIONALLY

CANTERBURY

Northbourne Court

A258

A257

A252

Chilham Castle

A28

A20

1

Godinton Park

Sissinghurst Place

Sissinghurst Castle

The Grange, Benenden

Hole Park

Great Dixter

A21

A28

A229

A262

B2086

A229

A27

A2100

BATTLE

A262

A21

A26

B244

B2096

A265

A259

B2095

B2059

Oakenwood

B2163

A26

A21

A228

A228

A2610

3

Crittenden House

Owl House Gardens

Scotney Castle

Bedgebury National Pinetum

A267

Batemans

Michelham Priory

Charleston

Manor

A259

A21

TUNBRIDGE WELLS

A267

A21

76

A21

B2027

A21

4

Emmetts

A25

Chartwell

B2026

A269

Hever Castle

Penshurst Place

Hall Place

Sheffield Park Gardens

Wakehurst Place

Beeches Farm

Borde Hill

A272

A275

B2026

B2028

A22

A264

3

Nymans

CRAWLEY

A23

B2114

A272

A264

A281

2

Heaselands

Leonardslee

A24

A24

A283

Parham Park

A27

Highdown

A29

A284

Arundel

Sutton End

1

Dunsborough Park

Polesden Lacey

A24

A25

A26

B2039

Winkworth Arboretum

Coverwood

Hascombe Court

A3

A246

2

A281

A3100

A3

B2127

A24

1

Grayswood Hill

A283

B2131

GUILDFORD

ZONE 2

The Kentish Weald
and
the South Downs

ALTHOUGH THE COUNTY of Kent lies on the side of England farthest from America, it has close associations with it; and it will be of interest to American visitors, if they do not already know, that in one garden (that of Northbourne Court) is the ruin of the house where Sir Edwin Sandys drafted the constitution of Virginia. Another link is Chilham Castle, built in 1616 for Sir Dudley Digges, whose fourth son, Edward, went to Virginia as a colonist. John Tradescant II visited him at his York County home in 1654 on one of his plant-hunting expeditions. Canterbury was the scene of much support for Virginia. Captain Samuel Argall, a skipper who went to and from the first Colony regularly, promoted a 'Plantation', selling fifty acres for £12 10s od a time. Tradescant senior had two plots, which he bought in 1610.

There are many place-name links, among them Dover, Kent, and Dover, New Hampshire; Canterbury, Kent, and Canterbury in New Brunswick; Rochester, Kent and

Rochester, New Hampshire, the county of Sussex with a sister-town in New Brunswick.

Apart from any links, Kent and Sussex are two fine counties with many exciting gardens, some the settings for great castles, others equally attractive of only a few acres; the famous 'Sissinghurst', created by the late Victoria Sackville-West and her husband Sir Harold Nicolson, is a happy combination of both – a series of intimate and charming gardens with a castle tower as their background. And there is the remarkable Chalk Garden planted by the late Sir Frederick Stern at Highdown.

The countryside is the rolling Weald which is contained in Kent, Surrey, Hampshire, and Sussex, and in this Zone we take you into the first two counties and the last (seventeen, sixteen and fourteen gardens respectively), so on your way to these you will see a goodly part of this lovely corner of England. Kent is famous for its 'White Cliffs of Dover' (pure chalk), for hops, oysters and cherry orchards, and for the thousands of sheep that graze on the Romney Marshes behind the coast. Surrey nestles in the beautiful hills of the North and South Downs, with some spectacular scenery around Hindhead. Sussex, a maritime county on the south coast, has many antiquities – Roman camps, earthworks and burial mounds, famous racecourses, rivers and woodlands. It all makes for an interesting series of gardens.

Bateman's

Zone Centre: Battle, Route 1

Owner: The National Trust

Rudyard Kipling's home for thirty-four years, Bateman's was given to the National Trust in 1939 by his widow, 'for all to enjoy', which is not hard to do, be you Kipling pilgrim or someone who just enjoys seeing an attractive garden. Only minor changes have been made since Kipling's time. The pond on the lawn which he made for his children to swim and boat in is now ornamental with water lilies and goldfish. New herb borders in his kitchen garden are an added interest, with a rose hedge screening what is still used for vegetables. At the bottom of the lawn his 'mad little torrent', the River Dudwell, which at flood-time used to invade his sitting-room, now has its banks planted with flowering shrubs for spring and autumn colour. The rest is as he left it: the path to the old mill where he made electricity for lighting the house, the rose garden he planted, the walled garden with its herbaceous borders where hollyhocks grow and all the familiar English garden flowers – Shasta daisies, the bright orange and yellow faces of Cone Flowers, tulips, spiraeas and delphiniums. Behind them, climbing up the wall, are the purplish-green Cup and Saucer flowers of *Cobaea scandens*. The maple tree he planted is still there, the alley of pleached pear trees, and the lime screens making an avenue down to the pond.

Bedgebury National Pinetum

Zone Centre: Tunbridge Wells, Route 1

Owner: The Forestry Commission

It is the dream of everybody who loves conifers to go at least once to the National Pinetum at Bedgebury. No one could ever be disappointed, and those who go knowing nothing about cone-bearing trees come away fascinated. The word Pinetum is an all-embracing term covering not only pine trees but spruces, yews, cedars, hemlocks, firs, cypresses, junipers, larches and sequoias, to name the main genera, because they all belong to the same botanical classification. Bedgebury is a garden of them, the wonderful conifers which are becoming more and more popular as people (even experienced gardeners) come to realise their decorative value, their tremendous variation of foliage, colour and shape, and as they realise, too, how dramatically a few, well chosen and well placed, can set off other plants. It is one of Bedgebury's functions to show people what conifers they can grow. It takes about three hours to see the Pinetum properly, one hour to walk round. Visitors enter by Thorn Hill on to Dallimore's Avenue, the great ride commemorating William Dallimore who was responsible for the first plantings in 1925 and who for twenty years supervised the building up of the collection. The trees are planted on the summits and slopes of two valleys running parallel till they join at the lake. The undulating land makes a perfect setting for them.

At the entrance to Dallimore's Avenue a map shows you where to find the different kinds of trees, and if you are new to conifer-viewing don't be appalled by the word Cypress. Mournful associations will flee when you see a hillside crowned by the one called Golden King, *Chamaecyparis lawsoniana*. There are two hundred-odd cultivars of Lawsonianas alone, and more than seventy of them are at Bedgebury. Standing on this grassy slope you gaze across to the tops of the great sequoias, spire upon spire ridging the skyline, and from there I will leave you to make your own way, to find your own favourites. I hope you will discover the Tiger Tail Spruce, which is very attractive, and the West Himalayan Spruce (*Picea smithiana*) with its long fringed foliage which most people think the most beautiful of all.

Beeches Farm

Zone Centre: Crawley, Route 2

Owner: Mrs Vera Thomas

It is a small and pretty garden of three-quarters of an acre, the setting for a sixteenth-century farmhouse. Appropriately chain-linked staddle stones are used for the balustrade of the sunken garden. In the centre of the lawn is a circular rose garden hedged round with yew rising to pillars at four entrances. The garden was started during the war and the rose garden added as a Victory garden. There are large herbaceous borders, one of moss roses and bourbons, and springtime cherries, daffodils and other bulbs.

Borde Hill

Zone Centre: Crawley, Route 3

Owner: Sir Ralph Clarke, KBE

This is the home of the world-famous camellia hybrid Donation. The original parent plant can be seen, with a plaque recording its birth date. Known among horticulturalists as a 'good doer' because it will grow in almost any soil, it is one of the very loveliest of all the camellias with its clear pink petals veined in darker rose. The twenty-acre garden (which does not include the park or woodland) was planned by the late Col Stephenson Clarke, CB, who formed an exceptional collection of rare trees and shrubs, many from the Wilson, Forrest, Farrer and Kingdon-Ward expeditions to China, Burma and Tibet. A book has been written about Borde Hill's trees, which are of such great botanical interest that the garden is managed by a Council on which Kew is represented, the Edinburgh Royal Botanic Garden and the RHS. An *Abies magnifica* and a *Pinus wallichiana* are the biggest in Britain. In the woodlands, where there is the largest collection of acers and oaks, are trees you can see nowhere else. What trees! Could any bole be more beautiful than the satin-red bark of the *Stuartia sinensis?* And what shrubs! There is a forty-foot-high dogwood growing like a tree, and a sixty-foot pink-flowered *Magnolia campbellii*. Gardenwise the place is a joy, with an immense lawn and a walled garden leading to glorious herbaceous borders, tiered topiary, paeony beds and dahlias. Growing against the house wall are two enormous magnolias, one a *soulangeana* cross planted in 1895, the other a *grandiflora* whose varietal name is rightly Goliath. Borde Hill is full of interest and the head gardener claims that 'two days *at least*' are needed to see it properly. But even an hour spent here is richly rewarding.

Charleston Manor

Zone Centre: Battle, Route 2

Owner: Lady Birley

What is it that gives a garden charm, that brings it back to memory with a smile? Whatever it is, the garden at Charleston Manor has it. Its owner is a painter, as was her late husband, Sir Oswald Birley, and their idea was to frame the garden in a design, with 'good composition, as in a painting'. It was laid out by the famous architect Walter Godfrey who gave it the yew-hedged terraces which step up a hillside. They face a magnificent tithe barn, with the lawn between. Plantings in the terrace gardens are designed to give a silvery effect against the dark yews, such as *Helichrysum lanatum*, *Coriaria maritinum*, white geraniums and white nicotianas.

But the garden's chief beauty is the roses. In a large border at the south side of the house are gallicas and bourbons – Souvenir de la Malmaison, La Baronne Prévoste, Variegata di Bologna, all in a cloud of blossom and fragrance. Continuing on, a wall is covered with climbing roses, and along it are the incomparable hybrid musks – the china-pink Felicia, and Cornelia 'which grows and grows and flowers and flowers' to Lady Birley's delight, with the old favourites Blanc Double de Coubert, Frau Dagmar Hastrup and many others. The path leads to a stretch of rough grass full of spring bulbs where more shrub roses grow, and on to an orchard where every apple tree has its climbing rose or clematis. The annexe of the house is here, a tea-cosy cottage set in a garden stuffed with flowers.

Chartwell

Zone Centre: Tunbridge Wells, Route 4

Owner: The National Trust

This is Sir Winston Churchill's garden, with its lake and island where he used to sit and paint, nearby his studio where many of his pictures hang. There is the little pool beside which he often sat to meditate and to feed his golden orfe from a blue-painted box. His blue-painted chair is beside it. In a second lake below still swim his black swans. The house is built on split levels and from its terrace you can

see the spectacular view he knew so well, a panorama of
Kent and Crowborough Beacon. At one end of the terrace
is the Marlborough Pavilion with murals and ceiling painted
by his nephew John Spencer Churchill. A path at the other
end leads round the lawn where Lady Churchill used to
play croquet, and on to the slope where the Golden Rose
Walk stretches before you, commemorating the Churchills'
golden wedding. Beech hedges line it, widening to encompass
a plinth surrounded by Peace roses. A plaque on the brick
wall at the end tells you that the greater part of it was built
'by Winston with his own hands'. As you enter Chartwell
you go into the rose garden where his pink favourites grow,
and if you are there in spring you will see by the front door
a big magnolia in all its glory. The gardener often had to
send blooms of it to London, because Sir Winston Churchill
loved its lemon scent.

Chilham Castle

Zone Centre: Canterbury, Route 1

Owner: The Viscount Massereene and Ferrard, DL

Inigo Jones built the castle for Sir Dudley Digges in 1616.
John Tradescant the elder, who accompanied Sir Dudley to
Russia two years later – the first botanist to visit that country
– designed the garden, and there still remain vestiges of
his work. There are two mulberry trees dating from his
time, slips of which were sent to Sir Dudley's son Edward

39

in America; and on the lawn is the huge evergreen oak planted on the day the castle was begun. The mulberries grow in a walled garden, the top half of which could have been the old parterre. Leaning over a high wall are vast old yews, and growing against it is the oldest wistaria in England, perhaps not Tradescant's (although in his 1656 garden list he indicates some sort of pea-flowered plant of this nature), for the introduction date of the wistaria is never given as earlier than 1724. It was 'Capability' Brown who made the lake in the woodland and who redesigned much of the garden. His three terraces descend from the castle, with sweeping views of the Kent countryside and with herbaceous borders on the two lower levels. At the sides brick steps lead down in wide curves to the lawn.

Crittenden House

Zone Centre: Tunbridge Wells, Route 3

Owner: B P Tompsett, Esq

When a man who owns a garden has planted it himself, and when that man is a plant hunter of the Himalaya who knows a good thing when he sees it – expect to find something out of the ordinary. And here it is, a four-acre garden full of interesting things. Well laid out, too. Mr Tompsett planned it on labour saving lines, eliminating hedges except where they were needed for shelter, with no digging of beds (they are mostly peated down), no annuals and few biennials. Shrubs are therefore a feature, and these he chooses for contrast in foliage and form; but there is a rose garden, and he has introduced roses into the shrub beds to give colour throughout the year. Not that Mr Tompsett likes great splashes of colour everywhere: he prefers it on a slow time scale, by which he means natural planting and mixed borders where the sequence of bulbs, rhododendrons, lilies and so on follow each other through the seasons till autumn brings out the berries and bright leaves. He started the garden in 1956, inheriting three large ponds choked with weeds and a tangle of overgrowth that almost hid the house. The soil was impossible. Because of iron mining operations there was no topsoil in some places and wet clay in the rest. He had to import thousands of tons of fresh soil. When planting he followed the contours of the land and ponds, and he was careful to leave the best of the native flora – the primroses and bluebells, foxgloves and spotted orchids, the honeysuckle that grew up the trees, and the wild roses. The result, created by this connoisseur of good plants who feels for each one almost as if it were a human being, is a garden completely satisfying, and perhaps your visit may coincide with one of the evenings when it is floodlit – an added enchantment.

Emmetts

Zone Centre: Tunbridge Wells, Route 4

Owner: The National Trust

This is entirely a shrub garden. It is tucked away among trees, its four and a half acres sloping down to a bluebell dell half a mile long. It was planted around 1894 by Sir John Lubbock, friend of Sir Joseph Hooker, Darwin, T H Huxley and all the great scientists of the day. Each shrub stands alone, to be admired for itself and not as part of a mass effect. Among them are specimen trees, the fastigiate Dawyck beech whose branches grow upwards like a Lombardy poplar, an *Acer davidii* about thirty-five feet tall. This is one of the snake-barks and the winter sun on the red tips of its twigs is an enchanting sight. The *Sorbus vilmorinii* will fascinate you whether you see it in summer with its fernlike foliage, or in autumn when its berries change to pink and then white. In July and August clethras spill their fragrance. But this is to name only a few of the treasures to be found at Emmetts. If you like shrubs, you will find many more.

Godinton Park

Zone Centre: Canterbury, Route 1

Owner: A Wyndham Green, Esq

A formal garden this, of ten acres with masses of exquisite topiary and elaborate yew hedges trimmed to match the Flemish gables of the house. It takes three to four weeks to clip it all: at the corners the hedges are ten feet thick. What a delightful place is the Pan Garden, with old Pan himself in the centre! He is surrounded by high box-edged beds filling a circle enclosed by four yew walls. The main pleasure garden leads down to a pond by way of a big sweet chestnut tree, carpeted in spring with crocuses, and past an open rose garden and shrub and herbaceous borders. The gravelled avenue here of cherry and sorbus trees is lined with rose plots. At Easter millions of daffodils make golden lakes in the wild garden with narcissi, crocuses, snowdrops and fritillaries. The Italian Garden is also full of bloom in spring with small plants such as rock phloxes, pinks and aubrietias. Behind them are summer borders and roses on the walls. Up the centre is a canal framed in grass and at the far end a pergola echoing the one at the entrance whose pillars are four stone figures hardly visible among tumbling cascades of white and pink clematis.

Grayswood Hill

Zone Centre: Guildford, Route 1

Owner: G L Pilkington, Esq

There was a rose border where roses wouldn't grow properly. It had steps leading round and out of it in a sort of rock garden. So they planted it all with dwarf conifers, adorable little fat golden *lawsoniana*, and tiny *parviflora* pines, white-tipped sequoias to fan round the feet of slightly bigger dwarfs blue-foliaged, green-foliaged. The transformation was not surprising, for although many kinds of trees grow at Grayswood – a magnificent cut-leaf beech on the lawn, for instance, and a fine specimen of the tulip tree – conifers take pride of place. A *Pinus montezumae* is now the largest in the country. The garden was started by a tea planter in 1890. He sent home plants by the hundred, and conifers fascinated him. The present owner has increased them to what amounts to a pinetum (his dwarf collection is one of the best) and some years ago he bred one of his own, a beautiful thing which I hope will have many progeny. The house is on a terraced plateau girdled by flowering shrubs for spring, acers and others for autumn. In spring you will find a blaze of azaleas and the blooms of choice rhododendrons all round the place. Standing on the terrace the view over the Weald of Sussex to Chanctonbury Ring, Leith Hill and Box Hill is superb, and below, beyond the sloping grass, a haze of blue hydrangeas is like a mist in front of the trees – more splendid conifers all mixed up with eucryphias that bloom in October.

Great Dixter

Zone Centre: Battle, Route 1

Owner: Mrs Nathaniel Lloyd

The accent is on the unusual, and the aim is to provide colour over a long season and to create effective plant associations. It is a plantsman's garden. It is also everybody's garden, five acres of fascinating topiary and yew hedges which, with low stone walls, divide the garden into a series of smaller ones. The manor house is fifteenth century and half-timbered, and its restorations and the garden were designed by Sir Edwin Lutyens. It therefore reflects Lutyens' classical touch. Hence the beauty of the hedges with their pillared doorways and niches; hence the decorative segmented steps leading up to a pair of mulberry trees, with tiny circles of grass at each level; and hence the series of surprises as you come upon one secret garden and then another— Lutyens was masterly at contriving this effect. He died in 1944 and, with the war over, Mr and Mrs Lloyd surveyed his once-lovely lawn where Victory had been dug for in cabbages and potatoes. Mr Lloyd made a sunken pool with borders around, designing the new garden on the medieval dictum – 'Balance without symmetry'. It is their son Christopher

45

who is now the plantsman-gardener. He mixes all kinds of plants together, because that is how they grow naturally, and puts in dramatic touches of variegated foliage, the grass *Arundo donax variegata* and the sword-leaves of a particoloured yucca to break the fuzz of too much soft green. Where you and I might grow a clump of montbretias he plants the arresting *Crocosmia masonorum* whose flower stems branch out and are even more vividly orange. And how few people grow the Wand Flower or Angel's Fishing Rods, tall bending stems bearing pink and magenta bells. There is not a corner at Great Dixter that is not superbly planted.

Hall Place Gardens

Zone Centre: Tunbridge Wells, Route 2

Owner: The Lord Hollenden

The focal point is the large islanded lake approached by a lawn sweeping down from the house and leading first into plantings of good shrubs and then into woodland, the walk round the whole garden taking up to two hours. Plenty of seats are provided to let you enjoy the views up and down the water, where you may see the Crested Grebe and Tufted Duck. The shrubs are in rich variety. They include the beautiful *Zenobia pulverulenta* with its large lily-of-the-valley flowers scented like aniseed, and the evergreen 'laburnum' *Piptanthus laburnifolius*, both from the Himalaya;

Osmanthus delavayi, a gem from China with fragrant white jasmine-like flowers in April, and the always fascinating *Garrya elliptica* with its long green tassels. Three little stone bridges with metronome finials cross the water at its narrow ends, the first draped with the pink *Clematis montana.* Here in early summer you are greeted by drifts of primulas companioned by *Spiraea arguta,* known as 'Foam of May'. The balustrading of the second bridge is purple with *Wistaria sinensis.* Everywhere the underplanting is lavish – here a big group of salmon-pink azaleas, there rhododendron hybrids like Sensation and Tally Ho, camellias and primroses, trilliums and lilies, with the Spring Bank a mass of daffodils in April. Crossing the third bridge we come out on the Old Drive where there are some good trees, an impressive Incense Cedar, a rare single-leaved ash, a well-grown *Pyrus salicifolia* with its silver leaves. The woodland and lake are not all of Hall Place. There is a large rose garden with pergolas rioting with Maiden's Blush and Emily Gray, the old Dorothy Perkins, the new Danse de Feu and Parade; and the Dutch Garden hedged round with yew and full of tulips in May, paeonies in summer, followed by dahlias grown to show standard and planted in colourshadings. There are good water lilies in its pool. Hall Place has been open to the public only since 1967 and is not yet well known. It deserves to be, for the garden is good all the year.

Heaselands

Zone Centre: Crawley, Route 2

Owner: Ernest Greverus Kleinwort, Esq

This is a heavenly place with great splashes of lawn sloping down to a stream where begins the woodland, planted sparingly at first so that you see reflected in pools a leaning trunk or a scarlet acer or the green pyramid of a conifer. You climb up into it, an expanse cathedral-like with straight uncluttered boles rising from its floor. Under its leafy roof grow more than three hundred species and hybrid rhododendrons, and then you suddenly see nothing but camellias, or ahead of you a blaze of azaleas where the sun spills through. You enter Heaselands by a new drive. The old drive is the way out, and surely you must slow up as you go, for a beautiful garden has been made of it, featuring an old ditch turned into a stream which drops from pool to pool. There are huge beds of *Darleyensis* ericas set in the greenest of grassland with attractive groups of shrubs and trees. Both formal and informal gardens are planted as beautifully as if each view were a picture. There is the Little Rose Garden full of Pernille Poulsen and Chanelle, the garden round the swimming pool walled in with red roses, and not least the rockery of Sussex sandstone at the front door which is mainly devoted to dwarf conifers and crowds of Mr Kleinwort's two thousand deciduous and thousand evergreen azaleas.

Hever Castle

Zone Centre: Tunbridge Wells, Route 2

Owner: The Hon Gavin Astor

It was Mr Astor's father, Viscount Astor of Cliveden, who created the garden at Hever, a quite fabulous garden of a hundred and fifty acres, not including the twenty-five-acre lake by which you can sit, either in the beautiful Tea House or on its balustraded piazza commanding a view of its whole length. The thirteenth-century moated castle was Anne Boleyn's home where Henry VIII courted her; between it and the lake is the Italian Garden with its fantastic array of statues, Roman columns, cinerary chests, busts and lions collected by the then Mr Astor when he was United States Minister in Rome. They date back to the first century AD and illustrate the complicated transition from paganism to Christianity of the Greek, Asiatic, Etruscan and Roman civilisations. The long border where they stand is bedding-planted with polyanthus and wallflowers, then begonias, petunias and fuchsias, but against the wall are flowering shrubs such as magnolias and forsythias, with clematis, wistaria and virginia creeper reaching out to drape garlands round the statues. Outside the castle end of the garden are eight columns, seven in Imperial porphyry and one in white marble, buttressing a dark yew hedge behind a Half Moon Pond which reflects a statue of Venus and Cupid. Flanking each side are groups of the beautiful Rosemary rose. On the south side of the Italian garden, running east and west along its entire length, is a pergola of stone columns roofed with wistarias, vines, honeysuckle and clematis. Even more spectacular is the Gallery of Fountains in the long aisle beside it with mossy scrollwork bays and carved heads. It was inspired by the Grotto of a Thousand Fountains in the Tivoli Gardens near Rome. Close to the castle is the Chess Garden where a double row of bishops and pawns, rooks and the royal pair stand rather crowdedly together awaiting the opening gambit. Across the way in another yew enclosure is the White Rose Garden. There are more rose gardens, and a Blue Corner leading up to a garden of immense herbaceous borders. At the top is the Cascade and above it the Golden Stairs which take you back to the castle.

Highdown

Zone Centre: Crawley, Route 1

Owner: The Corporation of Worthing

This is the famous Chalk Garden created by the late Sir Frederick Stern, the great horticulturalist to whom the RHS awarded their highest honour, the Victoria Medal. He started it as an experiment, to see what would grow on the chalk soil of the Sussex Downs, first putting in herbaceous plants and shrubs, and then trees. Having taken a small subscription in Reginald Farrer's expedition to northern China, and the plants raised from this seed doing so well, he was encouraged to try other seed from collectors in the Far East – Wilson, Forrest, Kingdon-Ward, Rock, Ludlow and Sherriff. The result is a garden full of fascinating things, the more interesting because some of them are prospering amid the sheer unadulterated white chalk of an old quarry. Here grows *Acer cappadocium* var. *sinicum* collected by Wilson about 1901. The tree is now over thirty feet tall. Another tree there is an original *Davidia vilmoriniana*, called the Pocket Handkerchief tree because of its long pure white bracts. The bare chalk pit is now covered with vegetation, and if you did not know it you would think that everything was planted in an enviable soil. The garden is laid out in no formal style. Pleasing walks broaden into lawns and narrow again between mixed groups of trees, shrubs and herbaceous plants of all kinds, and bulbs. The flowering year never ends, for even in the dullest of October days the bright crocus-like Sternbergias (too rarely grown) make a splash of gold, and in the same month the first snowdrops are out – *Galanthus reginae algae* – with the purple flowers of *Crocus media* and the sulphur-yellow spikes of *Mahonia lomarifolia*. Sir Frederick was an expert on bulbs. He bred daffodils, naming them after the Sussex villages around: Broadwater, Goring, Amberley, Handcross. He also bred the fascinating Wedding Day rose which comes out white and fades to pink, and grew his own tree paeonies and lilies: he started the RHS Lily Group and was chairman of it. Protective hedging, as in the big flat garden on from the quarry, is of pittosporum (which could be made more use of in gardens) with its curly leaves of pale shiny green, a green like no other. In front are great masses of blue agapanthus. There are some exquisite features: along one path a sheet of anemones like a colourful Persian carpet, along another nothing but blue anemones.

Hole Park

Zone Centre: Battle, Route 1

Owner: D G W Barham, Esq

A very beautiful garden originally laid out by the grandfather
of the present owner who continues his work, continually
improving and extending it. It is done in a happy mixture
of the formal and the informal, with a woodland garden and
broad expanses of lawn sheltered by walls and the decorative
yew hedges which are a feature at Hole Park enclosing a
series of gardens with spectacular views across the Kent
countryside. There is exquisite planning of detail, such as
the concave curve of the swimming pool which fits in –
across a stretch of lawn – to the convex curve of the Vineyard,
a central pavilion winged by vine-covered pergolas. Mr Barham likes 'colour' plants. The sunk garden is grey and
blue enlivened by bedding plants in the gaps, in spring a
blaze of tulips. Outside it, left and right, are two long borders,
one all blue and yellow, the other filled with paeonies, roses
– Nevada, Iceberg, Frühlingsgold and Frühlingsmorgen
repeated all along – and grey-leaved plants such as anapholis
and senecios. At the end of this border is a figure of the
Eagle Slayer with a dead lamb at his feet, the work of John
Bell and a copy of the 1851 Exhibition piece now in Bethnal
Green Museum. The North Walk, where high beech
hedges shelter camellias, leads to The Policy where autumn
colours are a speciality. Set in the grass are mounds of

heathers backed by a huge bank of rhododendrons forming a wall of bloom in spring. On the fringe of the woodland are trees and shrubs such as the pink-flowered Judas tree, eucryphias, cornuses, fothergillas and sulphur-yellow brooms. A *Tsuga canadensis* is reputed to be the best in Britain. Among azaleas, viburnums and the pink-belled Elizabeth rhododendron you climb up into the undulating woodland where there are magnolias, maples, rhododendrons and azaleas, with sheets of daffodils and bluebells, and primulas down by the stream. Here all is peace and birdsong. A really delightful garden in which you will love to wander.

Leonardslee

Zone Centre: Crawley, Route 2

Owner: Sir Giles Loder, Bt, VMH

A pilgrimage place in May when the rhododendrons are in bloom, among them the famous Loderi hybrids made by Sir Edmund Loder, grandfather of the present owner. The Loderi have their own special garden reached from the daffodil lawn by taking the topmost path. Here are many of the original specimens of the famous hybrid whose parents were *R fortunei* (introduced by Robert Fortune in 1855 and the first Chinese species rhododendron known here) and the Himalayan *griffithianum* discovered by Sir Joseph Hooker in 1849. They are tree size and a magnificent sight

53

with their thousands of huge trusses of sweet-scented flowers ranging from pink to pure white. Since then many varieties have been bred: Pink Diamond, King George, Fairy Queen, Pink Coral and Glory of Leonardslee, and it is never questioned by anyone that Loder's White is the best of all white rhododendrons. The garden is not merely a collection of these wonderful shrubs as a sort of living museum: they are beautifully planted in a woodland valley with a chain of lakes. The view down to the valley and across to the South Downs is hazed with the misty colours of birches and larches from which soar American redwoods and wellingtonias. In glades and open stretches the sun spotlights the vivid hues of azaleas, and there is a rock garden where the Kurumes are dazzling. There are other flowering shrubs. Camellias have their own Grove and Walk; and among the magnolias a sixty-foot-tall *campbellii*, Hooker's 'Pink Tulip Tree', is a wonderful spectacle in bloom.

Nymans

Zone Centre: Crawley, Route 2

Owner: The National Trust

A garden is never great just because it is well planned and well planted, however good the architectural features, however unusual the flowers in its beds and borders. It must be more than a show place, which Nymans is, but Nymans has something else. Now the property of the National Trust, it was for many years the home of the talented Messel family. Ludwig Messel bought the property in 1887. Among his friends were Sir Edmund Loder the great breeder of rhododendrons, William Robinson the landscape gardener, and Miss Ellen Willmott. They all lent a hand in designing the garden. The little Temple near the pinetum was the work of Alfred Messel, his architect brother, and the glorious herbaceous borders in the Wall Garden were designed by Gertrude Jekyll, a family aunt. They are typical of her exquisite colour combinations and are graced by a set piece of topiary round an Italian fountain. Everywhere you go at Nymans you have the feeling that this is somebody's home. There are such personal touches, which you find nowhere else, like the 'basket' on the lawn made entirely of winter jasmine and filled with hydrangeas. In a woodland are Loder rhododendrons and Leonard Messel camellias and magnolias. In the garden of old-fashioned roses are some given by Miss Willmott. And of course Nymans is the home

55

of the beautiful Nymansay eucryphia which in August and September covers itself with a mantle of white scented flowers.

Owl House Gardens

Zone Centre: Tunbridge Wells, Route 1

Owner: Maureen, Marchioness of Dufferin and Ava

In 1522 it belonged to the Abbot of Bayham. In 1948 it was bought by its present owner. It stood in a field, a half-derelict farmhouse to which led so many wires of one kind and another that her friends named it Cat's Cradle Hall. It is now an extremely attractive cottage in a twenty-seven-acre garden with a woodland in which a pool reflects autumn-colouring maples, a pieris which sends forth such flower-like pink shoots; the rosy plumes of astilbes, bright azaleas and a *Cornus kousa* bloom-laden as if with snow. All through the woods are rhododendrons. A feature is the broad grass ride bordered unusually with shrub roses and with violets and crocuses, primroses and daffodils, and red and blue anemones. Sackloads of lily-of-the-valley have been planted in imitation of the woods of Compiègne where they grow wild and are called Les Langues de la Neige. The ride leads on to grassland where stands a little white wrought-iron temple, and nearby are two orchards filled with daffodils.

Just by the house is a pretty rose garden where new and old favourites mingle: Peace and Blanc Double de Coubert, Queen Elizabeth, Cornelia and hundreds of others. Winding shrub borders shelter the lawn sweeping half round the house. And all over the place are owls. China owls live along the window sills; a stone owl peeps at you from its plinth in the wood; two ornament the rose-bowered entrance gate. Part of the wisdom of the Owl House is the fact that all the entrance money goes towards the upkeep of the nearby Oast House where a changing population of five arthritic patients come for a 'fortnight's paradise'.

Parham Park

Zone Centre: Crawley, Route 1

Owner: Mrs P A Tritton

As you walk towards the walled garden, leaving the massive Elizabethan house behind you, a scent greets you that always arouses exclamation. It comes from the insignificant white-flowered *Clematis flammula* bowering the wrought-iron entrance gates. On the left as you enter are five charming cupids with green moss hair. No neglect: the moss is encouraged. The large square garden of four and a half acres is beautiful from early spring with bulbs under the orchard trees. Then two thousand tulips come into bloom with wallflowers, followed by chrysanthemums and dahlias.

57

Large borders of roses are edged with the deep blue Hidcote lavender, and twin herbaceous borders three hundred yards long are a glory. The walls are covered with climbers, a bewildering number of different ones. You are allowed to walk through the peach and orchid houses and another where pot plants grow. From here you go into the pleasure ground where a lead Neptune looks over the lawn to a pond.

Penshurst Place

Zone Centre: Tunbridge Wells, Route 2

Owner: The Rt Hon Viscount de l'Isle, vc

It is situated in the part of Kent known as the Garden of England, and here is a garden essentially English, colourful with a wealth of flowers and having the most exquisite hedges of battlemented yew ten feet tall. You enter the garden by a herbaceous avenue full of lilies of all kinds, irises and phloxes, evening primroses and verbenas, scarlet potentillas, Red Hot Pokers (and yellow ones as well), scabious, delphiniums and lupins and almost every English border flower you can think of, in a display that keeps you lingering. By the lovely fourteenth-century castle a *Ginkgo biloba* glows like a yellow candle against a tower, and from here you look down into the parterre garden of roses and box. At the end of the grass terrace is a window in the wall commanding a wide view of the park. Below are the entrance gates where yellow roses and blue clematis grow. These are the house colours, which are often repeated in the garden borders and corners even when roses are used, when the choice is Blue Moon and Honeymoon. Opening off the parterre are two lovely borders by Lanning Roper, soft pinks and blues mingling with yellows and grey-leaved plants, with the taller William Lobb moss rose – crimson turning to slate-blue – and white buddleia, lilies and yuccas. At the ends of the borders are standards of the grey-leaved willow, *Salix repens*. Blue geraniums are used as a ground cover. This is one of a series of enclosed gardens opening off each other in almost bewildering number. It is the aim of Lord de l'Isle to make Penshurst the show place of the south. I have seen few I liked so much and few so beautifully kept. The colour effects are sometimes spellbinding: the lily pool with nothing but white water lilies, its surface on a sunny day red with goldfish; a blue and yellow border, I remember, of *Salvia patens* and primroses, wistaria, blue clematis and the yellow buttons of artemisia; the four beds of pink Elizabeth of Glamis roses underplanted with pink antirrhinums and edged with Woodii pinks; the avenue of standard roses, and the pool where the scented Water Hawthorn blooms from April till the frost.

Polesden Lacey

Zone Centre: Guildford, Route 2

Owner: The National Trust

The immense lawn in front of the house is one of Polesden Lacey's charms. It is studded on each side with cedars, and from it you can appreciate the spectacular sight of two *Clematis armandii* whose flowers make a white band fifty yards long above the ground-floor windows. It was once the home of Richard Brinsley Sheridan who is commemorated in a long Walk overlooking Ranmore Common. Wrought iron gates lead into an attractive walled garden and you must not miss seeing the aubrietias growing in the chequerboard squares of the wall to the left as you enter. Four rectangles are traversed by a long pergola covered with rambler roses, among them François Juraville, Excelsa and Emily Gray. Beneath are beds with Étoile de Hollande, Frensham, Grandmère Jenny and other beauties with four beds of hybrid musks – Penelope, Buff Beauty, Felicia and Cornelia. The paved paths are edged with lavender and there is a long border of lily-of-the-valley and another full of aquilegias and delphiniums. Here, too, there are three small yew-hedged gardens, one of lavender and Regal lilies, the second of lavender only and the third of bearded irises. Outside, the whole length of the wall is a long herbaceous border overhung with a continuous array of climbers. Beyond is a parrotia garden where three specimens of *persica* cover an area of fifteen square yards and grow forty feet high.

Scotney Castle

Zone Centre: Tunbridge Wells, Route 1

Owner: Christopher Hussey, CBE, FSA

A more romantic place would be hard to find than moated Scotney Castle and the nine acres surrounding it. Its long history dates back to c 1338, and in the earliest records, of 1137, there is a Lambert de Scoteni whose residence was probably one of the two islands enclosed by the moat (Scot Ney). It was last lived in by Mrs Edward Hussey II in 1836, great-grandmother of the present owner, though the estate bailiff continued to use the Tudor portion till 1905. The rest was 'ruinated' and is preserved as an Ancient Monument. If you know anything about Mr Christopher Hussey's love of the picturesque you can imagine that the gardens around it are in keeping. In a sort of blissful combination of the old and the new he uses modern plants to highlight, with a splash of colour to draw the eye to a focal point. Otherwise things are much as they were in the time of his grandfather who planted on the ideas of William Robinson's 'pictorial naturalism'. You gain the castle from a bridge across the moat, to find a spill of roses round a Venetian well-head. In the ancient ruin a vast wistaria drapes itself half along a wall. Old windows frame vistas. A semi-wild viburnum long ago took up residence here in a corner. It is now immense and in early spring its starry clusters are a mass of fragrance. The moat was easy to plant. *Osmunda regalis* ferns dip down

61

to the water's edge, and along by the boat house a view from the bridge is made dramatic in autumn by the huge yellow leaves of polygonum reflected in the water. The trees are magnificent, most of them planted more than a century ago. A *Sequoia sempervirens* is 126 feet tall, a Sitka Spruce 91 feet. A group of three *Thuya plicata* trees have a circumference of 240 feet, and a 132-foot *Pinus ponderosa* is among the tallest known. Willow gentians have naturalised themselves in the shade. But the history of Scotney goes back farther even than 1137. Up in the woodlands where you wander among rhododendrons, always catching glimpses of the romantic castle from a different angle, you can see the floor of the Wealden Sea, the fossilised ripples of its sand and the footprints of an iguanodon who walked there in the Jurassic Age 135 million years ago.

Sheffield Park Gardens

Zone Centre: Crawley, Route 2

Owner: The National Trust

Nowhere are the autumn colours more wonderful than at Sheffield Park, which is delectable enough in spring when the trees round its big lake are coming into leaf, the silver barks of birches hung with shimmering young green and the grassland alight with daffodils turning to a haze of bluebells. When the Third Earl of Sheffield died in 1909 Sheffield Park was bought by Mr Arthur G Soames, and it was he who in the next twenty-five years created the beautiful scenes you can see today. The lake was already there, indeed a chain of five falling one into the other, the work of Lancelot ('Capability') Brown. Mr Soames extended his original design and transformed the whole place with exquisite plantings of broad-leaved trees and conifers, rhododendrons and other flowering shrubs. His contrasts of form and colour make Sheffield Park one of the loveliest places in England. The gardens cover 142 acres. Summer sees the eucryphias white with their scented flowers. The water lilies open into stars of white and pink and red. Big blue-headed hydrangeas invade the shade of the woodland where all his trees are now mature, the *Picea breweriana* he planted for the grace of its drooping sleeves, the nothofagus – Chilean cousin of our native beech – the White Cypress and the Chinese juniper. But it is in autumn that Sheffield Park comes into its full glory, when the fothergillas, amelanchiers and acers flame with rich reds, the green leaves of the birches turn to gold and the Swamp Cypresses to bronze, contrasting strikingly with the dark green of Monterey pines, wellingtonias and the still columns of the Incense Cedars. It is the nyssas which are the most startling, pyramids of scarlet leaves among bright green ones. Wherever you look they arrest the eye. Sheffield Park is famous for them, for nowhere can you see nyssa trees like them, and up in the woodland there is a lovely sight, an avenue of grass between two carpets of blue gentians that roll away into the trees. It is an unforgettable spectacle.

Sissinghurst Castle

Zone Centre: Tunbridge Wells, Route 3

Owner: The National Trust

Everybody falls in love with Sissinghurst. Its six acres of intimate little gardens seem a sort of dream come true, with their clouds of roses over archways and walls, climbing up trees and pulled down over hazel hoops. There is the White Garden with its lead statue of a vestal virgin under the weeping branches of the silver-leaved pear tree; the gaiety of the Persian carpets of spring bulbs bordering the pleached lime walk in patches of blue muscari, chequered fritillaries, daffodils, dog's tooth violets, scillas and the vivid scarlet of *Anemone fulgens* all mingling together; and the other colourful carpet under the nuttery of Kent cobs and filberts – thousands of polyanthus primroses blooming from early April till the second week of May. You can see the whole garden from the top of the tower which has a view over a wide stretch of the Kentish Weald. You will notice a small circular lawn immaculately hedged with yew and radiating out in four paths. This is the Rondel, so-called from the local name for the round floor of an oast house where the hops are spread to dry. It divides the rose garden into four parts, and on the east side of it is a charming cottage with lead-paned windows where a Madame Alfred Carrière rose smothers a wall in white. This is an orange and yellow garden where tiger lilies are a feature. Leading out from here is the Moat

Walk and at the far end of the nuttery the herb garden. Unusual herbs like orris root, clary and woad (whose dye was used by the ancient Britons) are grown. Outside it is a small thyme lawn of *Thymus serpyllum*, the close-growing kind. The famous White Garden is on the opposite side, to be reached by a long yew walk. It lies at the foot of the Priest's House, with the castle tower in the background, and there is not one plant in it that is not white or grey or silver. It was Victoria Sackville-West and Harold Nicolson her husband who rescued Sissinghurst, and between them they created its gardens on the lines of 'the strictest formality of design, with the maximum informality in planting'. They loved their garden and made their dream of it come true.

Sissinghurst Place

Zone Centre: Tunbridge Wells, Route 3

Owner: Mrs Lindsay Drummond

This is an entirely different garden to that of Sissinghurst Castle. Here a spacious lawn greets you on which is an eighty-foot-high Durmast Oak that covers a quarter of an acre: five hundred years old, it is the finest in England. A ruined part of the house is attractively used for growing tender plants such as *Abutilon megapotamicum, Coronilla glauca* and all sorts of colourful things. Round the lawn are various small gardens, a tiny yew-hedged rose garden forming an ante-room to the lawn where a statue of a Roman lady stands in a pink sea of azaleas, a knot garden of roses close by the Oak and, hidden among trees, the rock garden. There are many shrubs, one hundred different kinds.

Sutton End

Zone Centre: Crawley, Route 1

Owner: Mrs Holland

The garden was started in 1922 but looks as if it had been there much longer, so ancient appears the big jumbly hedge opposite the mixed iris border. Close to the house is a brick-paved rose, tulip and lily garden where all sorts of other plants grow as well. Mrs Holland likes the old shrub roses for their perfume and soft colouring, and here grow the hybrid musks Felicia and Vanity, china-pink shading to yellow and rose-pink perpetually flowering. She delights in growing quantities of *Iris stylosa* against the wall, and the lilies are everywhere – crinums, Headbourne hybrids, blue-headed agapanthus, pink Nerines and the pretty pink schizostylus. A wide grass path goes down to the stream garden by way of a rock garden and a herbaceous border. Bridges cross the water into woodland where rhododendrons grow. You join the lawn again by a grand old shrub border where a Preston lilac is a smother of pink in early summer. Along by the waterside is a little border full of precious small bulbs – anemones and cyclamen, tiny irises, dog's tooth violets and Angel's Tears, and round the pond are dogwoods, azaleas, bamboos, ferns, hostas and primulas. If you come in May you will hear nightingales sing. It is that sort of garden, a peaceful place tucked away in a little world of its own.

Wakehurst Place

Zone Centre: Crawley, Route 3

Owner: The National Trust

Coming down the grass way from the car park the first tree you will notice is the Chinese Larch which puts on a beautiful bronze-gold dress in autumn. Behind it is the tall thin spire of a *Picea omorika* and beyond is a Swamp Cypress. They are typical of Wakehurst's beauty, a magnificent collection of trees and shrubs covering five hundred acres, of which about a hundred and seventy are open to the public. Although the property of the National Trust, Wakehurst Place is the country extension of Kew Gardens, chosen for its variety of soils in which almost every kind of plant can grow. So here in ideal conditions are forty acres of rhododendrons to enjoy. You will find them at the top of The Slips and in the Westwood growing on the steep hillsides of a ravine where, at the bottom, a small stream runs along to Westwood Lake. Growing among the rare and interesting trees is a grand magnolia (*campbellii*) more than sixty feet in height and probably the tallest in Britain. It is a fairly long walk to the lake but you can cut back half-way along the rock outcrop (a fascinating bouldered overhang). The Heath Garden is one of the most interesting parts of Wakehurst, where Sir Gerald Loder who re-created the gardens planted many of his original introductions from Australasia and South America. There are rare myrtles and malvas, and a conifer from Tasmania (*Athrotaxis selaginoides*) practically identical with fossil specimens found in the Isle of Sheppey. The steep-sided valley called The Slips has a little stream running down the middle. Here the trees are underplanted with thousands of bulbs, and if you go in spring you must try to find on the left side of the stream's bank the purple-flowered *Lathraea clandestina*. As its name suggests it is a parasite and grows here on the roots of a maple. Wakehurst is full of interesting things and is beautiful besides.

Winkworth Arboretum

Zone Centre: Guildford, Route 1

Owner: The National Trust

You go to Winkworth Arboretum for one of two reasons: to wander along pleasant paths through beautiful glades and woodlands, or to study the many fascinating specimen trees. There are unique collections of maples, oaks – including some rare ones – and sorbus, of which the Rowan is the common example. Mainly it is a natural oak and bluebell wood, but it has one of the oldest beech trees, planted in the reign of Queen Anne. You will find a map at the entrance showing where the various groups of trees are. There is the Styrax group where the Liquidambar trees glow red in autumn, and the hillside which cascades with cherry trees, dancing with blossom in spring. Among the birches are uncommon ones like *Betula papyrifera* from Europe and North America, with their silvery papery bark. Over 132 genera are represented in the arboretum, which covers ninety-five acres. It was the creation of Dr Wilfrid Fox who gave it to the nation in 1952. At the bottom of the valley are two lakes, one for swimming and the other for fishing.

Also open is

MICHELHAM PRIORY **(Zone Centre: Battle, Route 2. Owner: The Sussex Archaeological Trust)** which is interesting chiefly for its setting. Where the parts of the Priory no longer exist, white bricks mark the outlines. There is a very small all-white rose garden, but it is mostly lawns sweeping round the Priory inside the moat, with a large mixed shrub and herbaceous border.

Open occasionally are :

THE GRANGE, BENENDEN **(Zone Centre: Battle, Route 1. Owner: Captain Collingwood Ingram)** is a famous seven-acre informal garden with trees and shrubs collected by its owner in Japan, Spain, Alaska, New Zealand and other parts of the world. He breeds his own rhododendrons and has evolved his own race of polyanthus.

COVERWOOD **(Zone Centre: Guildford, Route 2. Owner: C G Metson, Esq)** is an enchanting place one thousand feet up in the Surrey Hills, with four lakes, woodlands full of magnolias, camellias and rhododendrons, a bog garden, and a spectacular terraced rock garden packed with azaleas which climbs to a viewpoint.

DUNSBOROUGH PARK **(Zone Centre: Guildford, Route 2. Owner: C F Hughesdon, Esq)** has rose, valley and stream gardens and four beautiful herbaceous borders, two parallel with the house and extending the line of the terrace. The rock and water garden is in 'natural' style and follows the course of a stream.

HASCOMBE COURT **(Zone Centre: Guildford, Route 1. Owners: Mr and Mrs C G Jacobs)** is a garden most beautifully laid out with classic herbaceous borders and a pool garden, with some magnificent trees. A Japanese garden on a hillside has an unusual thatched summer-house curving along the bottom. Sir Edwin Lutyens designed the terraces.

NORTHBOURNE COURT **(Zone Centre: Canterbury, Route 1. Owner: The Rt Hon the Lord Northbourne)** has a ruin in the garden of the house where Sir Edwin Sandys drafted the constitution of Virginia, ruins in which are little gardens and nooks planted with climbers. A beautifully planted terraced mount is at the end of the lawn which is overlooked from the house side by an unusual loggia perched thirty-six feet above it. Through from the loggia is an 'ecological garden' where chalk-loving plants find a natural home. A most fascinating two-acre garden.

OAKENWOOD **(Zone Centre: Tunbridge Wells, Route 3. Owner: Mrs H Sterndale-Bennett, RI)** is a charming two-acre garden full of the flowers Mrs Sterndale-Bennett loves to paint: hellebores, magnolias and camellias – of which twenty varieties prosper in peat beds on a lime soil. There is a pretty rose garden and a birch copse surrounded by ericas. Shrubs and shrub roses, irises, dahlias and chrysanthemums make a long flowering season.

ZONE 3 Wessex

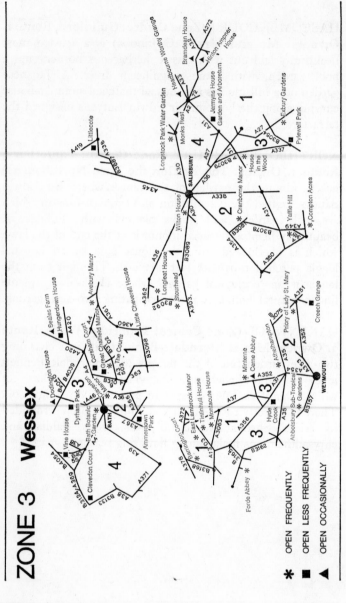

* OPEN FREQUENTLY

■ OPEN LESS FREQUENTLY

▲ OPEN OCCASIONALLY

ZONE 3

Wessex

THE COUNTIES OF Hampshire, Wiltshire and Berkshire were
the first settlements of the West Saxons, and by the early
years of AD 800 their kingdom had spread into Somerset,
Dorset and Devon. In Wessex is to be found a wealth of
natural beauty: spacious chalk uplands reaching into
Wiltshire and crowned by Inkpen Beacon; the massif of
Salisbury Plain with its rolling green lands extending through
Cranborne Chase into the Dorset Downs. There is beauty
of stone – Bath stone of fine golden grain with which the
entire city of Bath is built, mellow oolite from the Doulting
quarries which made magnificent Wells Cathedral, a stone
so easy to work yet becoming so hard with exposure that the
galaxy of saints, martyrs and kings decorating its west front
are today as perfect as they were when they were carved in
1242.

All this has a bearing on gardens, accounting for walls
of local Bath stone in one, paths of native granite in another,
the differences of soil in turn dictating in general 'the things
that grow best'. Some of England's greatest gardens are to
be found in this part of the west, Stourhead surely the
loveliest of all with its spring and autumn glories in trees
ranging round a three-armed lake, and such small gardens
as East Lambrook Manor where if you do not learn a dozen

lessons in good gardening you are no sort of gardener at all!

Let us now take you to Salisbury, Bath and Weymouth, convenient centres from which to follow the roads to Avebury, once England's capital, whose Manor and enchanting garden are in the midst of the greatest Megalithic Stone Circle in Europe; to Montacute, and to Longleat (where you can see lions as well as the gardens Queen Elizabeth knew in 1584), to gardens new and gardens old in England's most ancient kingdom.

Abbotsbury Sub-tropical Gardens

Zone Centre: Weymouth, Route 3

Owner: The Strangeways Estates Ltd

The designation 'sub-tropical' is no misnomer, for here in Abbotsbury's famous gardens, lush with exotic trees, bamboos and palms, you might be far from England – especially when the peacocks, wandering about you, spread their splendid tails. The magic touch of the Gulf Stream is the answer, for Abbotsbury is close to the sea (the nearby swannery shelters in its quiet creeks and reedy pools Britain's largest colony of swans, more than a thousand of them). Camellias, a tender plant from China and Japan, grow here to enormous size and jungle-like density, and in April and May when they are covered with their pink, white and red blooms, it is worth driving miles to see them. So, too, the rhododendrons and magnolias, and when this wealth of colour is over other flowering shrubs continue the sequence. The fifteen acres of Abbotsbury include a walled garden and water garden, but most of it is informal, a place to wander among interesting trees and plants from all over the world.

Ammerdown Park

Zone Centre: Bath, Route 2

Owner: The Rt Hon the Lord Hylton

What a wealth of love and planning went into this garden! Laid out in the Italian Renaissance style its thirteen acres are the product of that perfect partnership – Sir Edwin Lutyens the architect and the great gardener Miss Gertrude Jekyll. Some gardens seem to turn their backs on the houses they belong to. Not so Ammerdown which is an extension in spirit of the James Wyatt house built in 1788. It was Lutyens who designed the beautiful Yew Garden with its circling twelve-foot-high hedges, bold square-topped walls with rounded niches cut to exquisite perfection. It was Miss Jekyll who planned its knot beds with colour and texture designs. What could be more effective against the dark yew background than her geraniums among silver leaves, pink-flowered through to velvet-petalled scarlets? The stillness of this enclosure is enlivened by a jet fountain playing into a round stone pond. From here a path leads to the small stone

75

orangery with its five round-headed windows, a path flanked by globes of box and by standard lilacs, the steps up to it made fragrant with rosemary. Another path leads to the rose garden, with an astrolabe among them, the entrance to it bowered in *Vitis coignetiae*, scarlet-leaved in autumn. A late autumn border is one of Lady Hylton's joys and will be yours too if you see the garden at that time of year. A little rock garden almost completes our circle back to the house. There are besides four acres of shrub garden and a woodland where small cyclamen scatter the ground with patches of pink and white, and an avenue of apple and cherry trees. I have not mentioned the view: it looks across a park and beech woods to the Mendip Hills.

Athelhampton House

Zone Centre: Weymouth, Route 2

Owner: Robert Cooke, Esq, MP

The medieval house, legendary site of Athelstan's Palace and Thomas Hardy's Athel Hall, has been a family home for eight hundred years. Around it are ten acres of most attractive formal and landscaped gardens laid out by Inigo Thomas and balanced by riverside and woodland scenes. Focal point is the Corona with its tall obelisks leading to four different courts: the entrance court, the private garden, the White Garden through which flows the River Piddle, and the

Apollo Garden where stands the fine white marble group Il Giuocatore from the 1862 Exhibition. The Lime Alley protects a walk bordered with flowering shrubs. A raised walk leads to the Great Terrace with its Italianate pavilion. There is a beautiful wrought iron gateway, 30,000 square feet of clipped yew hedges, and a fifteenth-century dovecote with a thousand nesting-holes. Among the unusual trees and shrubs are rhododendrons from Florence Nightingale's home at Embley Park. Five hundred delphiniums borrow all the blues of the sky in June, and a two-hundred-year-old *Magnolia grandiflora* is something to wonder at. Lilies and irises, eucryphias with their white clouds of flowers, abutilons and tree paeonies, are some of the plants to admire.

Avebury Manor

Zone Centre: Bath, Route 1

Owner: Sir Francis Knowles, Bt, FRS

Of its romantic five-acre garden and sixteenth-century house reconstructed from a twelfth-century monastery, R C Hutchinson the novelist said: 'Whatever memories of England you carry away, let this be uppermost. For this, to me, *is* England.' You will agree, for from the moment you enter by the pretty wrought iron gate, here are all the things you expect to see in an English garden. Its setting is ancient England. You have just come through Avebury village, England's oldest capital, and have wondered at the standing stones surrounding it. They form the oldest and greatest Stone Circle in Europe. From prehistory you step into the first of seven flowery gardens, the Monks Garden which leads to the south lawn and a magnificent clump of topiary which, believe it or not, is mainly formed from only two box trees. A seventeenth-century armillary sundial stands in the centre of the lawn, and another on the East Lawn. The intricate clipped box hedges will arouse your interest: they copy the pattern of interlocking lozenges decorating the ceiling of the Manor's drawing-room. And because no English garden is complete without its lily pool, here you will find one, with fountains to cool the summer's day. A columbarium in the grounds dating back to the sixteenth century is today inhabited by white fantails – they probably greeted you with a flurry of wings as you approached the house; and in recognition of its primeval setting the owners of Avebury Manor graze in the park Soay sheep from the western Hebrides, the ancient breed of the Bronze Age. More modern are the dahlias which are a speciality of the garden, the Mexican plant named in honour of the Swedish botanist Dahl, and if you come in May you will be rewarded by the blaze of colour made by the ten thousand tulips of named varieties planted here each year. The garden was begun in 1560 and evolved by a succession of owners. The collection of herbs in the Long Border remind us how important these were in the days when sameness of food was disguised and enlivened with the help of dill and coriander, cumin and Good King Henry.

Barrington Court

Zone Centre: Weymouth, Route 1

Owner: Sir Ian D Lyle, DSC

When you hear that this garden was developed (in 1922) mainly from cattle yards, you will surely be surprised. For today it is a real English colour-garden and on a massive scale. The glowing brick walls of the old yards form a series of gardens and are ideal backgrounds for graded colour-schemes, massed effects in borders eighty yards long by six yards wide. There are lily, rose and iris gardens, and a shrub garden. Following the bulbs and other springtime flowers carpeting the orchard are lavish displays of colour through to dahlia-time. In keeping with the sixteenth-century house the paths are stone-flagged or of Tudor brick laid in herring-bone patterns. You must see the ten-faced sundial standing on the lawn, and if you are looking for a plant to make a bright patch in dense shade, see the bronze-leaved vermilion *Impatiens petersiana*, a gay 'Busy Lizzie'. Other bronze-leaved beauties here are canna lilies and *Ricinus gibsonii*, the annual copper-leaved castor-oil plant, merely a few of the interesting things to be seen at beautiful Barrington Court.

Bath Botanic Gardens

Zone Centre: Bath, Route 4

Owner: The City of Bath Corporation

No stay at Bath is complete without a look at its Botanic Garden, which is in the Royal Victoria Park three-quarters of a mile from the city centre. From mid-April to mid-May is the best time to visit it, although it is interesting at all times of the year. Originally a private garden, it was taken over by Bath Corporation in 1887 to house a collection of over two thousand plants from the garden of C E Broome, FLS, of Batheaston. Since then considerable additions have been made and it now has one of the finest collections of lime-loving plants in the country. A pond and a stream with a waterfall make refreshing features on hot summer days, and you must see the unusual sundial and Temple of Minerva built of Bath stone. Though classed as an informal garden it has herbaceous borders and alpines besides good trees and shrubs.

Claverton Manor

Zone Centre: Bath, Route 2

Owner: The American Museum in Britain

This is America in Britain. In the Greek Revival house are completely furnished rooms of the seventeenth, eighteenth and nineteenth centuries, every chair, table and utensil brought from the United States. There is also a fascinating Folk Museum. Outside is the Colonial Herb Garden which was the gift of the Southampton, New York, Garden Club, with forty different kinds of aromatic, culinary and medicinal herbs. A key plan mounted on a board makes it easy to identify them. Down a flight of steps is the George Washington Garden representing part of the First President's garden at Mount Vernon. It was the gift of the Colonial Dames of America, and here behind its white palisade fence with 'Adam' vase finials are to be found a host of American plants, many of them originally brought to England by John Tradescant the younger, who in the seventeenth century made three plant-hunting trips to Virginia. His treasures included *Monarda fistulosa*, the wild bergamot of American woodlands, aquilegias, michaelmas daisies and cardinal flowers. Here you can see them and many more, forming an old-time link between the New World and the Old. A memorial note is the ivy trailing over the balustrading of the stone steps leading down to the garden: it came from Washington's tomb. There is a good collection of shrubs including the beautiful pink-berried *Pernettya mucronata,* and a long border of shrub roses – what scent in the world compares with theirs! Around are fifty-five acres of parkland with well-grown trees. There is a glorious view across the Avon Valley.

Clevedon Court

Zone Centre: Bath, Route 4

Owner: The National Trust

The fourteenth-century manor house has a terraced garden laid out by Sir Abraham Elton IV about 1775, though the octagonal summer-house is dated 1720. Under the terrace walls are well-planted herbaceous borders, and there are mature specimen trees – chestnuts, holm oaks, hollies, pines and an especially fine plane tree. The shrubs are mainly spring-flowering from April, and from then till September it is a pleasant place to visit. Its nine acres spread across the south slope of a hillside.

Compton Acres

Zone Centre: Salisbury, Route 2

Owners: Mr and Mrs J R Brady

This fifteen-acre garden is deservedly popular with the 150,000 people from all over the world who visit it each year. It is itself cosmopolitan, for here you will find a Roman and an English garden, an Italian garden, a Palm Court, a semi-tropical glen, rock and water gardens and a heather dell; with a Japanese garden authentic in every detail, as Japanese visitors delight to discover, down to the guardian frog placed exactly in the position best to ward off evil spirits. Here grows the curious Twisted Willow (*Salix matsudana tortuosa*) and here you can see in May and June the crimson lantern-shaped flowers of the unfortunate shrub which bears two quite different names – *Tricuspidaria lanceolata* and *Crinodendron hookerianum*. In fact, taxonomists declare, its correct name should now be *Crinodendron patagua*. But by any name it is beautiful. Compton Acres boasts that its seven unique gardens are the finest in Europe. They are so planned that only one can be seen at a time. I found each enchanting. The Glen with its rock and water gardens is a joy of trees and tumbling streams ending in a chain of small lakes. In spring sheets of bulbs cascade down its length. The trees are tropical and sub-tropical, among them mimosas, Brazilian jacarandas, Australian gums and the Chilean Fire Tree. They are underplanted with Himalayan rhododendrons. Next, in complete contrast, is the English garden with its lawns, herbaceous borders and cherry trees, with a very English view of Poole Harbour below and the Purbeck Hills beyond. What could be called the Scottish garden is next door, with a wonderful collection of ericas keeping up a sequence of colour throughout the year. The Italian garden is a splendid affair with a Long Canal, balustrading, vases, carved stone fountains, and thousands of goldfish. Long flanking beds either side are filled with a thousand rose bushes backed by thirty-two stone columns garlanded with clematis. The gardens are rich in statuary: a God of Wine sculpted in Carrera marble, a magnificent bronze depicting 'The Death of the Centaur', the famous 'Wrestlers' of Herculaneum. In the Palm Court, so small and peaceful, so green and still, is the sad bronze of the dying Spartan soldier who brought the news of the defeat by the Greeks in the Pass of Thermopylae. But there is a happier note, too, in this garden, a beautiful Venetian wishing-well carved from a solid block of stone. For all the coins thrown into it go to deserving charities, and every year the sum of about £500 is collected. I cannot think that anyone visiting Compton Acres will come away disappointed: whatever nationality you are, at least one (but surely all) of its gardens must make you glad you came here, so many are the beauties of each, so rare the genius that created them all.

Corsham Court

Zone Centre: Bath, Route 3

Owner: The Lord Methuen, RA, FSA

The noble park and gardens were laid out by Lancelot ('Capability') Brown and Humphry Repton as a distinguished setting for the Elizabethan mansion with its magnificent Georgian State Rooms added in 1760. If you come from Africa or are interested in the beautiful plants of that country you will find them here in a collection made by the owner of Corsham Court, Lord Methuen, who also specialises in mecanopsis, crinums and primulas. There are some rare flowering trees, a good specimen of the lovely Tulip Tree, and many flowering shrubs.

The Courts, Holt

Zone Centre: Bath, Route 1

Owner: The National Trust

Here we find seven delightful acres of formal and woodland gardens designed in 1921 by Lady Cecile Goff. While old roses and old English plants are a special pride, there are dramatic features such as the magnificent vine pergola massed alternately with *Vitis rubra* and *V coignetiae* which in autumn make flames of bright bronze and copper-red. What a simple idea to adopt for the back of a large border: pine poles with a length of thick rope. Take note too of *Pyrus salicifolia* 'Pendula', a small weeping tree which would grace any garden with its silvery willow-like foliage and cream-coloured flowers. Interesting trees are a *Liriodendron tulipifera*, which unfailingly flowers its 'tulips' every June; a *rubra* form of *Robinia pseudacacia*, the tree named after Jean Robin who was arborist to Henry III of France; and an *Acer griseum* with its fascinating oily brown bark. Gardeners are now choosing trees decorative not only for leaf or flower but for the joy of varied boles. Hence the Snake Bark birches and others. The Courts has good viburnums and its herbaceous borders are lovely. There is some very old topiary, of what I call the 'jumbly' type, originally perhaps trimmed into the shapes of bears, and some of the pieces here, charmingly rotund, can still be distinguished as such. But I would not for the world have them trimmed back strictly to bear-shape: they are so much nicer as they are. There is a pond with water lilies, and around it the scented stateliness of lilies. The lawn is a pleasant place, an English lawn at its best. Of the thousands of visitors who come here every year the biggest number are Americans, Australians and South Africans, all of them admirers of the greenness they find in Britain. No wonder they fall in love with The Courts.

Cranborne Manor

Zone Centre: Salisbury, Route 2

Owners: Lord and Lady Cranborne

A magnificent beech avenue leads to one of the loveliest manor houses in England. It was originally built as a hunting lodge for King John. In the early years of the 1600s the garden was partly laid out by John Tradescant the elder, who was head gardener to Lord Salisbury at Hatfield. He made new borders and replanted much of the garden, introducing to it some of the hundreds of new roses he had been buying on the Continent for Lord Salisbury who also owned Cranborne. To this day Cranborne is a place of roses. A Mount and a grass-terraced descent to a stream (probably the 'grandstand' of a tilt-yard) still remain from the old days, and a bowling alley between yew hedges. The series of gardens have evolved under the guidance of Lady Cranborne who is a devoted gardener. The Mount, for instance, she has turned into an unusual rose garden and, although now surrounded by a yew hedge, it still commands the 'fair prospect' for which purpose it was originally made. Here Lady Cranborne grows many of her favourite old roses – President de Sèze, Madame Hardy, Pale Pink Moss, Proliferé de Redouté, Variegata di Bologna, and the Great White Rose brought by John Tradescant. There are old-fashioned climbers like Gloire de Dijon with its unending succession of double golden-buff flowers deliciously tea-scented. The soil at Cranborne is poor chalk, but species roses thrive here, too. The Sweet Garden is one of Lady Cranborne's favourite corners, full of flowers and herby savours, a delight even in winter with so many evergreen and grey-foliaged plants. A Garden Centre has been opened where you can buy many of the roses and plants you admire in Cranborne's lovely borders.

Creech Grange

Zone Centre: Weymouth, Route 2

Owner: Lt-Col A R Bond

In keeping with the Tudor manor house geometrical flower beds echo the past, and the beautiful grounds look up to Creech Barrow. There are some fine trees in the nineteenth-century woodland which has been opened up and planted with rhododendrons and azaleas. Ponds and cascades and a Long Canal are an added interest, as are the stately peacocks for which Creech Grange is famed.

Dyrham Park

Zone Centre: Bath, Route 3

Owner: The National Trust

To appreciate fully the Dyrham of today you must look at
the Dyrham of the past, viewing the grand rolling parkland
after studying the 1712 engraving by John Kip (which you
can ask to see). This shows the great seventeenth-century
lay-out by George London who was superintendent of
Charles II's royal gardens, with a grand cascade on the
hillside facing the east front of the house, and an elaborate
arrangement of terraces, avenues, geometrical borders,
fountains and a Long Canal. Changing fashion swept
formality away. In 1800 Humphry Repton was called in to
recast the landscape into the romantic mould, which is how
we see it today. For three years Repton was busy, removing
the barriers of seventeenth-century iron railings (all but
those in the West Garden, which date back to 1694) and the
stiff parallels of hedge and alley. He did not entirely succeed
in removing the contours of the grand cascade, and if you
stand at the bottom of the garden looking past the house to
the hillside you can still faintly see its outlines. A modification of the landscape expanse is being planned by The
National Trust to whom the property now belongs. The
house was built by Talman who also designed the ornate and
massive Orangery facing the Old Deer Park, and this you
must see for the delight of looking at a wall entirely covered

with a blue cloud of plumbago. As well as the Kip engraving there are delightful Flemish tapestries of old gardens to be seen and enjoyed.

East Lambrook Manor

Zone Centre: Weymouth, Route 1

Owner: M H Boyd-Carpenter, Esq

As it was created by the late Mrs Margery Fish, you would expect to find unusual plants here and come away fired with ideas, in which case you will be right. Mrs Fish described it as a 'jungle' garden, meaning that weeds here have a poor time of it vying with the abundance of underplanting and ground-cover plants (which leave hardly an inch of naked soil), on both of which she was an authority. She also made a speciality of 'foliage' plants and those with variegated leaves. Flower arrangers love it and often beg for seed heads or for a leaf or two of her beautiful Lambrook Silver Artemisia to add an unusual note. It is only a small garden of an acre and a half, of what is called the informal cottage-garden type, but you can wander in it for hours, there is so much to see. It is indeed a plantsman's garden, and what a joy to come across such old-fashioned things as the double primrose – Jack-in-the-Green or Hose-in-Hose. There are special collections of hellebores, euphorbias, primroses and snowdrops, with a herb garden and a terrace garden, in all a perfect setting for the small fifteenth-century manor house. You come away from it with the feeling that you want to rush back and see it all over again.

Exbury Gardens

Zone Centre: Salisbury, Route 3

Owner: Edmund L de Rothschild, Esq

When any serious gardener, amateur or professional, points to a rhododendron and pronounces the name 'Exbury', you know you are looking at something good. For Exbury Gardens are the home of the great de Rothschild hybrids, and here you can see them growing in the family's two-hundred-and-fifty-acre woodland near Southampton which is part of a larger estate. It was the late Lionel de Rothschild who started it all in the 1920s. It took a task force of two hundred and fifty men to clear the area he wanted to plant. In May 1922 he set about creating his garden, putting in the whole of the key plants himself. Basically it was rhododendrons, azaleas, magnolias and camellias, a spring garden, though there is plenty of colour in autumn from acers, berried shrubs and colouring trees. There are now a million plants in the garden, including twelve hundred hybrids of which nearly five hundred have been named. In May, at their best time of flowering, as many as 36,000 people come to see them. No wonder, for the walk through this rhododendron woodland is a sequence of joyful surprises as you come upon Charlotte de Rothschild and Mouton Rothschild, Exbury Naomi and Exbury Fabia in their springtime glory: Charlotte with heavy trusses of fourteen flowers on long red-stained stalks, the throat of each whitish pink bell speckled with chocolate, frilly lobes completing her dress; Mouton with bright red waxy flowers; Fabia an attractive orange-pink; and variations of Naomi, pale pink to rich rose with undertones of yellow. And to see gorgeous-flowered rhododendrons reflected in the pool at Exbury is something not to be missed.

Forde Abbey

Zone Centre: Weymouth, Route 3

Owner: The Roper Family Trust

Surrounding one of the loveliest houses in England, a perfectly preserved Cistercian abbey unaltered and complete, are fifteen acres of superb gardens and lakes on the River Axe. They were begun a century ago when many interesting trees were planted. Rock and water gardens and herbaceous borders were added early in this century, but it is due to the work of Mr G D Roper, the present owner, that the beauty of the gardens has come to fulfilment. It is true to say that no shrub, tree or other plant is forgotten that can provide a link in his design of colour, form and texture, either as an individual or as part of the general effect. Unusual conifers are a feature and underplanting is lavish: there are for instance three acres of *Crocus versicolor* and in the same woodland a sheet of anemones. Azaleas and rhododendrons make a bold display. A splash of blue in the shade brings you to admire a group of willow gentians, while a magnolia with two thousand flowers is evidence of the gardening skill given to each plant. There are many fascinating features such as the Beech House Mr Roper planted in 1932. Cottage-shaped and on the edge of a pond beloved by wildfowl it has a 'window' cut for bird-watchers and provides a perfect hide.

Great Chalfield Manor

Zone Centre: Bath, Route 1

Owner: The National Trust

If you would like to see something of an English garden complementary to a fifteenth-century manor house, a visit to Great Chalfield will provide you with this happy experience. The moat and fish pond linger on from early days, and they are now attractively planted as bog and water gardens, providing a peaceful setting. Both house and garden have been saved for the nation by the National Trust.

The House-in-the-Wood, Bartley

Zone Centre: Salisbury, Route 3

Owner: Mrs H E Spink

This is a garden-in-a-wood too – it is in the New Forest – and on acid soil, hence the great displays of rhododendrons and deciduous azaleas which are a speciality here with other choice ornamental shrubs and trees. In moister places drifts of primulas have naturalised themselves, as have the beautiful blue-faced meconopsis. It was here that the many pink forms (known as the Bartley strain) of the candelabra primrose (*Primula pulverulenta*) were produced. The garden was made by Hugh Dalrymple who created out of the original woodland the walks where you can wander and the glades where shrubs could be grouped in massive plantings. The garden's year begins early with a wonderful show of naturalised daffodils.

Hungerdown House

Zone Centre: Bath, Route 3

Owners: Major and Mrs Egbert Barnes

One of the most delightful corners in Wiltshire is this four-acre garden originally designed by Percy Cane as a setting for the charming Regency house. From the paved terrace here you will notice at once the alpine wall where, without stooping or bending, the gardener may happily weed and plant. Steps lead down to a lower terrace whence the garden slopes into semi-woodland where clematis runs riot and young sorbus trees promise colourful leaves and berries for many an autumn to come. If you like species and old shrub roses, herbaceous borders flowering as profusely in autumn as in summer, and wish to see the exquisiteness of a Japanese cherry walk, here you will find them. A small wild garden has been specially planted for autumn colour. But in fact you will find it quite as attractive from May onwards. The terraces make good vantage points for views overlooking the valley of Bristol's Avon and the Marlborough Downs. The whole is a garden of great interest and commendable for the use made of different levels, and you will long remember those clematis throwing mantles of blue, pink and purple over branches, poles and shrubs. In spring, if you come then, you will find the grassland under the sorbus trees a carpet of crocuses, daffodils and bulbocodiums.

Hyde Crook

Zone Centre: Weymouth, Route 3

Owners: Major and Mrs P R A Birley

The garden was laid out in 1936 by W J Bean, the shrub expert of Kew, and Dr Wilfrid Fox of Winkworth. As might be expected it is therefore an informal woodland garden which you will see at its best in April when the Japanese cherries are in flower with magnolias, camellias and azaleas, and daffodils and narcissi carpet the woodland slopes. Other flowering trees and shrubs add up to a garden superbly planted for colour and effect, and there are two orchid houses well worth seeing.

Jermyns House Garden and Arboretum

Zone Centre: Salisbury, Route 4

Owner: H G Hillier, Esq

This is Mr Hillier's own garden, as distinct from his world-famous nurseries, so you can imagine that it contains his special favourites which, among the shrubs, are rhododendrons (here planted in their series), camellias and magnolias, and, among the trees, conifers, of which he has more than a thousand varieties dwarf and tall in his arboretum. In all there are at Jermyns between thirteen and fourteen thousand different species of plants. The garden is 'a home for plants'. Design is secondary (although the prospect from the front of the house is most attractive with its islands of shrubs, scree slopes and heathers rising up from the lawn). Plants come to him from all over the world. He puts them in just the situation they adopt in their native lands – shade or sun, shelter or out in the open, and in the soil that is right for them. There are two magnificent borders, two hundred and sixty yards long, where in eleven pairs of bays herbaceous plants alternate with roses. Each is backed by hollies of sixty different sorts. The scree, peat and bog gardens, with their moisture-loving plants, alpines and ericas, add interest and colour throughout the year. The visitor can see it all in a mile-long walk. Garden and arboretum cover an undulating area set in an out-lie of the New Forest surrounded by glorious beech trees.

Littlecote

Zone Centre: Salisbury, Route 4

Owner: D S Wills, Esq

Entirely unspoilt countryside in the beautiful Kennet
Valley is the setting for Littlecote which hides itself away
among wooded grounds. There is a large walled garden with
an inviting trout stream nearby. A Tudor mount is a relic
of the first garden there, for the historic manor house dates
back to *c* 1490.

Longleat

Zone Centre: Salisbury, Route 1

Owner: The Marquess of Bath

The gardens of the great Longleat have evolved through the centuries, the rural simplicity of the one created by Sir John Thynne (builder of Longleat in the sixteenth century) being replaced by elaborate parterres embellished with statues and fountains by Lord Weymouth, after whose death the place became a wilderness of unclipped hedges and over-grown paths. The third Lord Weymouth called in 'Capability' Brown and under his direction the formal gardens were swept away. We see it today as he planned it, the park an almost perfect example of his work, and the series of lakes with the small waterfall which replaced the canal or Long Leat. During the last war the garden had to be neglected but it has now been skilfully replanned with ornamental formal gardens, yew hedges and a pleached alley. And still remains the old orangery at the end of the formal gardens.

Longstock Park Water Gardens

Zone Centre: Salisbury, Route 4

Owner: The John Lewis Partnership

Every visitor to Longstock must feel when he comes upon it that he has made a personal discovery of this lovely aquatic place, so seemingly natural it is in its woodland setting, so apparently uncontrived by the hand of man. Yet here a liquidambar has been purposely planted behind a stretch of water long enough to reflect its full length when in autumn it blazes with colour, and there a distant planting of scarlet-twigged dogwoods draws the eye across a pool scattered with the white flowers of the water hawthorn. Paths follow a series of pools and small lakes, crossing by plank bridges rivulets which feed the nearby Test, so that at all times you can walk beside or be surrounded by water richly fringed with moisture-loving plants. There are bold groups of the giant-leaved *Gunnera manicata,* rare hostas, *Scirpus albescens* from which mats are made, and the golden grass named after E A Bowles of crocus fame. The water is gemmed with flowers of many species of water lilies, and beneath them swim enormous golden orfe. As a variation you may wander through the protective woodlands, predominantly oak and underplanted with rhododendrons, azaleas and other calcifuge shrubs, and carpeted with bulbs from early spring. A feature here are groups of the giant lily *Cardiocrinum giganteum,* ten feet tall, which takes seven years to flower and then dies. Forty different kinds of primula make brilliant patches of colour by pathway and waterside.

Minterne

Zone Centre: Weymouth, Route 3

Owner: The Lord Digby

This large shrub garden in a beautiful valley is famed for its rhododendrons of which at least one thousand different species (both Himalayan and Chinese) and hybrids are grown. They were developed by that most successful cultivator of the genus, the late Lord Digby, who was chairman of the RHS Rhododendron and Camellia Committee. The setting is among beech woods planted in the late eighteenth century. With magnolias, azaleas and Japanese cherry trees you will find a springtime wander through these woodlands unforgettable.

Montacute

Zone Centre: Weymouth, Route 1

Owner: The National Trust

The magnificent and beautiful house was begun in 1588 by Thomas Phelips. It can be seen from afar, dominating the landscape, its local Ham Hill stone weathered to honey-brown. The Elizabethan period lingers on in the balustraded forecourt garden on the north-east side with its two exquisite Tudor pavilions that are among the most perfect examples that remain to us. Gardeners at Montacute are aware of this heritage, and in the herbaceous borders planned by Victoria Sackville-West 'We match the colours to the stone of the house'. One of the finest macrocarpa hedges in the country can be seen here: it is one hundred and forty years old, and ranged round the greenest of lawns are ninety-four sentinel Irish yews.

Priory of Lady St Mary

Zone Centre: Weymouth, Route 2

Owners: Mr and Mrs J E Greenwood

As you can guess from its name this garden has old roots, so to speak, and there are plenty of old walls to use for climbing roses and clematis, while ruined parts of the Priory have been used to create little hidden gardens. Wide lawns (weed-free and velvet) slope down to the River Frome where pink hydrangeas are massed. There are four hundred different flowering shrubs, and a heather garden flowering in summer and winter. Unusual is the planting of interesting brooms among them. On one side running down to the river is a wide border with 'foliage' shrubs, silver plants and sedums. On the other side a herbaceous border has happy touches such as the silver leaves among delphiniums and sidalceas. There is a small and charming white garden hiding behind hedges in the angle of two walls, and those who like clematis will have plenty to admire, for there are fifty different kinds cascading everywhere. Even the walls of the boat house are decked with colour where a wistaria and a vine ramble together.

Pylewell Park

Zone Centre: Salisbury, Route 3

Owner: William Whitaker, Esq

Forty acres·of delightful woodland enclose a lake one mile in circumference, and it is all very romantic with an enchanting little wooden bridge spanning the mother stream. The garden stretches down to the Solent which you can glimpse at the bottom of a long grass ride. Pylewell is famous for its rhododendrons. It has a twenty-six-foot-tall *falconeri,* one of the great species rhododendrons brought back from the Himalayas in the last century by Sir Joseph Hooker, and a fine hybrid named 'WFH' after a former head gardener who raised it. Its leaves are dark and glossy, its flowers orange-scarlet. On the way to the lake you cross a stretch of sloping grass where date palms grow, so happy in their surroundings that they have multiplied themselves by root shoots. If they look rather odd in such an English setting as Pylewell their presence indicates the extreme mildness of the climate here which is almost frost-free. It was Mr Whitaker's father, William Ingham Whitaker, who developed the garden after he inherited Pylewell in 1892. He was one of the leading gardeners of the day, as the mature beauty of Pylewell shows evidence. Thirty different species of camellias are grown, eucryphia trees with their showers of white blossom, scarlet-fingered embothriums and many other beautiful flowering trees and shrubs.

Stourhead

Zone Centre: Salisbury, Route 1

Owner: The National Trust

The house was built in 1722 for Henry Hoare the banker, and he it was who created this masterpiece, transforming 'a barren waste' into what Horace Walpole described as 'one of the most picturesque scenes in the world'. The beauty of his great landscape garden is unforgettable, whether seen in spring or early summer when the rhododendrons are in bloom, or clothed in its autumnal glory of flaming acers, beeches, nyssas, swamp cypresses – beauty twice given when form and colour are reflected in the water. For the heart of Stourhead is its three-armed lake which was formed from old fish ponds. A walk goes round it all the way, unrolling a panorama of splendid trees and vistas framing temples and other conceits of a great garden placed unerringly where they will best please the eye. A stone bridge across one finger of the lake leads to the Temple of Flora and to the grotto with its mighty River God whence flow the springs which are the source of the River Stour. You follow on to the rural thatched Watch Cottage, and to the Pantheon designed by Henry Flitcroft who took his inspiration from the Pantheon at Rome. Here are statues of a Muse and a Dionysos, and in its inner hall the Hercules by Michael Rysbrack, a Flora by him, a marble figure of Livia Augusta from Herculaneum, and other figures. 'Few buildings,' wrote Horace Walpole, 'exceed the magnificence, taste and beauty of the Temple'. Beyond, an iron bridge leads you to a fourteen-acre lake made by Sir Richard Colt Hoare and on to the circular Temple of the Sun. The walk round Stourhead with time to examine these artifacts and marvel at each vista is a pleasant hour's stroll which surely must be an hour stolen from paradise. For this is not only one of England's greatest gardens, it is supremely the Dream Garden come to reality.

Tintinhull House

Zone Centre: Weymouth, Route 1

Owner: The National Trust

It is sheer delight, a series of small gardens in four acres beautifully planned and planted. It was made by the late Mrs F E Reiss and given by her to the National Trust. Garden leads to garden, from the terrace with its wall climbers and stone pots filled with *regale* lilies and hydrangeas to the White Garden and the formal garden with its pool, loggia and flanking borders backed by yew hedges. Mrs Reiss chose each plant with loving care, to add to the right place something definite in colour, form or texture. Each border has its own individual character, one triumphant with bright clear colours, another dreamy with pastel tints. Her mixed borders are truly so, shrubs, flowers and foliage-plants, ornamental grasses and even small trees, all living happily together. The whole is a successful demonstration of how a modest space can be used effectively to provide all we ask of a garden – peace among flowery loveliness, where nature and a good gardener have worked together to create a living tapestry.

Vine House

Zone Centre: Bath, Route 4

Owners: Prof and Mrs T F Hewer

The two acres of this labour-saving 'natural' garden are notable for the fact that they contain many plants collected by the owners, Professor and Mrs Hewer, in Europe, North Africa and the Middle East (Turkey and the Lebanon). Shrub-bordered lawns lead into a wooded glade and water garden. There are special collections of *Paeonia lutea* × *delavayi* hybrids, tree paeonies up to five feet tall with saucer-shaped flowers of deepest crimson blooming in May; primulas, which flower from March till September, and hundreds of cyclamens in the shade of great yews.

Wilton House

Zone Centre: Salisbury, Route 1

Owner: The Earl of Pembroke

On the twenty-five acres of magnificent lawn stands the finest collection of cedars in Britain, many of them planted by British and visiting royalties. You can read their names on plaques. The oldest has weathered two centuries. The extent of lawn puzzled one Australian who, while full of admiration, remarked: 'But – my, what a waste of land!' For it pastures no sheep or deer. Beyond, an elaborate Palladian bridge spans the River Nadder. Covered with an Ionic colonnade with small temples at either end, it was built in 1737 by the 'architect Earl', Henry Herbert ninth Earl of Pembroke and his protégé Roger Morris. The river is fast-moving and is a trout stream. Nearby grows a beautiful Golden Oak (*Quercus pedunculata* var. *concordia*), the best specimen in the country. There are other interesting trees such as a Scented Ash, and along by the river are plantings of choice shrubs: *Dipelta yunnanensis,* its flowers cream-coloured with orange markings, a pieris also from Yunnan, the shrub whose young shoots of pink and scarlet never fail to attract attention. And no collection of shrubs would be complete without a *Rhus cotinus,* the Smoke Bush or Wig Tree, especially the purple-leaved variety which at Wilton makes a handsome bush. A most decorative archway, to the right of the house at the end of a long walk, is the Holbein Porch (built in 1553 which once stood in the forecourt and served as the entrance). Students and architects can apply to examine it. There is a long border of viburnums and sweet-smelling plants, and a good herbaceous border against a fine wall which is a favourite subject for photographers, especially when the climbers are in bloom and the leaves of the delightful *Actinidia kolomikta* are splashed white, pink and green. A garden to see and enjoy.

Yaffle Hill

Zone Centre: Salisbury, Route 2

Owner: Cyril Carter, Esq

First let me explain, if you do not already know it, that a yaffle is a woodpecker, and as you come down the woodland drive to the house you can see a very gaily painted one above the front door. The house is modern, built in 1930 by its present owner, and the garden he created demonstrates hearteningly the growth that can be obtained in a short span of years. It is mostly informal with grass paths winding round plantings of unusual trees and shrubs, particularly conifers (*Abies pinulosa*, the Sikkim Spruce, grows here), rhododendrons, azaleas and heathers. A speciality is the range of eighteen different species of sorbus, including *S rochiano*, the last one to be introduced from China. The setting is a slope of the hills north of Poole Harbour. See its six acres at their best in spring for the flowering shrubs, and in autumn for the blaze of coloured leaves and berries. Another collection is of dwarf conifers, and there are some interesting alpines grown both outside and in a cold greenhouse. Do not miss seeing the Dell before you leave. Its unbelievably well-grown trees are another example of what can be done well within a lifetime.

Also open is :

DODINGTON HOUSE AND PARK **(Zone Centre:
Bath, Route 3. Owner: Major S F B Codrington)** where
you will find a magnificent 'Capability' Brown park designed
as a setting for the James Wyatt Regency mansion. Wherever
Brown worked he created a lake, and here there are two, one
flowing into the other over a cascaded waterfall. A large
number of fine trees complete his picture. There is a small
rose and herbaceous garden. A new house-plant exhibit in
the large conservatory will be a permanent and enjoyable
feature.

Open occasionally are :

BRAMDEAN HOUSE. **Zone Centre: Salisbury, Route 4.
Owners: Mr and Mrs C H Feilden)** whose three-acre
garden is beautifully planned and planted, full of charm and
colour. Contemporary with the early Georgian house it
began life in 1742, but its present owners have added greatly
to its interest and have in fact re-created it. A wide daffodil
walk through the orchard is a delight in spring, and in summer
the four long wide borders which form the garden's main
axis are a tapestry of colour and texture most carefully
chosen, tall silver-leaved thistles (*Onopordon arabicum*)
complementing the blue of Pacific delphiniums, creamy
Spiraea gigantea side by side with blue-mauve and pink-
mauve campanulas. This is typical of the whole garden.
Every corner is satisfyingly planted, and there are roses
enough to keep a Redouté busy for a lifetime. I saw Bramdean in drenching rain, but I think of it glowing in sunshine.

CERNE ABBEY **(Zone Centre: Weymouth, Route 3. Owner: Pamela, The Lady Digby)** is important for its herbaceous borders and flowering trees and shrubs including rhododendrons, which can be enjoyed from March onwards. In the grounds are the remains of a fifteenth-century guest- and gatehouse.

HEADBOURNE WORTHY GRANGE **(Zone Centre: Salisbury, Route 4. Owner: Diana, Lady Strathcona)** is a three-acre plantsman's garden originally made by the Hon Lewis Palmer, FLS, VMH, who achieved excellent results on a cold chalk soil. A rich variety of plants make each season interesting, and cyclamens, one speciality, flower almost all the year round. Principally it is the home of the famous 'Headbourne Hybrids', a hardy strain of the blue African Lily developed by Lewis Palmer.

HINTON AMPNER **(Zone Centre: Salisbury, Route 4. Owner: Ralph Dutton, Esq)** is one of Britain's great gardens to be seen if you can. A classical beauty of lay-out and ornament in the French and English styles, planted by a connoisseur. Favourite old flowers and new ones, with a large selection of lime-tolerant shrubs and shrub roses. There are good trees.

LITTLE CHEVERELL HOUSE **(Zone Centre: Bath, Route 1. Owner: Joyce, Lady Crossley)** has a five-and-a-half acre garden laid out one hundred and fifty years ago but recently replanted with unusual shrubs, herbaceous and rock plants. There is an exceptionally fine *Stranvaesia davidiana salicifolia* and a collection of eleagnus of different kinds.

MONKS REST **(Zone Centre: Salisbury, Route 4. Owners: Brigadier and Mrs P R Henderson)** is a tiny half-acre garden whose merit is that it demonstrates what can be done on chalk. It is botanically interesting and full of unusual plants, some from the Watson and Furse expeditions. Alpines are grown in raised beds and there are special collections of hostas, foliage plants and alliums.

SEALES FARM (Zone Centre: Bath, Route 3. Owner: Lt-Col R B Moseley) has two acres landscaped and planted from 1958, attractive features being its rock and water garden and a large herbaceous border. Duck enjoy this garden, too: the collection of water-fowl includes forty different species.

ZONE 4   Devon and The Cornish Riviera.

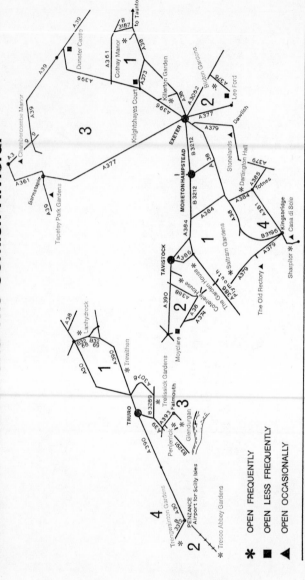

* OPEN FREQUENTLY

■ OPEN LESS FREQUENTLY

▲ OPEN OCCASIONALLY

ZONE 4

Devon and the Cornish Riviera

DEVON, CORNWALL AND the Isles of Scilly – here are romantic names, conjuring up pictures of smugglers (and the road to Land's End passes Jamaica Inn, made famous by Daphne du Maurier), of holiday coves where the blue Atlantic meets the red rocks that bastion Devon's rich ploughlands, of the Moor with its granite tors so terrifying to our ancestors, of luxuriant vegetation where sub-tropical plants grow as in their native homes.

Cornwall and Devon are rhododendron country, and almost every garden features these beautiful shrubs from the Himalaya and China. Yet each garden is different. There are hundreds and hundreds of kinds ranging in colour through the entire rainbow, white to deepest purple; yellows, reds, oranges; and to see them at Killerton, for instance, is a quite different experience from seeing them at Trewithen, growing on a hillside in one, in woodland glades in the other. Equally, of course, you could say it was camellia country, or magnolia. . . .

Again the garden at Tresco is different: it is in the realm of the fabulous, for here you will see plants that grow nowhere else in Britain. As a collection of exotics it is unrivalled – it is unbelievable – and all in the setting of an island fifty miles out in the Atlantic where longshore waters are sapphire. To reach Tresco is simple, by boat if you choose but far easier by helicopter and the ferry from St Mary's.

You will notice as you drive along the Bodmin road lonely fort-like towers here and there in the hills, with winding machinery. They are for tin and copper mining operations. China-clay, too, is mined in Cornwall, most of it for export to America. Otherwise it is all Devon cider and green lanes, and Cornish clotted cream.

Bicton Gardens

Zone Centre: Exeter, Route 1

Owner: The Clinton Devon Estates

This is a garden to spend the day in with the children; where to take Granny; where to see fine old trees, some the largest of their kinds in Britain; where if it rains you can dive into Tropical, Temperate and Cool glasshouses to see a collection of desert plants such as flowering cacti, and the exotic bougainvillea and Bird of Paradise plant, lemon trees, pineapples, ginger and pepper; where you can wander for hours in woodlands and by lakeside; where, besides, you can enjoy a really beautiful garden, part of which was designed by André Le Nôtre who also planned the gardens at Versailles. Bicton covers forty-three acres and the best way to get an overall view is to take a ride on the little narrow-gauge railway. The manor of Bicton was granted by Henry I to John Janitor for looking after the gaol at Exeter Castle. More recently the Rolle family lived here, and it was Henry Rolle, created Baron Rolle of Stenenstone in 1748, who made the Italian Gardens on Le Nôtre's design. This is the long greensward you see, enclosing a rectangular pool with a four-tiered fountain bounded on three sides by a canal fed from the lake in the park. No flowers grow here, though plenty grow elsewhere in herbaceous borders and beds. Its beauty is the peaceful green setting and the charm of the lead shepherd and shepherdess who stand there. A museum of shells at the top of the garden will interest you. The display cabinets are lit inside to show them in all their colours, and looking at the exquisite pink Queen Conch you feel you are glimpsing a garden of the sea.

Cotehele House

Zone Centre: Tavistock, Route 2

Owner: The National Trust

The terraced garden looks down a valley to the River Tamar, a steep valley that is a natural rockery planted with dwarf rhododendrons merging into bigger ones and into glorious trees. You reach it by a short tunnel in the garden, emerging into a scene breathtaking with colour. Following the path you come upon a curious stone dovecote shaped like a beehive, and reaching the bottom the Tamar is before you. In spring the slopes on the south side of the house are a sea of daffodils. There are interesting trees. In the upper garden where Neptune presides over a pond are a Golden Ash and a Tulip Tree. Pink and red roses make a wonderful display. Elsewhere there is a Chinese Coffin Tree, and you can see many uncommon shrubs against the garden wall – a mimosa (*Acacia dealbata*) usually grown indoors, and the famous Macartney rose with its large single white flowers. Camellias follow the daffodils and are in bloom here for six or seven weeks. One of the most attractive features of the garden are the terraces where bands of flower colour light up the grey old stone of the house. The wall supports two large magnolias, *M soulangeana* and *M rustica rubra,* the first white, the second stained with rosy purple. Cotehele is a fortified manor house dating back to the fourteenth century. It was the home of the Edgcumbes, famous in history for their courage.

Cothay Manor

Zone Centre: Exeter, Route 1

Owner: Mrs Astley-Rushton

A topiary and roses garden typically English in character, it was laid out in 1926 by Col Reginald Cooper on the architectural feature of a long yew corridor with gardens opening off it: herbaceous on the left, roses on the right where a bronze-leaved violet grows, irises and hellebores, more roses, and a kitchen garden. From the terrace of the house stone steps lead down into a pretty little fountain garden of clipped box knot beds. Below, the grassland slopes to the River Tone where in open woodland carpeted with bulbs many good shrubs have been planted. Cothay Manor has been described as 'the most perfect small fifteenth-century country house that survives in the Kingdom'. The approach to it is idyllic: you drive up to see it mirrored in a large pond full of ornamental ducks. The rest of it nestles among flowers. Lawns and a courtyard garden complete an attractive picture.

Dartington Hall

Zone Centre: Exeter, Route 4

Owner: Dartington Hall Trustees

This is basically a spring and autumn garden, but it is interesting all the year round for its highly individual features. It was planned in 1933 by Mrs Beatrix (Max) Aarrand, the American counterpart of Miss Gertrude Jekyll. Part of the mansion goes back to the fourteenth century and there is a tiltyard made by John Holland, Duke of Exeter, who was half-brother to Richard II and a jouster of international fame. Mr and Mrs Elmhirst who founded Dartington as a cultural centre have turned the tiltyard into an open-air theatre. Its rectangular grassed terraces are spectacular, and the row of twelve Irish yews known as the Twelve Apostles which stand on one side of it look almost as if they were queueing to get in. Around it are trees and shrubs chosen for their autumn colouring, such as red oaks, parrotias and maples, and opposite the house is a large heather garden through which a wide flight of stone steps goes up into the hillside. Spaciousness is the keynote of the garden, where serpentine paths trick the measure of distance and vistas carry the eye forward – to the little Temple, to a view of the Hall or a glimpse of a piece of sculpture. A glade leads to an ancient terrace lined with four-hundred-year-old Spanish chestnuts, at the end of which is Henry Moore's *Reclining Woman*. After the war Percy Cane was called in to remake the garden. He used the natural contours of the land to create architectural features, such as the viewpoint over miles of countryside which was turned into a circular eyrie. Plant material was chosen to accentuate the same natural features, good specimens of ornamental trees to balance the mature specimens of native trees. The Dell is full of azaleas and the woodland of rhododendrons. Because of the mild Devon climate tender hybrids can grow out in the open, such as crosses of the fragrant Lady Alice Fitzwilliam and Princess Alice rhododendrons. Dartington Hall has even produced its own, a form of *R augustinii* with flowers that are almost true blue.

Dunster Castle

Zone Centre: Exeter, Route 3

Owner: Mrs G F Luttrell

The massive turreted and battlemented castle, dating from 1070, is setting enough for any garden, and because this is the mild West Country you find lemon trees, date palms and other sub-tropical trees growing with hardier ones such as the attractive Handkerchief Tree because of its large white flowers which are really bracts. The River Avil passes the grounds with a picturesque old mill beside it. Herbaceous borders are bright with blue and yellow flowers – blue anchusas and agapanthus lilies, yellow achilleas and solidagos, centaureas and echinops, and the grey-leaved anaphalis dotted with yellow buttons. The gardens surround the high tor on which the castle stands. They are famous for magnificent views.

The Garden House, Buckland Monochorum

Zone Centre: Tavistock, Route 1

Owner: Lionel Stanhope Fortescue, Esq

You come along the drive to the square solid house which gives not a hint of what lies behind it. A pleasant lawn, a few nice old trees and banks of shrubs. Then you go down a path beside a high wall, open a little gate and turn – to see a torrent of flowers cascading in steep terraces to your feet. Thus you can see the whole garden either from the bottom, where there is a most decorative fourteenth-century tower, or from the top. The tower has a granite spiral staircase and is all that remains of the old vicarage in which the former Abbot of Buckland was installed after the Dissolution. In summer it becomes a mound of clematis and roses. The age of the original terracing is unknown. Certainly the garden is an old one, but the main planting was begun by the Fortescues in 1945. They have used a variety of hedging to achieve different effects and made architectural use of the quick-growing *Cupressocyparis leylandii*. The rectangular terraces have grass paths backed by borders. Exploring them is a floral adventure, for among the more familiar perennials are tender plants suited only to a climate like Devon's. The flowering shrubs add up to an extensive collection and include good forms of rhododendrons and azaleas, camellias, deutzias, skimmias and philadelphus. In the more shaded parts of the garden meconopsis and primulas grow. Effective use is made of agapanthus and varieties of day lilies. It is a garden beautiful from spring to autumn, from March when *Erythronium tuolumnense* in the Dog's-tooth Violet family makes bright patches of yellow starry trumpets branching from lily-of-the-valley leaves. The setting is the small valley of a stream running into the River Tavy.

Glendurgan

Zone Centre: Truro, Route 3

Owner: The National Trust

Scenically this is perhaps the most beautiful of the Cornish gardens, though in saying this I run the risk of being flatly contradicted, for they are all beautiful and each has its individual appeal. Certainly no walk to any Cornish cove could be more lovely, winding through a woodland of grand trees punctuated with flashes of colour from the rhododendrons for which Cornish gardens are famous. On the way down is a two-hundred-year-old laurel maze which, believe it or not, is one and a quarter miles in and out! Then there is the little islanded lake, once the delectable spot where the Fox children used to picnic. Glendurgan was laid out by Alfred Fox in the 1700s and has been cared for by successive generations of the family including the present Mr P H Fox. The height of some of the trees bears witness to their good planting: an eighty-six-foot-high *Taxodium distichum pendulum*, the weeping form of the beautiful Swamp Cypress which first came to England in the seventeenth century, a sixty-foot-high *Acer campestre*, commonly called the 'Hedge Maple', its foliage turning a clear yellow in autumn, and among the conifers a sixty-five-foot-tall Chinese Fir of emerald green foliage which in autumn turns a gorgeous bronze. There is a wealth of magnolias and rhododendrons, and some of the camellias are over one hundred years old. You will see them in the Camellia Walk. The end of the woodland path leads you to the tiny village of Durgan, a handful of houses round a little cove on the Helford River estuary, and coming back on the other side of the stream children will delight in the Giant's Stride, a sort of maypole where for generations children have swung on ropes. Continuing on you will find glorious herbaceous borders.

Killerton Garden

Zone Centre: Exeter, Route 1

Owner: The National Trust

This is a garden of beautiful lawns sweeping into a hillside, with magnificent views over the Devon countryside to the heights of Dartmoor. It is planted with shrubs and trees which are not just 'shrubs and trees', for many were grown from the original seeds sent home from the great plant-hunting expeditions of the last century and this, new and exciting things like the Arboreum rhododendrons which grow to tree size and cover themselves with blooms through all the pinks to startling blood-red. I remember one at Killerton decked out in pink and looking as pretty as a Christmas tree. There is a *Sequoia wellingtonia*, the Big Tree of America, which grows high up on the hillside here. It too came from the original packet of seeds, and it is worth climbing up to see it, especially with the bonus reward of superb views from the Dolbury where you can trace the remains of late Iron Age earthworks ringing the crest of the hill. When Walt Disney drew a Cork Tree he had it hanging with champagne corks. Here you will see the real thing in *Quercus suber*. There is a group of them; and when the sun shines on their trunks, the corky bark turns bright gold. Killerton is packed with beauty like this. It was all started in 1825 by Sir Thomas Acland, helped by his tenant Robert Veitch who was to become the famous nurseryman responsible for introducing so many new plants to this country (his first nursery was at Killerton). Since then every generation of the Acland family has made its contribution to the garden. One is the rock garden, made in a quarry, where you will see a curious stone pillar: it came from the Giant's Causeway in County Antrim and was brought back stone by stone. Among the trees is a specimen of *Chamaerops humilis,* the only species of palm native to Europe: its home is Spain, Sicily and North Africa. Alongside the terrace is a big herbaceous border, at its best in July, the terrace itself a sea of colour with dwarf flowering shrubs and such ever-green plants as the big-leaved bergenias which put forth their handsome pink spikes in the earliest spring days, lavenders and Cotton Lavender, the beautiful white-spired *Yucca filamentosa* and *Y flaccida* from the south-eastern United States. Before you the lawn stretches away in spaci-ousness to the trees, with glorious mounds of rhododendrons smothered in bloom in the spring, a season when Killerton is full of flowers – camellias, magnolias, azaleas, sheets of daffodils and showers of cherry blossom. The rhododendrons start in February and go on till July when the eucryphias one after the other join the pageant, snowy with bloom till the berries and leaves start to colour.

Knightshayes Court

Zone Centre: Exeter, Route 1

Owner: Sir John Amory, Bt

It is a garden in a wood, a truly lovely garden, and a family garden where the present owner's grandfather – who rode to hounds – cut a topiary frieze the length of the terrace, accurately depicting a fox fleeing from the advancing pack. The garden is still in the making. Sir John and Lady Amory are ardent gardeners who never cease planning and planting fresh beauty. When Sir John hears of a new tree or shrub he does not rest till he has a specimen growing – and thriving – at Knightshayes. You go past informal beds of dwarf shrubs – patches of white azaleas and heathers in beds fringing a lawn, and up into the woodland where in early summer you can see four hundred blue poppies out at once in a glade. There are blue anemones, hellebores and trilliums, a mass of periwinkles white, blue and purple, a *Magnolia salicifolia* that is a pyramid of white blooms; and here the trees act as props for climbing roses, and there you will see the pink snowflake flowers of a *Rhododendron pentaphyllum*. It is the loveliest garden in a wood I have ever seen. Other plants are chosen for the beauty of their bark, such as *Acer senkaki* which is pink all winter. Below the terrace, grassland goes far down the garden as a home for groups of rare rhododendrons and shrubs. Not forgetting the collection of trough gardens, the little scree garden bright blue with gentians from Christmas onwards, and in the formal gardens one with a circular pool surrounded by battlemented hedges lying below the woodland and reflecting a mirrorful of colour.

Lanhydrock

Zone Centre: Truro, Route 1

Owner: The National Trust

Lanhydrock was originally one of the many possessions of the great Priory of St Petroc at Bodmin. In 1642 the present house replaced the old monastic barton, but you can still see the monks' holy well and their tithe barn, parts of which date from the fifteenth century. The modern garden was made about 1860, and replanting began in 1930 when flowering shrubs and flowering trees were added to the existing plantings, one of which was the tree-like *Rhododendron arboreum*, the shrub introduced into England in 1820. It has found itself so happy in Cornwall and Devon that it seeds almost as freely as a weed. People in the next-door county call it the 'Devon Pink'. In Cornwall it is known as 'The Old Cornish Red' and it grows all over Lanhydrock in great outsize bushes of glorious colour. There are twenty-two acres of garden and two hundred acres of woodland, with wonderful views as far as Dartmoor. Everything is grown to exhibition standard in the formal and informal gardens and in the woodland where rhododendrons and magnolias make a specially gorgeous show: in 1968 Lanhydrock won an RHS silver-gilt medal for the best display of flowering shrubs, trees and climbers. Magnolias grown are *M veitchii*, *M acuminata* – called the 'Cucumber Tree' because of the shape of its fruits – which has sweet-scented canary-yellow flowers, and *M mollicomata* whose flowers are like large rose-purple water lilies. It is worth a special pilgrimage in spring to see them. In the Higher Garden grow many of the summer-flowering shrubs and there is a small garden below laid out by Lady Robartes a century ago, full of roses and familiar flowers. In the 1930s an old greenhouse there was converted to a pillared shelter. It is hung with clematis.

Lee Ford

Zone Centre: Exeter, Route 2

Owners: Mr and Mrs B M Lindsay-Fynn

If you visit Lee Ford in the spring you will come up the drive to be greeted suddenly by a sea of daffodils almost lapping the old grey stones of the house. All the opening times have been chosen to let visitors see the garden at the height of its various flowering seasons. During March and April camellias, rhododendrons and magnolias are all out with the bulbs, the rhododendrons following on to June when

131

brooms are in flower with laburnums and lilacs, displays of arum lilies, flowering shrubs and roses. The apple orchards are a lovely sight. September brings the dahlias. Begonias and hydrangeas, lilies and roses are still in flower. There are walks through woodland glades of fine beeches, turkey oaks, elms and chestnuts, and there you can see many of the beautiful rhododendrons. The forty acres include both formal and informal gardens.

Moyclare

Zone Centre: Tavistock, Route 2

Owners: Mr and Mrs Louis Reid

This is a garden with a personality, a small garden of one acre in which the dedicated Mrs Reid grows a bewildering number of familiar and uncommon plants. There are eighty different kinds round the fairly small lawn including such decorative things as the scarlet-flowered embothrium, an ornamental crab, a green-tasselled *Garrya elliptica*, a *Pinus radiata*, an *Enkianthus campanulatus*, a six-year-old euca-lyptus raised from seed and the blue-foliaged *Cedrus atlantica* – all worth growing. In her 'Half-circle and Plunging Bed' she has ninety more, everything from the succulent *Sedum spectabile*, hostas and heathers, azaleas and camellias, to a *Myrtus luma,* that beautiful red-barked myrtle from Chile, and growing on and against the house are twenty-four different climbers and wall shrubs. Yet nothing is cluttered, though because Mrs Reid does not like the red Devon earth as a background she grows a variety of ground-cover plants which all merge happily together. And there is a bit of every sort of garden, round the far side even a strip of woodland. It is well laid out and full of ideas, as her use of bamboo sticks, leaves and all, woven through pig netting as a wind filter, and her placing of an *Eleagnus glabra* (with bronze undersides) beside an *Eleagnus macrophylla* (with silver undersides). A shrub I liked very much was of her own growing, her 'Pink Pearl' sport of a *Berberis darleyensis*. The Reids started the garden in 1927 on a bare plot of field, one-third of an acre. In 1936 they added an L-shaped piece and planted a *Pinus insignus* which now towers above the other trees. It shows what can be done.

Penjerrick

Zone Centre: Truro, Route 3

Owner: R Trench-Fox, Esq

A valley garden with a view of Falmouth Bay, it slopes gently down into woodlands where rhododendron bushes and trees look bright as a flock of parrots. Tree ferns here and there add another exotic note, and I shall always remember the Elysian scene of one Dicksonia sheltering under its feathery umbrella a host of white and chequered fritillaries.

133

There are exquisite corners in this garden and long stretches of beauty. There is the towering weeping Nothofagus (in the lower part of the garden, to which you cross by a bridge over the road), which is now the biggest in the country. Most of the twenty acres are woodland. In its shelter and in the mild Cornish climate no camellia needs to be cosseted. Year after year the magnolias put forth their blooms, shell-like and fragrant, and in summer and autumn the little philesia its rosy-red flowers. The white hoheria from New Zealand is another tender plant growing happily here, with the azara from Chile; and only in a garden like Penjerrick can *Dacrydium franklinii* thrive, a spruce-like tree from Australasia. The house and its terrace, bordered by small and larger rhododendrons and many other flowering shrubs, face the length of the woodland where all these treasures grow.

Saltram Gardens

Zone Centre: Tavistock, Route 1

Owner: The National Trust

People start coming to Saltram in daffodil time. There is a long straight avenue of limes whose grey columns are the perfect foil for their drifts spread around and for the white ribbons of narcissi lining the path. It leads up to the octagonal garden house known as The Castle, and in the other direction to the great house which is the largest country house in

Devon and Cornwall, though it has not been lived in since the 1750s. Its 291 acres are of park and woodland except for the formal garden with its herbaceous border 165 feet long by 15 feet wide where the flowers, including the interplanted shrub roses, are all of soft pastel shades. There is an orangery which really is what its name says. Oranges and lemons grow in tubs there and in summer are taken outside to be lined round the paving. It was begun in 1773 and finished two years later when orange trees were imported from Italy. By 1811 they were immense. In 1789 before they arrived, Queen Charlotte and the two princesses Augusta and Elizabeth visited Saltram for a twelve-day holiday. Fanny Burney who was Keeper of the Queen's Robes recorded in her diary the time spent 'very serenely in my favourite wood'. Commemorating the place there where she sat is Fanny's Bower. It commands a glorious view northwards up the valley of the Plym to the distant tors of Dartmoor.

Sharpitor

Zone Centre: Exeter, Route 4

Owner: The National Trust

This is a garden perched above the Salcombe estuary.
Standing in it and looking over the sapphire waters far below,
you cannot help feeling that it is all not quite real. The
house and the six acres of garden surrounding it are at the
very top of a steep winding road. Opening a handsome
wrought iron gate the beauty of the garden bursts upon
you. The head gardener will tell you it is a botanist's garden,
which is to say that each plant is worth looking at and that
most of them are out of the ordinary or grow specially well.
He will show you the forty-foot-high Camphor Tree and
will point out with pride the enormous *Magnolia campbellii*
which blooms in the second week of March. He will take
you along the path where the palm trees grow and a banana
tree which, however, does not bear fruit even in this balmy
Devon climate. There is an unusual euonymous from the
Himalaya (*fimbriatus*), coloured copper-pink and gold, and
a border of deep purple hellebores from Greece. The garden
steps down in a series of steep informal terraces clothed with
bloom. Above them a stone-pillared pergola balustrades a
formal garden of lawn with borders full of tender plants.
Just below in a special raised bed grows the magnificent
magnolia, visible far out at sea.

Trelissick Gardens

Zone Centre: Truro, Route 1

Owner: The National Trust

The sixteen acres of Trelissick's gardens give a tremendous feeling of spaciousness, with its expanse of lawns, wide avenues of beeches and oaks, and great plantings of species and hybrid rhododendrons, camellias, azaleas and magnolias which you can see in the hanging woods. The gardens go right down to the River Fal, which is always to be glimpsed through the trees. There are collections of astilbes and hostas, those moisture-loving plants becoming increasingly popular, the first for its plumes of bright pink and crimson, the other for its lovely mauve sprays of delicate flowers, some with variegated leaves. There are thousands of daffodils, anemones and other bulbs in the spring.

Trengwainton Gardens

Zone Centre: Truro, Route 4

Owner: The National Trust

The drive to the gardens is a first hint of Trengwainton's beauty. A small stream, once probably not more than a ditch, has been widened into pools joined by a series of little cascades and its banks planted with bright kingcups and mimulus, primulas and astilbes. Behind are broken clumps of bamboo, groups here and there of birches and rhododendrons, with gaps between to let your eyes wander into the woodland where there are bluebells and primroses, and later the beautiful Himalayan blue poppy. In the clearings rhododendrons catch the sun. The gaps become solid with them. Trengwainton is famous for these gorgeous shrubs, especially for the large-leaved species such as the incomparable *sinograwde* with its enormous trusses of creamy flowers, for *falconeri* with its beautiful rust-coloured undersides to the leaves, and for the tender species *maddenii* series whose flowers are funnel-shaped and waxy in texture, and often sweetly scented. Two other tender rhododendrons grow here which are usually only to be found in greenhouses: *R ciliicalyx* and *R taggianum,* the first with lovely wide-open white or pale rose-coloured flowers, the other pure white with a splash of yellow in the throat. There are hundreds of others, and though primarily a rhododendron garden in a natural woodland setting, there are Asiatic magnolias and mimosas and other Australasian shrubs rarely to be seen in inland gardens, with exotic tree ferns and plants such as the 'Cape Heath', *Erica canaliculata*. Some of these grow in a series of gardens enclosed on three sides by walls, with a path on the fourth side looking into each. Here in one grows the fascinating Chatham Isle Forget-me-Not, its waxy flowers of an intense blue, and you can easily find the red Australian Bottle Brush, the Japanese Bitter Orange, and the New Zealand ramarana which is a myrtle, for they are all clearly labelled. The view from the top of the garden is of St Michael's Mount and the Bay in which it lies. The garden was formed in the nineteenth century, but since 1926 Sir Edward Bolitho has transformed it. In his hands it has become one of Britain's loveliest gardens famous for the wealth of good plants he grows.

Tresco Abbey Gardens

Zone Centre: Truro, Route 2

Owners: Lt-Commander and Mrs T M Dorrien-Smith

Off the coast of Cornwall beyond Land's End lie the delectable Isles of Scilly, among them Tresco where between 1834 and 1872 Augustus Smith created a sub-tropical garden of sixty acres on a wind-blown peninsula. He arrived to find nothing much more than a granite hill and the solitary arches of Tresco Abbey built in AD 964. Round the ruin he laid out a small formal garden and built to the west a twelve-foot wall to shelter it, with a lower wall to the south. The plants flourished. He extended it and planted it with seeds he collected in distant lands. They all prospered and today Tresco is the most remarkable garden anywhere in the British Isles. His trees are now one hundred feet high. Nothing I could write could convey the astonishing beauty of the Tresco gardens, the fantasia of the plants and the exuberance of their growth, where palm trees are not self-conscious exhibits but growing as naturally as in their own warm climes. It is astonishing, for instance, to see cinerarias growing out of doors; to look for the first time at the red aerial roots streaming from the New Zealand *Metrosidaros tomentosa*, the great Pohoutakawa Tree; to come upon a group of red-pokered African aloes and absurd house leeks with flowers like the trunks of baby elephants. To illustrate how things grow, an *Echium pininanum* once produced a towering flower spike twenty-three feet long! It is a borage from the Canary Islands. Parts of the gardens go by the name of the countries whose plants grow in them – Mexico, Higher Australia and Lower Australia, so if you are interested in the flora of these countries you can see them concentrated there. The gardens are traversed by two great cross-walks – the Long Walk, and the Lighthouse Walk which has a dramatic view seawards down the Neptune Steps and on past the forty-foot-high ilex hedge which bisects it. At the foot of the steps two Canary Island date palms form an exotic archway. The Middle Terrace is where you will see the most interesting assembly of sub-tropical plants and where you will find lily ponds overhung by cordylines bearing their long fragrant flower trusses. Climbing up trees are a giant honeysuckle from Burma and the west Australian *Kennedya nigricans* with its somewhat sinister jet-black flowers. Above is the Agave Bank where one species grows and grows till it is forty years old and ready to produce its forty-foot-high flower spike, by which time its leaves have a wing-span of eighteen feet. This is the sort of weirdness you find at Tresco. Its lovelier beauties are in the clouds of mimosa blossom out at Christmas when England may be thick with snow; in the lacy-looking casuarinas; in the shining red boles of the *Myrtus luma* trees; and the silvery-grey stems of eucalyptus with their leaves grey-blue against the sky. I was told that July was a lovely month at Tresco. I saw it on an April day when surely it could not have been more beautiful.

Trewithen

Zone Centre: Truro, Route 1

Owner: Mrs Alison Johnstone

This lovely place is a personal garden, laid out by the great horticulturalist, the late G H Johnstone, OBE, VMH, who was an authority on Asiatic magnolias. He grew them with other wonderful shrubs in his woodland, skilfully cutting a series of paths into it and within it, so that visitors could enjoy seeing them. One of his most successful plantings was the handsome *M sargentiana* var. *robusta* with its petals rosy-crimson on the outside, paler within. Through the years he developed his own forms of different plants, from the wall shrub ceanothus producing the famous 'Trewithen Blue' which all gardeners show you with pride if they possess it. His 'Trewithen Orange' is a lovely example of his work on rhododendrons, and he was a great breeder of daffodils. He inherited Trewithen in 1908. There was only one shrub in the garden. Today it is a storehouse of treasures, one of which is his astounding specimen of *Rhododendron macabeanum* which Mrs Johnstone declares is 'the most photographed plant in England'! Certainly no one who sees it in April, a tower of soft yellow blooms, could resist taking a picture of it. Whatever Mr Johnstone grew he improved, carrying on the beauty of a species with his own variations. To walk into his woodland and see them all, to wander along paths bordered with daffodils that have new and exciting differences of colour and petal, is to share part of his adventures in gardening. So as to carry on the colour when the rhododendrons and camellias are over there is a delightful formal garden full of summer flowers.

Also open are:

CHAMBERCOMBE MANOR **(Zone Centre: Exeter, Route 3. Owner: L C L Pincombe, Esq)** which is in a beautiful setting of shrub and herbaceous borders. Lovely all the year round and with a herb garden.

THE OLD RECTORY, THURLESTONE **(Zone Centre: Tavistock, Route 1. Owner: R C Lake, Esq)** has four worthwhile acres of long herbaceous borders, island borders of flowering shrubs, lawns and trees. It is full of unusual plants and there is always something to see.

STONELANDS GARDENS **(Zone Centre: Exeter, Route 4. Owners: Mr and Mrs Gerald Moore)** is a large informal garden originally landscaped by 'Capability' Brown and then 'improved' by Humphry Repton. There are rhododendrons, azaleas, magnolias, cherries and maples, with river walks and fine trees in the woodland.

TAPELEY PARK GARDENS **(Zone Centre: Exeter, Route 3. Owner: The Christie Estate Trust)** was the home of the late John Christie who founded Glyndbourne; the gardens designed by his mother, the late Lady Rosamond Christie. They are in Italian style with terraces and statuary, and there is a magnificent view from the bowling green of the estuary of the Tor and Torridge rivers and the surrounding country. There are extensive woodland walks and many rare plants.

Open by special appointment:

CASA DI SOLE **(Zone Centre: Exeter, Route 4. Owner: Dr G Barker)** which is nicknamed 'Little New Zealand' because of its many Australasian plants including forty-six species of eucalyptus. Dr Barker has evolved a method of retaining rainwater, much needed in this exciting 1-in-3 gradient garden which overlooks the Salcombe estuary. He specialises in camellias and has over one hundred named varieties.

ZONE 5 The Cotswolds and Shakespeare's Country.

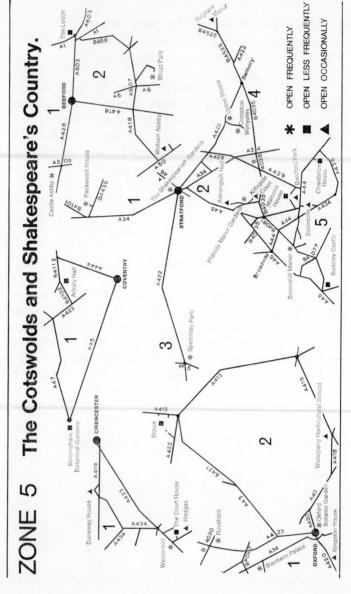

OPEN FREQUENTLY ✳

OPEN LESS FREQUENTLY ■

OPEN OCCASIONALLY ▲

ZONE 5

The Cotswolds and Shakespeare's Country

THE COTSWOLDS MEAN to those who know them a series of lovely old villages and market towns – Burford and Broadway, Chipping Campden and Chipping Norton ('Chipping' means market) – all built of the same golden stone as the city of Bath, and nestling in the valleys of gentle green hills. Sheep walks and arable fields bounded by dry-stone walls complete the country picture. You know by the very charm of the place that you are in 'the Cotswolds'.

Different is Shakespeare's Warwickshire with its black-and-white half-timbered houses. The fertile valleys of the Avon, the water meadows of its tributaries, the hedgerows of elm and stout English oak – this is the very heart of rural England. Shakespeare's Forest of Arden once covered a large part of the Midlands: enough is left in untouched stretches of woods and mossy corners to evoke the romantic scenes of *As You Like It*. Curious that only thirty miles away from Stratford should be Blenheim, birthplace of England's greatest son of modern times, Winston Spencer Churchill.

Oxford, from which centre you may be visiting Blenheim,

has been a town since Anglo-Saxon days and a seat of learning since the twelfth century. With the Dreaming Spires of its thirty-one colleges it is one of the world's most beautiful cities, its university Britain's oldest. It lies among meadows at the meeting place of the Cherwell and the Isis rivers, and in Magdalen Meadow you can see a rare sight in spring: a chequered-purple carpet of the Snake's Head Fritillary, first brought to England in the seventeenth century by John Tradescant the younger, from Virginia. At the Bodleian Library is to be seen the first guide to a Stately Home, the vellum book illustrated by Alexander Marshall showing the orchard fruits Tradescant's father grew at Hatfield House when he was gardener there in 1609–14. Just over Magdalen Bridge is the Oxford Botanic Garden, also Britain's oldest, where plant material is grown for some of the most advanced studies on plant diseases and genetics.

Admington Hall

Zone Centre: Stratford, Route 2

Owners: Lt-Col and Mrs G Horton

A delightful four-acre garden worth seeing for the pleasing simplicity of its lay-out. The spacious lawn reaches towards a small woodland where a lake reflects fine trees and the house itself, which is part seventeenth century and part Georgian. There grow great clumps of ligularias with their bold ragged-petalled golden flowers, some with green leaves, others with bronze. Between lake and house flows a small stream whose banks are gaily lined with all sorts of moisture-loving plants – tall yellow *Primula florindae,* mimulus, irises, with small groups of acers behind, a spread of green juniper to weld them and some dwarf conifers to give miniature height. In and around the woodland and along the walk behind the stream daffodils and other bulbs are a glad sight in spring, and by the house is a paved rose garden where one hundred varieties are grouped round a sundial and the deep blue clematis Beauty of Worcester drapes the wall. Set in the lawn are a pair of double herbaceous borders full of colour till the year's end. Canna lilies and *Lobelia cardinalis* and red and purple thistles with variegated leaves are arresting company for double white delphiniums, fuchsias and verbenas, penstemons and that classic flower of architecture, the acanthus. Shrubs mingle with them.

Arbury Hall

Zone Centre: Coventry, Route 1

Owner: F H FitzRoy Newdegate, Esq

The historical setting is part of the garden's attraction, for Arbury Hall is connected with many interesting people: Sir Richard Newdegate who in 1805 gave the Newdegate Prize for English verse; Mary Fitton, sometimes identified as the 'Dark Lady' of Shakespeare's sonnets, and Mary Ann Evans, better known as the novelist George Eliot who was born at a farm on the estate. All of them knew this garden well. It is attractive. Along by the lake is a bog garden planted for spring and early summer flowering, and there is an Easter Garden full of bulbs and alpines, a Bee Garden of shrubs and paeonies. Every year a ton and a half of bulbs are added. After them come the rhododendrons and azaleas – there are some good species rhododendrons in the wild garden. An old ruined orangery makes a picturesque background in the rose garden where terraced steps go down to a small lily pool with lead figures.

Birmingham Botanical Gardens

Zone Centre: Coventry, Route 1

Owner: The Birmingham Botanical and Horticultural Society Ltd

There are many interesting features about this botanic garden. It is less than a mile from the Bull Ring centre of Birmingham and much used by city workers as a lunchtime lung. The enterprising society which runs it takes every opportunity to interest them in their own gardens by planting the very best 'modern' trees and flowering shrubs, unusual hedges as alternatives to dreary old privet – *Cupressocyparis leylandii* for a quick-growing conifer, berberis for its berries and autumn leaves, rose hedges for their scent and Purple Plum for constant colour. In the large rock and water garden are good moisture-loving plants – a host of new primulas of all colours, pencil junipers for bringing height to the scene, varieties of water lilies to grow in your own pool. There are glorious beds of roses, all the new varieties, and lectures to attend in a glorified potting shed. In the collection of plants you can light on many new things. A second feature is the BBC Gardening Club Garden where for so many years Mr Percy Thrower has been seen on television working through the seasons. It is Everyman's dream garden with every sort of border and device for making the small garden useful and the envy of the Joneses. The Gardens are also interesting because they were laid out, in 1829, by John Claudius Loudon, one of the greatest chroniclers of plants that ever lived. His lawn sweeping down to the bandstand and his overall design have not been altered, and the Society has done what Loudon would have done – kept abreast of the times. An imaginative place and a lesson to many a botanic garden.

Blenheim Palace

Zone Centre: Oxford, Route 1

Owner: His Grace the Duke of Marlborough

Anybody who knows anything about Sir Winston Churchill knows he was born at Blenheim, that great and beautiful winged palace designed by Sir John Vanbrugh and the gift of the nation to John Churchill, First Duke of Marlborough, for his victory at the battle of that name. While surveying the Queen's bounty of the two-thousand-acre Woodstock Park to choose the site for the palace, Vanbrugh was also mentally designing the gardens. Everything must be the greatest. He had a romantic mind and it occurred to him that a Grand Bridge must span the marshland between the new edifice and the approach from Woodstock. To him the tiny trickle running through it was a river. It was not until 1764 that the river actually flowed, or rather in the capable hands of Lancelot Brown became a great curving lake, still the most magnificent private lake in the country. Brown knew it even then and swore that the Thames, into which the little Glyme flowed after joining the Evenlode, would never forgive him. Vanbrugh laid out a Great Parterre nearly half a mile long and as wide as the south front. Queen Anne lent her gardener, Henry Wise, to create it and an army of labourers moved in to build a battle scene all carried out in brick, stone and topiary. There were fountains as well, and the taste of the day pronounced it splendid, all except Sarah

Churchill for whom Vanbrugh had to make a flower garden on the east front of thousands of irises, hyacinths, carnations, narcissus and Brompton stocks. When Brown came he swept the Great Parterre away: the ten-acre lawn you see today on the south front is his 'naturalising' handiwork. It was left to the Ninth Duke to create the great water terraces which with the lake are Blenheim's chief glory. He had thought of them for years. Now he chose Achille Duchêne to design them. The Bernini river-gods fountain on the second terrace was a scale model for the famous fountain in Rome's Piazza Navona, given to the First Duke and treasured by the Ninth. He made it the key to the design, and there they lie – like a great parterre of water, baroque stonework holding a series of pools, between each an intricate pattern of boxwork on gravel, with the Bernini fountain in a lake of its own below. Seen from the Long Library the water terraces are a stupendous spectacle, and the lake seems to run from the edge of the top. As the Duke told Duchêne: 'It is certainly a stroke of genius on your part bringing the water line up to the first terrace. I certainly should not have thought of this idea myself, and I doubt if any English architect would have.'

Castle Ashby

Zone Centre: Bedford, Route 1

Owner: The Marquess of Northampton, DSO

One of the loveliest of gardens surrounding a stately home, whose date of building – 1624 – you can read on the parapet of stone letters, with the Latin of the verse beginning: 'Except the Lord build the house . . .' Three Marchionesses made the gardens and 'Capability' Brown had a hand in it too. He increased the size of the Park, where he put a sunk fence or ha-ha, and built the dairy and the temple against the Menagerie. It was the Third Marchioness who in 1860 laid out the present terraces, built the Italianate glasshouses and turned the old kitchen garden into an Italian garden. Her terraces are one of the most beautiful features of Castle Ashby. The balustrading copies the idea of the parapet, and here the letters read: 'Consider the lilies of the field, how they grow. They toil not, neither do they spin.' In reading the verse from Matthew you turn all the way round, and thus see the pattern of the lawn, a great square of green in which intricate designs are carved and filled in with gravel. From here you can see 'Capability' Brown's lake and close to it his temple which in the evening sun lights up in gold. A companion terrace is laid out with beds shaped like four great silver hand-mirrors. *Senecio greyi* and *Statice lanata* are used to simulate the silver. A fountain, like some pretty ornament on a lady's dressing table, is between each pair of mirrors, and in the centre is a huge bed of roses. From here you look over to the fourteenth-century parish church which is in the grounds, and to the north for miles down the valley of the River Nene. The protective woodlands around are of magnificent beeches two to three hundred years old, one a massive weeping beech with four great trunks. In spring it is like a waterfall with its pale green leaves. In spring too the floor of the woodland is carpeted with flowers – snowdrops and daffodils, bluebells, anemones, primroses and fritillaries. Under one chestnut with a 144-foot spread grow aconites and thousands of Martagon lilies. The back of the house is quite different to the front, for here is the Italian garden with its clipped yews and straight path lined with box pyramids interplanted, as it were, with vases filled with senecio. It leads to the beautiful orangery and it is all framed in a Roman archway. Going the other way you come to a series of gardens walled by box hedges ten to twelve feet high (twenty-five feet thick at one corner). Here grow shrubs, roses and all the summer flowers.

Chastleton House

Zone Centre: Stratford, Route 5

Owner: Alan Clutton-Brock, Esq

The house is connected with Robert Catesby, one of the three rascals implicated in the Gunpowder Plot. The present garden was made almost a century later, and remaining from that period is a unique collection of topiary objects and figures. The rest of the garden is informal, but there are lawns with slanting herbaceous borders and a very good collection of alpines in troughs. The setting is the side of a Cotswold hill commanding a beautiful view over a valley.

Compton Wynyates

Zone Centre: Stratford, Route 4

Owner: The Marquess of Northampton, DSO

Part of the garden is enclosed by the moat, and a very pretty part it is: a lawn surrounded by glorious mixed borders of flowering shrubs and shrub roses, herbaceous plants and a small tree here and there. So there is scent and colour all the season, with the fragrance of the crimson Roseraie de l'Hay, the mauve and white Mary Queen of Scots, and the deep rose-pink of Louise Odier. In spring it is a sight with polyanthus and bulbs everywhere and pink apple blossom. From here you can see Compton Pike, the stone spire at the top of the hill. It was one of the network of beacons ready to give warning of the landing of the Spaniards at the time of the Armada. On the north side of the house is a great stretch of lawn, behind which a slope rises up in a series of grass terraces, all that remains of the old tiltyard made in the reign of Henry VIII, and on the lawn are fifty topiary pieces in pawn shapes and tiered pyramids. They were designed and kept clipped by the present Marquess's father. Here and there among them are hoops of roses and ornamental vines, with rose beds, some pink, some red, and other plots between them in the grey and yellow of santolina, the deep blue-purple of Hidcote lavender and white clouds of forget-me-not. From here you get a wonderful view of the pink brick castle and its spiralling chimneys. The five acres of Compton Wynyates are sheer delight.

The Court House

Owner: Mrs John Wooldridge

This cottage garden is an example of how quickly a garden can be made. It was started in 1961 when it was just some old trees, dumps of bottles, tins and rubble. The Wooldridges had it all ploughed up and Mrs Wooldridge began planting, planning as she went along, choosing shrubs and trees for their beauty of foliage, flower and berry and sequence of interest through to autumn colouring, with 'foliage' plants so that even in winter all was not bare or devoid of colour. Scent too came into the picture, of course, so species roses, shrub roses and musk roses had their place among good modern hybrids. The one and a half acres were perfectly flat: Mrs Wooldridge contrived variation by breaking up the expanse with different heights of trees, shrubs and flowering plants, so that the skyline and borders had different levels, and she would have nothing niggly. So she planned big mixed borders as an introduction to the whole, ranging round two sides of the lawn at the front. Neither are the plantings patchy. The result is a sense of spaciousness. Her choice of plants went always to the unusual: roses like Miss Wilmott, pale pink with frilled edges, purple monardas, variegated weigela, buphthalmum – the large rayed flower supposed to resemble the eye of an ox. She uses contrasting colour effects as well as graded colours and

156

abhors the bare boles of trees. 'Cover their legs', is her rule, so she plants 'plenty of stuff in front'. There is hardly space for another plant: even the roof of a shed is a creamy cloud of Mile-a-Minute vine. Yet nearly all the garden faces north!

Hidcote Manor Gardens

Zone Centre: Stratford, Route 2

Owner: The National Trust

The famous garden at Hidcote Manor was the creation of an American, the late Major Lawrence Johnston, in the first forty years of this century. It is famous because it is so utterly perfect in all its parts, in the way it is laid out in a series of gardens each showing a different facet of the art of gardening, famous too for the lavish plantings of good things. In the Stilt Garden you will find screening hornbeams clipped as immaculately as poodles, and this goes for every piece of topiary and hedge in the formal gardens – the Pillar Garden, for instance, with its round-topped columns of English yew, while the area known as 'Westonbirt' is a half-wild woodland planted specially for autumn leaf-colour and berries, with the Stream Garden meandering along its fringe. The sound of water draws you over a little bridge where a pink burst of astilbes greets you. The path divides to form an island of attractive shrubs including the pink lace-cap hydrangeas becoming more and more popular for shaded places. The

157

curving path leads on through a glade brimming with yellow-flowered plants, and there is a bank where such homely little ones as Creeping Jenny are allowed to grow. Splendid yellow foxgloves stand against the greens of shrubs merging into trees, and the path ends at an enormous cherry, *Prunus sargentii*, in spring a cloud of single pink blossoms. In between are sheets of blue meconopsis, ferns, azaleas, the delicate sprays of purple thalictrums and golden epimediums, with here a corner filled with lilies, all jostling each other in happy confusion. There is a White Garden with a tapestry hedge of yew and box, the famous Red Borders where not only the flowers range through every shade of red – roses, the Cardinal Flower, dahlias and so on – but the trees, such as the red-leaved plum and the purplish-leaved hazel, the *atropurpurea* berberis with its rich bronzy foliage in spring and summer turning to a glittering red in autumn. And there is the Camellia Corner, the Pine Garden and Mrs Johnston's Garden (she was his mother) which is almost entirely devoted to yellow-flowering plants. You can see it is something of a garden, and where lavender grows it is, of course, the one raised here – 'Hidcote' of compact growth and intense blue spikes. Major Johnston gave Hidcote to the Committee formed in 1949 under the auspices of the National Trust and the Royal Horticultural Society for the preservation of gardens of outstanding merit. Not all gardens can be accepted. Hidcote was the first.

The Lodge, Sandy

Zone Centre: Bedford, Route 2

**Owner: The Royal Society for the
Protection of Birds**

This is the six-acre garden and one-hundred-acre Reserve of
the RSPB. It once belonged to Arthur Wellesley Peel,
Speaker of the House of Commons and son of Sir Robert
Peel, the statesman who founded the modern police force.
It was the last owner of the house, Sir Malcolm Stewart,
who laid out the Italianate garden – the balustraded terrace
with its classic pool, the walk under the stone-pillared
pergola hanging with vines and wistaria, and the small
walled garden with its canal pool. When the RSPB bought
The Lodge a few years ago much of the garden was in a
state of neglect. It has since been restored, at no great cost
but that of labour-of-love on the part of the devoted staff.
And what is exciting is that it is now gradually being replanted with such things as shrubs bearing berries known
to be the food of various bird species. So, as you walk
through the garden, into the woodland glades and down to
the old rockery where some of them are growing, you will
be able to list them for your own bird visitors: they are all
clearly labelled. The idea was explored by the Society some
time ago and much research done on the subject.

Malcolm House

Zone Centre: Stratford, Route 5

Owner: Mrs Fleischmann

Look for no spectacular terraces, lake or topiaried lawn, for this is an intimate garden where you strike up a friendship with almost every plant. Mrs Fleischmann has put great thought into placing them, so that each acts as a foil to the other. When she came here in 1954 it was a jungle: it is now full of interesting plants and the collection of old and rare roses she has made over the years. She has even grown her own – a sport of Souvenir de la Malmaison; and the 'Wedding Day' rose Sir Frederick Stern gave her (which opens yellow, turns white, then pink) now almost covers the tree up which it grows. How few Gloire de Dijon do you see nowadays, that lovely climbing tea rose with its tea-coloured petals of wonderful fragrance. Here is one on the wall of the house, and growing in the bed below the entrancing Natalie Nypels that fades to cloudy pink. Dwarf campanulas, fuchsias, penstemons, lilies, hellebores – you will find them all here, with a Lancastrian rose and a wall glorious with clematis.

Oxford Botanic Garden

Zone Centre: Oxford, Route 2

Owner: The University of Oxford

This is the oldest botanic garden in Britain. It was founded and endowed by the Earl of Danby in 1621 and completed in 1642. John Tradescant, the king's gardener, would have been its first keeper but for his death in 1638. The post fell to an old Brunswick soldier, Jacob Bobart, who had a long black beard down to his waist. On gala occasions he decorated it with pieces of silver. But he was a good gardener, as was the younger Jacob who succeeded him, and many of the latter's plants – especially his West Indian ferns – are still growing in the garden. It is a beautiful place, and what is most interesting is that this oldest botanic garden claims to be the most advanced in catering for modern plant research. There is a fascinating collection of variegated-leaved plants, for which the garden has become quite famous, with over four hundred different types. Flower arrangers come to see them when looking for fresh ideas. The collection came about almost by accident. A few were grown as material for a line of study which was merely 'in pursuit of knowledge'. Out of it evolved three important practical results – demonstrating the structure of plants, viruses (most people thought that variegation was caused by a disease) and genetics. So far as we gardeners are concerned, we shall in future be able to buy variegateds that will not revert. In the garden too are rose beds showing the evolution of the modern rose, and a very fragrant and lovely evolution it is. Another unusual feature are the one hundred and twenty Family Beds arranged in taxonomic order on the Bentham and Hooker system, Oxford being the only botanic garden, it is believed, to depart from either Linnaeus's 'artificial' system or the Natural System. Mr J R Burras, the superintendent, believes that botanic gardens can no longer be 'vegetable museums': they must provide material suitable for modern research. So half-hardy perennials and tender annuals and hybrids are grown among the hardy permanent specimens. To you and me this means glowing flower colour everywhere. While visiting Oxford it is worth while poking your nose into some of the College Gardens. **Balliol** has an Elizabeth I mulberry, and it was at **St John's** that Reginald Farrer planted his rock garden. In its circular 'quad' are two magnificent nothofagus. **Magdalen's** Water Walks are lovely, and at **Trinity** you can see one of the best specimens of Catalpa in the country.

Packwood House

Zone Centre: Stratford, Route 1

Owner: The National Trust

Historic 'Pacca's Wood' was mentioned in a deed of 1190, and the 'Great Manciant House' was built in 1556–60 by William Featherston, yeoman. It lies in the romantic Forest of Arden. Between the years 1650 and 1670 William's grandson John Featherston set out the ninety pieces of topiary in the Yew Garden for which Packwood House is famous. Representing the Sermon on the Mount of Olives, it is an amazing spectacle. You come into the garden from across a lawn to see a host of immense conical yews crowding the ground. They are The Multitude. At the end is a raised path reached by a short flight of steps, and here are the twelve great yews of The Apostles, with four very large specimens in the middle known as The Evangelists. The Mount towers above and is crowned by the biggest yew of all, The Master. You can reach the top of the Mount by a spiral path hedged with box. You may have noticed as you came into the Yew Garden the niches in the wall just inside. They are 'bee boles' where the bee skeps used to be put. Cascading over the wall are falls of bright purple clematis. The Carolean Garden used also to have topiary: it is now just lawn but with two gorgeous herbaceous borders which are perfect examples of colour- and height-grouping, grandstands dazzling with bright flowers. At one end is a very pretty formal garden.

The terrace separating the Yew Garden from the Carolean Garden is always a ribbon of colour, varied each year, sometimes sweet peas and cosmos, when I saw it a rainbow of cherry pie, calceolarias and all colours of geraniums. You may think when you see the famous yews they are all alike, but, says the head gardener: 'Each is a personality.' He has tended them for twenty-two years, and when you look into their foliage you will find that some are of fine growth, some curly, some drooping their feathers, some upturned. Yet all are English yews.

Rousham

Zone Centre: Oxford, Route 1

Owner: C Cottrell-Dormer, Esq

There are few gardens where any trace of William Kent's work remains. In London you can see him as architect in such buildings as The Treasury and the Horse Guards in Whitehall. The garden at Chiswick which he designed for Lord Burlington is being restored to something of its former glory, but it is only at Rousham you can see his work untouched as he left it. With Burlington, Kent evolved the Palladian school of architecture, and it is not surprising that when he turned landscapist he should do so in the Italian manner. But his masterpiece at Rousham does not mean rows of pencilled yews leading to statue or lively fountain. He did not make that sort of Italian garden but the place of sylvan retreat Horace Walpole described as 'Daphne in little, the sweetest little groves, streams, glades, porticos, cascades and river imaginable. All the scenes are perfectly classic'. The scenes are still there: the cascades and ponds in Venus's Vale, the Cold Bath with its elaborate waterways, the seven-arched arcade known as Praeneste (from a likeness to the terrace of the Temple of Fortune at Palestrina, anciently known as Praeneste). The grass blows rough about the feet of his satyrs, with no flowers round them but the wildflowers. Where else is there a glade dedicated to Venus so primeval that imagination evokes the shades of ancient gods and goddesses? Nothing takes the eye away from the contours he created, the impact of the Mount on which stands his Temple of Echo, the lonely beauty of his Apollo. There is an older garden, by the house, tucked away behind high walls, where thousands of roses grow in knot beds about an old stone dovecote dated 1685. Through an archway is a lily pool, and a lavender walk leads to a clematis pergola and wide herbaceous borders.

The Shakespearian Gardens

Zone Centre: Stratford, Route 1

Owner: The Shakespeare Birthplace Trust

Everybody who comes to Stratford-upon-Avon to see where Shakespeare was born, to see the cottage at Shottery where he wooed Anne Hathaway, to see where he lived when he retired from his busy life as a London playwright, finds unexpectedly a series of beautiful gardens. It was a happy idea when his birthplace was bought for preservation as a national memorial, to lay out the garden as a place associated with all the flowers Shakespeare had mentioned in his plays. So you will find a medlar tree – 'You'll be rotten ere you be half ripe, and that's the right virtue of the medlar,' says Rosalind; and in *Hamlet* – 'There's rosemary, that's for remembrance . . .' In all, 125 plants recall Shakespeare's references to them: old-time flowers with old-time names – the Woodbine (the honeysuckle), Love-in-Idleness (the pansy), Mary-buds (the marigold), Eglantine (the sweet-briar), and the Gillyvor (the carnation). Colourful little borders run round the base of the house, and it is all very much what it would have been in Shakespeare's time, with bright green lawns patterned by the shade of a cedar tree ('as upright as the cedar') and by an oak ('The worthy fellow is our general; he's the rock, the oak, not to be wind-shaken'), and there are two great borders of perennials. Then there is **The Great Garden of New Place,** part of which was the poet's garden – his orchard and kitchen garden, it is believed – and part where the foundations of his house are preserved in an expanse of velvet lawn where grows an ancient mulberry claimed to have been grown from a tree planted by Shakespeare himself. You go through The Tunnell, the sort of 'pleached bower where honeysuckles, ripen'd by the sun, forbid the sun to enter' and into **The Knott Garden** which occupies another part of the garden Shakespeare tended and loved in the years of his retirement. It has been described as one of the most enchanting sights of Warwickshire and is a faithful reproduction of a typical Elizabethan garden enclosed by yew, of four 'knotts' or beds, each forming an intricate pattern interlaced with box and filled with the gayest of flowers. Looking down at the garden from the paved walk round its four sides is to see a mosaic typical of the garden needlework of Shakespeare's day. **Hall's Croft** was the home of his daughter Susanna and her husband Dr John Hall, one of the finest Tudor half-timbered houses in Stratford and only a few yards away from the parish church where Shakespeare is buried, and though the garden in its present form dates back no longer than 1950 it portrays period formality while still being homely and full of the trees and flowers he knew. A most beautiful garden has been created here. **Mary's Arden's House,** where Shakespeare's mother lived as a child, has a simple garden with a stretch of lawn where the old farmyard was. Borders fringe it, full of roses and lavender and things like Honesty, and in what used to be the rickyard grow the wildflowers Shakespeare described – 'the freckled cowslip, burnet and green clover . . .' It is at **Anne Hathaway's Cottage** that we really feel back in Shakespeare's day. The flowers crowd up to the very doors and windows, among them, fittingly, Sweet Williams. And you can see the orchard where William wooed his Anne. The clipped box in front of the cottage was growing in their day. While in the neighbourhood you can see **Charlecote Park** connected with Shakespeare in the alleged poaching incident. There is not much garden but fallow deer still roam in the parkland.

Snowshill Manor

Zone Centre: Stratford, Route 5

Owner: The National Trust

The garden slopes westward in three enchanting terraces against the background of the house with its honey-coloured Cotswold walls and roof. You look first from a parapet smothered with roses down to a lawn where a stone column bears an armillary dial. White doves are fluttering from the columbarium and you go down steps – but not yet to the lower terrace, for on the right a path beckons you to see the Model Village laid out on a sloping lawn, a little port with harbour and lighthouse, ships at the quayside and customs shed, houses and cottages climbing up into a miniature hillside. Next you go to explore the stable where there is a collection of old farm implements including a two-headed hoe used, Bob the gardener remembers, by his father. The effigy there of a bearded old man called 'Joseph' was carved out of a hollow tree. The long stable building forms the end of the terrace garden with its lily pool set in a little lawn and bordered round with all the old sweet-smelling flowers you can think of, candytuft and wine-coloured roses, old-fashioned things like ox-eye daisies and

thrift, with hollyhocks against the walls and yellow alchemilla flowing over the paths. You will notice the astronomical
clock against the north wall. It was restored by Bob's son
Peter from an old photograph. Opposite in a niche of the
dormer of the old stable roof is the figure he also repainted,
of the Virgin Mary. A motto above an old archway reads:

> *A gardyn walled al with stoon*
> *So fair a gardyn wot I nowhere noon*

and I am very much inclined to agree. The National Trust
advertisement merely says: 'Terraced gardens'. Don't be
misled by such modesty.

Spetchley Park

Zone Centre: Stratford, Route 3

Owner: Capt R. J. Berkeley, Esq

It can be called a large garden, and its twenty-eight acres
seem very much more, for it wanders off into open woodland by the side of a lake, the home of wild New Zealand
swans with black head and neck, Egyptian geese, barnacle
geese, barred geese and crested grebe which nest here every
year. On its far side stretches parkland scattered with fine
old trees as far as the eye can see, where white and red deer
roam. You enter by the old Melon Yard and go first into a big

169

walled garden where massive herbaceous borders line the walls. They are planted on the grand scale with an enviable variety of good things, quite astonishing and full of colour, as are the walls which you simply cannot see for the mass of climbers – honeysuckles, actinidias, lapagerias, plenty of clematis, of course, but unusual ones like the rare Texan, with the Chilean bignonia *Eccremocarpus scaber*, its tubular flowers like scarlet bells. The famous Miss Ellen Willmott was an aunt of the family and many of her plants grow here. You wander from one garden to another. Flowers and flowering shrubs are in profusion, and although these are formal gardens there is nothing really formal about them: they all seem to run into one another in mounds of bloom. There is a fountain garden with twenty-eight borders in a key pattern of yew enclosures, and you will find yourself suddenly on the lovely lawn stretching out in front of the summer-house where enormous blue agapanthus lilies grow in tubs on the paving. A woodland on the left is full of different meconopsis, primulas and rhododendrons, with specimen trees such as the Tree of Heaven and the Fossil Tree, and the little willow they call Harry Lauder's Walking Stick because of its tortuous branches. There is a wonderful cut-leaf beech and a cut-leaf silver birch, all sorts of fascinating pines. The woodland joins on to a new plantation of sorbus and other trees, and you go back to the house through great clumps of hydrangeas and handsome white yuccas. I haven't even mentioned the heath garden or the alpine garden where fritillaries have naturalised themselves, or the peacocks and Japanese quail. The Long Walk by the old moat is bordered in spring with crocuses and drifts of daffodils. There is the *Rubus giraldianus* you must find, for its stems are covered with pure white wax. This silver-stemmed thorny bramble with feathered foliage like an ash tree somehow sums up Spetchley Park – it is full of unusual things.

Stowe

Zone Centre: Oxford, Route 2

Owner: Stowe School

Celebrated for its beautiful eighteenth-century garden buildings, there are more temples and monuments at Stowe than in any other garden in Britain, and all are works of art. Four great landscapists in turn sited them in scenes of grandeur never since excelled – Charles Bridgeman who worked in collaboration with Sir John Vanbrugh the architect, followed by William Kent and 'Capability' Brown who entered service at Stowe as under-gardener in 1740 when he was twenty-four years old. The owner of Stowe was Sir Richard Temple, afterwards Viscount Cobham, who celebrated a reversal of bad fortune and his marriage to an heiress with the creation of the Stowe we know today. The seventeenth-century mansion built by his father called for something better than the setting of the formal gardens he inherited. He engaged Charles Bridgeman who was beginning to make his name as a landscape designer in the great manner, helped by his invention of the ha-ha or sunk fence which enabled him to free the landscape from enclosing hedges and walls. But it was Kent who really saw the ha-ha as the key to an untrammelled landscape and who was the real inventor of Landscape Gardening. He transformed the whole lay-out and created the Elysian Fields and the Grecian Valley. He smudged the Octagonal Lake into a more

natural-looking piece of water. By then young Lancelot
Brown was at Stowe and Sir John Vanbrugh busy designing
garden buildings. When Kent died Brown took over and he
it was who lifted the whole thing into splendour, unrolling
belts of woodland over the landscape and making the first
of his famous lakes. Around 1790 Stowe was complete. A
joke has been made about the vast number of its temples –
the Temple of Concord and Victory, the Queen's Temple,
the Gothic Temple, the Temple of British Worthies, to
mention only some of them. Lord Temple's family motto
was *Templa quam Dilecta* which a wag has translated as
'How delightful are thy temples'! They certainly are, and the
grand vistas are so contrived that standing by any one of
them you see two more. After the First World War Stowe
would have fallen to the housebreakers but for the happy
accident of a new boys' public school coming into being,
and it is due to the Committee formed for its preservation
that the garden buildings are one by one being restored.
As they come back to their original beauty under craftsmen's
hands – stucco and broken balustrades repaired, ceilings
repainted – each is being used by the school. How fitting
that the Elysian Fields, a quiet solitude among trees by a
small lake, should be the HQ of the school's Natural History
Society. In what more congenial atmosphere could the
Orchestral Section practise than in My Lady's Temple, on
whose portico the History Society stage their plays to an
audience sitting on the terraced grass.

Sudeley Castle

Zone Centre: Stratford, Route 5

Owner: G M Dent-Brocklehurst, Esq

A bird's-eye view of Sudeley would show the fifteenth-century towered and battlemented castle standing in a neat framework of garden where a dazzling carpet is spread. The carpet is the famous parterre garden made in 1837 by the Dent family, an intricate pattern of flowers bounded on two sides by huge yew hedges in double rows, the whole set in magnificent lawns with a border of topiary balls and pyramids. Sudeley is famous for its associations with Katherine Parr whose home it was after Henry VIII died and she married Sir Thomas Seymour. Part of the castle is in ruins, and up the walls of the banqueting hall climb lovely old moss roses, pale yellow against the Cotswold stone.

Upton House

Zone Centre: Stratford, Route 4

Owner: The National Trust

This is a garden of terraces on an enormous scale. From the house you cross a lawn velvet as a bowling green, and not till you come to the very edge of it do you see anything but a wide view of Warwickshire meadows rising to the skyline. The terraces lie in a steep coomb between, and right at the bottom is a lake. It is thought they date back to the reign of James II when Sir Rushout Cullen owned Upton House, and that they were completed in 1730. But the plantings are modern. Successive owners have added their contributions, another lake created after Sir Rushout's time and a classical temple by Sanderson Miller placed on its far side. Finally the Second Viscount Bearsted developed the gardens and just before his death gave them with his house and collection of pictures to the nation. To explore the gardens you go down a balustraded stairway at the right-hand corner. Upton House is famous for its white delphiniums with the 'bee', and has won RHS medals for it. The end of June is delphinium time here, and you will see them in the long herbaceous borders on the first terrace and in the border running down on the right. Another speciality are polyanthus: you must come in spring or early summer to see these. Find the Bog Cottage where a monastery once stood, where the spring-time bulbs are legion. This spot is the source of all the water that flows through the gardens. There is a little corner at the bottom of the terraces full of roses and thyme and heathers where a little leaden Pan pipes a silent tune, and you will come upon glorious shrubs, some at least in flower at every season, a springtime glory of cherry blossom pink and white. Among the masses of bulbs are unusual ones like the scarlet Jacobean Lily, *Sprekelia formosissima*, which means 'the most beautiful', which it certainly is. In few places will you see such stocks or such hedges of lavender. It is a garden great in flowers.

Westonbirt

Zone Centre: Cirencester, Route 1

Owner: The Forestry Commission

Not to have seen Westonbirt is like never having heard a Beethoven symphony. It is to have missed the sight of trees in their most kingly majesty, in all their variation of leaf and form and colour. To see it is to recognise with a stab of delight that trees have personalities as distinct one from another as the first dozen people you could go out and meet. Westonbirt Arboretum was founded by Robert Stayner Holford who began planting the trees in 1829 and established the fine old oaks you see today, the Scots pines and other conifers. The work was continued by his son and, following Sir George Holford's death in 1926, by his nephew, the late

Lord Morley. Since 1956 the Arboretum has been managed by the Forestry Commission. It extends to about 116 acres with five miles of walks, not counting the 175 acres of Silk Wood and the 100 acres of parkland. Westonbirt is not only a botanical collection of both conifers and broad-leaved trees, it is laid out as carefully as a garden, and surely there is no more splendid sight than the towering columns of the Incense Cedars against the changing colours of birch trees and maples. Broad grass rides make noble avenues to see them at their best, and if you are lucky – as I have been – you may catch a glimpse of a red fox slinking across a glade from his hide-out among the rhododendrons. For Westonbirt has become a woodland world with a wild life of its own. You will find your own beauties there, at whatever time of the year you go, perhaps in the Specimen Avenue where you enter the forest proper and where the great sequoias grow – the Redwoods of western North America, or in the Acer Glade where fingered leaves against the sky are like a ballet of hands, or in Silk Wood where a ghostly nothofagus wraps a cloak about itself; perhaps even in a single soft velvety crimson leaf of the shrub *Euonymus oxyphyllus* from Japan and China, which grows against a 'Triomphe de Boskoop' Lawsoniana with its overlay of silver frosting its foliage.

Wrest Park

Zone Centre: Bedford, Route 2

Owner: The Ministry of Public Buildings
and Works

It was Batty Langley who said that 'The Pleasure of a
Garden depends on the variety of its Parts'. In which case
pleasure awaits you at Wrest Park. It is lovely, with spacious
lawns, a chain of lakes, and all the devices the eighteenth
and nineteenth centuries invented to make a garden great.
So there is the French Garden designed as a miniature
Versailles with statues round a marble fountain, the Long
Water at the end of which is the Pavilion by Thomas Archer,
the ruinated Bath House with its Cascade and bridge near
the American Garden, and the column commemorating the
modification of the Great Garden by 'Capability' Brown.
When the estate was sold between the two World Wars many
of the garden ornaments were dispersed, but enough are left
in the beautiful setting to make Wrest Park still one of the
finest formal gardens in the country. In 1735 Batty Langley
himself designed the exquisite Bowling Green House now
restored by the Ancient Monuments branch of the Ministry
of Works to its former Palladian charm. On the way to it
you walk along by a 'canal', one of the chain of lakes surrounding Wrest Park's one hundred and fifty acres of
gardens and woodland. The Pavilion has famous examples
of the *trompe l'œil* device sometimes used in old gardens and

177

buildings to fake the real thing. Its circular walls are painted to represent panelling, its dome decked in false coffering, and below it is a frieze of all the worthies of the day. But all this does not convey the real beauty of Wrest Park, the loveliness of its green walks by the Long Water sheltering in its avenue of magnificent trees, the arresting sight of the Hunting Mound crowned by the statue of a horsewoman and her two attendants, all surrounded by eight blue-foliaged *Cedrus atlantica*. You can sit to admire her; there are four marble seats, two pink, two grey. Nor does it convey the excitement of all that is going on at Wrest Park today, not only in restoration work but in research, for this is now the home of the National Institute of Agricultural Engineering. Have you ever seen such a lawn? It too has been 'restored', and the roses growing in the garden by the house are as clean as a pin in their vigorous beauty. A magnificent garden packed with interest, containing, incidentally, Bridgeman's original ha-ha.

Also open are:

SULGRAVE MANOR **(Zone Centre: Stratford, Route 4. Owner: The Sulgrave Manor Board)** is the early English home of George Washington's ancestors and was presented in 1914 to Great Britain and America in celebration of their Hundred Years Peace. Gardenwise it is mostly pleasant lawns with cherries and lilacs and some flower borders.

WOBURN ABBEY **(Zone Centre: Bedford, Route 2. Owner: The Duke of Bedford)** consists of a vast English parkland and pleasure park, and a woodland full of pre-Hooker rhododendrons. Plans are afoot to restore the gardens to something of their former beauty and interest as conceived by the Sixth Duke who was a great horticulturalist and agriculturalist. There is a new Garden Centre.

Open occasionally are:

BATSFORD PARK **(Zone Centre: Stratford, Route 5. Owner: The Batsford Estate)** with a thirty-acre arboretum where over nine hundred species of shrubs, exotic trees and older plantings of 1860 grow in an open woodland setting. Spring and autumn are the best times to see it, spring for bulbs and flowering cherries, autumn for good colour.

DANEWAY HOUSE **(Zone Centre: Cirencester, Route 1. Owner: Oliver Hill, Esq)** overlooks Gloucestershire's Golden Valley. There is a collection of old French roses in the small garden, with interesting ornamental features and use of plants. There are peacocks, fantails and black swans.

HODGES **(Zone Centre: Cirencester, Route 1. Owner: The Hon Mrs A Strutt)** has a fascinating tapestry hedge of beech, holly, thuja and yew cut so that none intermingles. The four-acre garden, started in 1940, is charming, with perfect examples of a pond garden, rose garden, herbaceous borders and a woodland with cherries for spring beauty, lawsonianas for grandeur, white sorbus for autumn berries. Enjoyable from bulb time onwards.

KIFTSGATE COURT **(Zone Centre: Stratford, Route 2. Owners: Mr and Mrs J A F Binny)** is a fabulous garden of colour, old roses (well over one hundred different kinds) and effective plant associations. Nothing is done by halves – mounds of lace-cap hydrangeas, hedges of shrub roses, the famous *Rosa mundi* hedge, and *the* rose which grows and grows. See it in July, the unconquerable 'Kiftsgate' *Rosa*

G

filipes, with one hundred and seventy heads on one cluster. Roses grow here as nowhere else, fifteen feet tall, and not a hybrid in sight. Spectacular is the view up the ravine to the Palladian-fronted house, through a maze of flowering shrubs, bluebells, acers, lilies. Created by Mrs Binny's mother and still growing, like 'Kiftsgate'.

KINGSTON HOUSE **(Zone Centre: Oxford, Route 1. Owner: Miss Marlie Raphael)** is a plantsman's garden in a delightful setting of lawns and woodland. There are big groups everywhere of plants and fine trees, a large collection of rare shrubs and hellebores, coloured primroses and hostas. The woodland with informal plantings in open glades is enchanting. Lilies are a speciality.

SEZINCOTE **(Zone Centre: Stratford, Route 5. Owner: Cyril Kleinwort, Esq)** is the only garden of its kind in England, a Taj Mahal house and curving conservatory; a garden with a three-headed cobra swarming up a stone tree-trunk in a pool, a grotto with an enshrined goddess and even a miniature Taj tennis pavilion. Lakesides, streamsides and open woodlands are planted with richly coloured flowers and shrubs. Exciting! You might really be in India.

WATERPERRY HORTICULTURAL SCHOOL **(Zone Centre: Oxford, Route 2. Owner: Miss Beatrix Havergal,** MBE, VMH, NDH**)** is for women trainees only where in every type of garden they learn their profession. Formal flower gardens, a walled vegetable garden, a herbaceous nursery of propagation and display, and an alpine nursery where there is a very fine collection of plants.

ZONE 6 East Anglia.

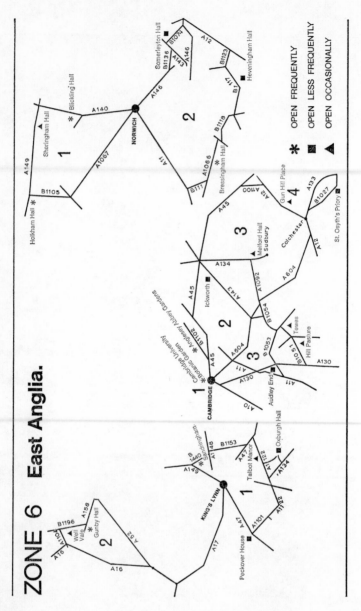

1 Holkham Hall ✳
Sheringham Hall ▲
Blickling Hall ✳
A149
A140
A1067
B1105

NORWICH
Somerleyton Hall ■
Blickling Hall
A146
B1136
A143
A146
B1074
A12

2
Heveningham Hall
B1123
B117
B1118
Bressingham Hall ✳
A1066
A11
B111

3
Melford Hall
Sudbury ●
A45
A134
A12
A100
Colchester ●
Gun Hill Place ▲
A133
B1027
St. Osyth's Priory ■
A604
A1092
A143

4

2 Ickworth ■
A45
A143
B1054
B1053
Jewes
Hill Pasture ▲
A130
A604
A11
A130

3 Anglesey Abbey Gardens
Botanic Garden
B1102
A45

1 Cambridge University ✳
CAMBRIDGE ●
A10
A11
A130
Audley End
B1051

1 Sandringham ✳
B1440
A148
A149
B1153
Talbot Manor ■
A47
A122
A17
KING'S LYNN ●
A1122
A134
Oxburgh Hall ▲

Peckover House ■
A47
A1101
A1122

2 Well Vale ✳
Gunby Hall ▲
A158
B1196
A16
A1104
A52
A16

✳ OPEN FREQUENTLY

■ OPEN LESS FREQUENTLY

▲ OPEN OCCASIONALLY

ZONE 6

East Anglia

THE SKIES OF East Anglia are wide and clear. They arc above lands almost purely agricultural, so that here one not only feels close to the things of earth but spiritually released into an immensity of freedom. A E Tomlinson, the Suffolk poet, put it well when he described its skies as 'half of Heaven spread before your eye'.

Geographically East Anglia comprises a portion of that rump of England bulging out from the Thames estuary. It is the easternmost part of the British Isles, and it is here, at Kessingland just south of the fishing port of Lowestoft, that the daylight comes earliest and the first rays of sunshine. Bypassed by the main stream of traffic it is out of the world and still unspoilt, a haven from frantic go-getting with a healing quality in its peace that is balm to mind and body.

The Zone covers the gardens of Suffolk (the South Folk), Norfolk (the North Folk), Lincolnshire, Cambridgeshire and those in part of Essex.

It is an ancient land (Boadicea ruled here) and it suffered the four invasions of the 'Eena, meena, mina, mo' – the Romans, Angles, Danes and Normans. The adventuring spirit of these invaders reflects in the sturdy independence of its people. East Anglia has produced great seamen, Nelson among them, and from its shores sailed many of the settlers of the New World: there are more East Anglian place-names in America than from any other part of England.

Though unable to boast a single decent-sized hill East Anglia is by no means dull. Its charms are elemental, the skies with their stupendous coloured sunsets and cloud effects, the waterways of Fens and Broads, sea and wandering rivers, lush meadows and tremendous fields. The quality of its light is unlike anything you can find elsewhere in Britain. Untarnished by smoke or fumes it is crystal clear. For this reason artists love East Anglia (they love it, too, for its picturesque pantiled and thatched houses. Constable painted its elms) and with much of its soil limy the flowers in its gardens have an added intensity of colour.

There are some fine gardens, Anglesey Abbey one of the best in Britain and the more interesting because it was created only as recently as 1926. Another gem is Hill Pasture, open only occasionally but worth waiting for, which applies to the remarkable garden at Talbot Manor owned by farmer and plant-hunter L Maurice Mason, whose collections of tender and hardy plants are incomparable. At Bressingham you will find uncommon plants in a setting of great charm, and Sandringham Gardens are of course those of the Royal Family.

We think you will like East Anglia.

Anglesey Abbey

Zone Centre: Cambridge, Route 2

Owner: The National Trust

This garden is something of a miracle, for most of it was made from 1926 onwards. On the grand scale with avenues and statuary it could have been conceived by Le Nôtre himself. Praise be, it is a great garden of our own times and entirely English, the creation of the late Lord Fairhaven who turned one hundred acres of flat Cambridgeshire meadowland into one of the finest gardens in Britain. He had the unerring eye of the true artist and he planted with a lavish hand: a Main Avenue over half a mile long of four rows of planes and chestnuts, the Warrior's Walk over three hundred and fifty yards long of a magnificent double row of larch and Norway spruce, and parallel to it the Emperor's Walk of Norway spruce alone. Radiating from these alleys he planted lesser avenues and at the intersections and far ends placed temples, urns and obelisks to catch the eye and lure you thither. It is a garden splendid with statuary, of masterly positioning and setting-off against clipped yew or copper beech hedge or framed in the enormous arc of the East Anglian sky, or against the still mirror of water. He laid great carpets of lawn and made an open temple of soaring stone pillars with Corinthian capitals from Chesterfield House, in the centre a copy of Bernini's statue 'David', stone lions to guard the entrance and yew hedges around.

He liked to surprise you now and then and planted two curving beech hedges with a wide grass corridor between, bordered on one side with a swathe of forget-me-nots. The curving blue and curving greens are irresistible: you just have to follow the path to see where it leads. Lord Fairhaven was a lover of trees as well as of statuary, and his favourite was a towering silver lime over a hundred years old. The Atlas cedar, the Algerian and Hungarian oaks were others, with the 'Keaki' of Japan and the Honey Locust. There are flower gardens, too, at Anglesey Abbey, three of them. One is the herbaceous garden planned by Major Vernon Daniell, a long curve joining the two ends of an L. The borders lie under ten-foot-tall beech hedges around a lawn. Key-pattern beds in a yew-hedged garden grouped round a Rysbrack figure of Father Time are filled in spring with two thousand blue and white hyacinths, in autumn glowing with Elsdon dahlias in brilliant reds and golds. The house was an Augustinian priory founded about 1130 and close to it is a beautiful rose garden of modern hybrids – pinks, whites, reds, yellows and even the lavender of Intermezzo – set out in square and rectangular beds enclosed on two sides by yew hedges, on the north side by a wall, by trees on the west.

Audley End

Zone Centre: Cambridge, Route 3

Owner: Ministry of Public Buildings
and Works

This is a minor Stowe, with exquisite Adam temples decorating fifty acres of superb parkland. The first thing you will see of it is a view of the great house from the beautiful bridge that carries the traffic to and from Saffron Walden. It was the work of Robert Adam in 1763–4. His next work was the Ionic rotunda known as the Ring Hill Temple, built in 1770–2 and set within the ramparts of an Iron Age hill fort. It commemorates the ending of the Seven Years War. Then came the beautiful little tetrastyle Ionic bridge temple known as the Tea House Bridge, built in 1783. Adam's last work at Audley End was the Corinthian pillared Temple of Concord erected in 1790–1 to commemorate George III's recovery from his first attack of insanity. Lancelot Brown had meanwhile landscaped the grounds, built a ha-ha to the London road and reshaped the River Cam to form a lake. His lawn in front of the house is one of the largest in England, seven and a half acres. Some of the trees he planted are now magnificent specimens, a Cedar of Lebanon in the Mount Garden dating back to 1762, a *Platanus occidentalis* to 1770, a wellingtonia to 1761, with fine oaks and chestnuts. One oak is indigenous here, self-sown in 1767 and called Lord Howard's Oak.

187

Blickling Hall

Zone Centre: Norwich, Route 1

Owner: The National Trust

To give you a taste of Blickling, this was said of it in 1777: 'The situation is highly pleasing; more so to me than any I have seen in the east; you admire Houghton, but you wish for Blickling; you look at Houghton with astonishment, at Blickling with desire. . . .' The writer was Hannah More, founder of the Religious Tract Society and author of the pastoral drama *Search after Happiness,* and certainly Blickling is pleasing from first sight – a broad walk bordered by lawns and yew hedges one hundred and seventy years old, cavernous inside, and at the end of it the perfectly proportioned Hall in rose-red brick with pinnacles either end of its three Flemish gables. Recorded in the Domesday Book is the fact that the manor of Blickling belonged in 1045 to Harold, Earl of East Anglia and King of England. The garden, on the north-east side, is distinguished for its topiary and unique raised borders, four of them grouped round a fountain. East Anglia is flat and these large borders create welcome levels. Striking is the use of big groups of *Lilium candidum* hybrids with their great spikes of white flowers, *Cicerbita plumieri* with purplish-blue clusters, beautiful pink tree mallows and varieties of day lilies in all their shades of apricot and bronze-gold. There are graceful Plume Poppies (*Macleaya macrocarpa*), the dramatic *Ligularia clivorum* of orange-

188

rayed flowers, and the Transvaal plant which looks like a bigger montbretia – *Curtonus paniculatus*. To the left of the lawn is a fantastic oriental plane which covers one thousand square yards. There are small-leaved limes and Turkey oaks all of great size, magnolias and mounds of rhododendrons. Beyond the lawn a straight path leads to a late eighteenth-century classical temple, and there is an elegant orangery dated 1781, with urns on plinths at the intersections of the paths criss-crossing the wooded park. To the north is a mile-long artificial lake shaded by magnificent trees. A delightful feature round two sides of the house is the dry moat planted as a garden, with hostas, camellias, Cherokee roses, Japanese anemones, clematis and climbing hydrangeas.

Bressingham

Zone Centre: Norwich, Route 2

Owner: Alan Bloom, Esq

To spend an afternoon at Bressingham is to most East Anglians a treat they look forward to every year. First and foremost it is the garden of that distinguished horticulturalist Alan Bloom who specialises in little-known and rare hardy plants, and heathers that will grow on a lime soil. The 'Cinderellas', he calls them, and if the younger members of your family are not so plant-minded there is the Bressingham collection of steam engines (always one or two of them to be seen in a great old barn with fly-wheels working) which on occasion emerge puffing and rumbling like iron dinosaurs to challenge visiting dinosaurs to a race across the field. There is also the Nursery Steam Railway which takes you by a two-acre lake round the perimeter from which you can see the garden passing in panorama. It is a most charming garden with irregular island beds and borders along lawn-like walks, and there is always plenty of colour from big groups of kniphofias, brilliant phloxes, the dramatic spires of creamy-white *Yucca filamentosa* and other plants in the large and varied collection. All, I may add, legibly labelled. A new raised bed for alpines was made in the winter of 1966–7, and as a long-term project trees were planted for a future woodland garden. There is a long curving sloping bed where alpine plants mingle happily with heathers, dwarf conifers and shrubs. In the fairly light soil 'rock plants' do well and are effective as frontal groups to the taller perennials. There are two pleasing features: the flint-walled hut with a coolie-hat thatch of reeds, and in the Dell – home of shade- and moisture-loving plants – a pretty flint bridge originally built to allow grazing cattle and horses into a meadow which is now part of the five-acre garden. Mr Bloom is always on the look-out for new Cinderellas. They are sometimes even wildlings. Planted at Bressingham they very often turn out to be good garden plants. He breeds them as new varieties and in this way nearly a hundred have been evolved and are now in cultivation. More than half have been given the Award of Merit by the Royal Horticultural Society.

Cambridge University Botanic Garden

Zone Centre: Cambridge, Route 1

Owner: Cambridge University

Time after time efforts were made to establish a botanic garden at Cambridge. John Gerard, whose *Herball* records some of our earliest introduced plants, tried in 1588. His plea got nowhere. Plans for a 'Physick' garden began to take shape in 1695, but the project was abandoned. It was not until 1759-62 that a botanic garden was established and presented to the University, but by 1827 its five acres in the city centre were 'utterly unsuited to the demands of modern science', as Professor John Stevens Henslow pointed out. (One of his pupils was Charles Darwin.) In that year he was seeking the expertise of Sir William Hooker (then Dr) of Glasgow University, as to the salary of a head gardener or curator, the acreage of Glasgow's Garden and the extent of Glasgow's greenhouses. In 1831 the present Garden of forty acres was acquired and in 1846 laid out by the triumphant Henslow. It is a pleasant garden with many attractive features: the Scented Garden made seven years ago so that blind people, too, could enjoy it; the Chronological Bed where the plants are arranged in the order in which they were introduced into this country from the days of the early plant-hunters; the beautiful limestone Rock Garden which is a very large one and laid out according to the areas of the world from which the plants came. There is also a special garden devoted to plants that flower in the winter. It is a long piece of ground laid out formally with shrubs and beds of heathers that will grow freely in a limy soil, and is one of the largest and most interesting collections of its kind in the country. A lake and stream with a water garden is another most attractive feature. There is a range of glasshouses including an Alpine House, with bays between where tender plants are grown in the open. Though the primary function of the Botanic Garden is, of course, to provide plant material for study and there are Systematic Beds where plants are grouped in their families, it is all beautifully landscaped among trees such as Cedars of Lebanon, conifers, poplars, oaks, sorbus and many more, with groups of flowering shrubs of all kinds and herbaceous borders. The largest tree, planted in 1846, grows by the Main Gate off the Trumpington Road, and if you come in there you will cross a river known as Hobson's Conduit. It commemorates Thomas Hobson of 'Hobson's Choice' fame whose dictum was 'This or none'.

While in Cambridge have a look at the College Gardens: **Christ's,** where there is a mulberry tree under which Milton used to sit; **Clare**, which has two quite distinct gardens either side of the River Cam, the Scholars' or Masters' Garden with a lovely stone bridge dated 1662 crossing to the Fellows' Garden, both with beautiful displays of flowers; **Emmanuel,** famous for its trees and swans, has colour borders of red and orange, and silver and white, a herb garden, shrubs and an outstanding *Metasequoia glyptostroboides* forty-two feet high, with fine beeches and a huge and famous liquidambar, in all ten acres; **Pembroke,** with rock gardens and dry walls, modern shrubs, herbaceous borders of mainly dwarf types, greenhouse and conservatory plants and a good collection of alpines.

Gunby Hall

Zone Centre: King's Lynn, Route 2

Owner: The National Trust

This – Tennyson's 'haunt of ancient peace' – is considered to be one of the nicest old-world gardens belonging to the National Trust; and growing in it, on the wall going up to the coach house, is one of the oldest roses in existence – a Reine Marie Antoinette whose single red blooms come in July. Another lovely old rose growing there is the Maiden's Blush, known in 1597 when it was recorded by John Gerard. Its semi-double flowers deepen from pink-flushed white to pale salmon-pink. You enter the garden through an archway with a clock above it and find yourself in a court-yard where a big beech tree grows. A small gate leads to a walled garden full of flowers. There are two herbaceous borders of nothing but yellow and blue flowers, and at the end is the Apple Walk. The rest is roses, modern hybrids but more particularly sweet-scented musks like the crimson Will-helm, and shrub roses like Nevada, pale pink buds opening to creamy white. A bigger walled garden of nearly two acres is a real French *potager* with straight rows of vegetables, fruit all round the walls – figs, peaches, plums, pears – and two wonderful herbaceous borders running down the centre which give a cycle of bloom from March through October to November. There is practically every perennial you can think of. Spring, too, is a lovely season at Gunby Hall with crocuses, daffodils, narcissus and grape hyacinths making splashes of colour in the borders and under the trees. Then comes the foam of blossom all along the Cherry Walk leading to Gunby Church. On the circular lawn are some big cedars, the oldest one hundred and eighty years old, and a copper beech nearly ninety years old, and at the end of the lawn near the Ghost Walk are carpets of the little September-flowering *Cyclamen neapolitanum*, which have naturalised themselves. It is a garden always gay from spring to autumn, from which in summer you come away feeling bathed in the scent of roses, one of which you will never forget, the massive Cupid whose yellow blooms are saucer-sized, in fact five inches across. This wonderful climber is forty years old and was raised from a cutting struck from the original plant.

Heveningham Hall

Zone Centre: Norwich, Route 2

Owner: The Trustees of the Heveningham Hall Estate

Lancelot 'Capability' Brown travelled far. In 1781 he came to Heveningham to design the lay-out of the park, gardens and surrounds of the handsome eighteenth-century house with its great Corinthian pillars on the north front. He prepared two plans, both of which are in the family's possession and which are on show. One scheme was for a chain of lakes in the valley below, but this was dropped in favour of a more simple lake, the stretch of water you see as you come along the road, with Heveningham Hall standing on the rise above. You come in through the stable yard and go at once into the formal garden which is on two levels sloping down to Irish yews and an Albertine rose covering a wall. A main feature are the two very large Cedars of Lebanon. There is an interesting border replacing the usual perennials. The soil is heavily lime and Californian Poppies and tree paeonies thrive in it, as does the silvery-leaved *Convolvulus cneorum* with its white funnel flowers striped with pink, the attractive *Carpentaria californica* which daily sheds a shower of white petals, *Viburnum tomentosum* of spreading branches and large heads of flowers with showy rayed florets, and the September-flowering *Parrotia persica* strikingly coloured in the autumn. Shrub roses find a place here, among them the large white Nevada and the beautiful Frühlingsgold. Behind, against the wall, is a Judas tree, a wonderful sight in flower, and a very large *Ceanothus dentatus*. Rambling over the wall is a white wistaria and the Riverbank Grape of North America, *Vitis riparia*, with its mignonette-scented flowers and glorious autumn colouring. On this level are Japanese cherries leading to an elegant orangery, the work of James Wyatt who also designed the temple facing it some distance away. He it was who made the interior of Heveningham such a beautiful place. There is a walled garden with thirty beds of modern hybrids and polyanthus roses, and here you will see a crinkle-crankle wall, typical of East Anglia and one of the finest examples. Not many gardens in East Anglia grow the beautiful eucryphia, but here the lime-tolerant *nymansensis* flourishes near a very old *Laburnum vossii*, with a twelve-foot-tall late-flowering *Magnolia sieboldii* whose pure white flowers have claret-coloured stamens, and a *nigra* magnolia whose flowers are almost as dark as a black tulip. There are some very fine trees in the park including oaks more than two centuries old.

Holkham Hall

Zone Centre: Norwich, Route 1

Owner: The Earl of Leicester, MVO, DL

This, of course, was the home of that greatest of all agricul-
turalists 'Coke of Norfolk', the father of modern agriculture
who introduced the rotation of crops system that saved the
land from impoverishment and the animals grazing upon it.
He inherited a bleak and sterile stretch of country where, if
there was 'one blade of grass, there would be two rabbits
fighting for it'. His eight hundred sheep had 'backs as narrow
as rabbits'. By digging up the rich marl lying underneath
the sandy surface and spreading it over the land, by growing
only two white crops in succession and then keeping the land
in pasture for two years, he was able to maintain a splendid
flock of 2,500 Southdowns and rear Devon cattle. He
planted woodlands and reclaimed more than a thousand
acres from the sea. After forty years the Duke of Bedford
declared: 'In all Europe I found nothing like England; and
in all England nothing like Holkham.' His services to
agriculture were rewarded: Thomas William Coke was the
first commoner to be raised to the peerage by Queen Victoria.
The park you will see was once washed by the tides. The
woodlands of oak, Spanish chestnut and beech were part of
the shingle-strewn desert he reclaimed. The handsome
spacious house with its Palladian front was designed by
William Kent in 1730, Kent's first major building. Four

great landscape designers were responsible for the gardens and the park. Kent extended his design of the house into the grounds and Humphry Repton laid out the park, 'improving' the earlier work of 'Capability' Brown. Finally the large formal garden around the house was designed by Sir Charles Barry. The main entrance is from the south, through the Golden Gates and a triumphal arch designed by William Kent's friend Lord Burlington. The park stretches before you and the beauty of 'Capability' Brown's islanded lake which is a sanctuary for wild-fowl. Beside it is Barry's beautiful terrace garden with its stone baroque work enclosing a fountain group of Perseus and Andromeda, with patterns of flowers in great beds, facing the Palladian south front. There is a special collection of polyanthus roses and among the perennials lilies and paeonies. The Arboretum is open to the public on special occasions. There are many fine specimen trees including the liquidambar, red oak and the beautiful cercidiphyllum, and many flowering shrubs.

Ickworth

Zone Centre: Cambridge, Route 2

Owner: The National Trust

The great eighteenth-century house is a most unusual one, a
rotunda connected by two curved corridors to east and west
wings. The gardens follow the same great curves with a
huge half-circle of lawn on the north side. The general
lay-out is a Victorian design of hedged walks among the
trees, glades cut through with hedges on either side and a
hedge round the whole perimeter. There is no formal
garden as such, though there are rose beds of floribundas
(the salmon-pink Dearest, shell-pink Ma Perkins, Lavender
Queen and the deep pink Plentiful) on the south side of
the house, with a long border on the north side full of
campanulas, groups of alchemilla, lavender, the handsome
Crambe cordifolia, globe thistles, shrub roses and more
perennials. A magnolia garden, mostly of *M soulangeana*, is
a joy from the end of April, and there are two other interesting features: the display of foliage plants in the large orangery
in the west wing, with flowering aralias and mimosas, and
the large tubs of big blue agapanthus put out on the steps
there in the summer; and in the house the huge pots of
bright blue Chimney Bell-flower and Canterbury Bells six
feet tall which are stood about the rooms. There are magnificent trees in the grounds – holm oaks, cedars and redwoods.
On the south side, if you are there in July or August, you

will notice a very attractive tree with large panicles of yellow flowers. It is a koelreuteria, named in honour of John Theophilus Kölreuter, professor of natural history at Karlsruhe who was famous for his researches on the pollen of plants. It was introduced from China in 1763.

Oxburgh Hall

Zone Centre: King's Lynn, Route 1

Owner: The National Trust

In fifteenth-century England you had to apply for permission to build, just as you have today. On 3rd July 1482 Edward IV granted a patent to Sir Edmund Bedingfield to build a manor house or hall at Oxburgh, with towers and battlements in the form of a castle. In fifteenth-century England people built moats round their manor houses or castles to keep bands of robbers at bay: it was a time of depression and the peasants were hungry. Oxburgh Hall still has a well filled moat, and this is the setting for the gardens you see today. The entrance is over a brick bridge with three great arches and through a grand tower which is almost like a tunnel: it is twenty-two feet long and thirteen feet wide. Above it soars the magnificent Gate Tower, eighty feet high, described by Pugin as one of the noblest specimens of the domestic architecture of the fifteenth century. The formal gardens occupy four acres and it is fitting that they should be laid out as a French parterre, for

199

although it was not made till about 1845 Sir Edmund Bedingfield's third son who inherited Oxburgh was knighted at Montdedier in 1523 in the wars of Henry VIII. The parterre is patterned with four great S loops converging on a circle and dotted with topiary. It lies in a great lawn on the east side of the house. There is an older link with France: the Bedingfield family were originally French, their ancestor being Ogerus de Pugeys, a Norman who came to England with William the Conqueror and was awarded the manor of Bedingfield. Castle, moat and garden are surrounded by thirty acres of parkland and trees.

Peckover House

Zone Centre: King's Lynn, Route 1

Owner: The National Trust

From 1772 when the Georgian house was built this was the home of the Peckover family. Gardens evolve, and this one did until Victorian times. It still has its colourful Victorian beds and borders, its conifers and evergreens. There are summer houses including an outstanding example decorated with motifs derived from treillage. In 1752 or 1754 a curious tree was introduced into Britain from China, the *Ginkgo biloba* or Maidenhair Tree. At Peckover grows one of the largest in the country. There is also a large Tulip Tree, a beautiful cut-leaved beech and a *Sophora japonica,* a round-headed tree introduced in 1763 which in August and September produces large bunches of rather small creamy flowers. As an exotic note the orange trees in the conservatory always bear fruit. The Great Exhibition of 1851 was a great source of statuary: dozens of English gardens furnished themselves with figures from it. One group exhibited there found its way to Peckover, made of Cararra marble and representing a boy and a dog. It was the work of Franck Gand in 1843. Peckover House is on the North Brink of the River Nene.

St Osyth's Priory

Zone Centre: Cambridge, Route 4

Owner: Somerset de Chair, Esq

It was the 'done' thing even in Tudor times for a visiting royalty to plant a tree. Thus at St Osyth's did Queen Elizabeth I plant a holm oak. She visited St Osyth's on two occasions, on a summer progress of July 1561 when she stayed here two days, the 30th and 31st, and in 1579 when she arrived on the 29th August and stayed for three days. The first occasion was marred by a great thunderstorm which began about eight o'clock in the evening of the 30th and lasted till ten, when so much rain tumbled down 'that the people thought the world was at an end and the day of doom come'. With the ground in a sodden state, perhaps the holm oak was planted on her second visit. It is not the only ancient tree in the Priory garden: a Lombardy poplar was brought from Italy by the Third Earl of Rochford in 1758. You can see both trees today. A feature of St Osyth's is the magnificent fifteenth-century gatehouse elaborately decorated with flint. It is said to be unexcelled by any other monastic remains in the country. Inside the Priory walls to the right is an interesting rose garden in four squares within a square, each having a circular bed in the centre and four paths radiating from it. A path through the yew hedge on the north side leads to the topiary garden where there is an aviary. In the deer park beyond the ha-ha you really can see deer. A water garden and beautiful old trees on lawns complete the sense of peace which makes St Osyth's such a delightful place to visit. The thirteenth-century chapel and the Abbot's Tower can all be seen with the ruins of the old monastery.

Sandringham

Zone Centre: King's Lynn, Route 1

Owner: HM the Queen

Sandringham has been the private home of four generations of sovereigns. King George V called it 'Dear old Sandringham' and wrote that it was 'the place I love better than anywhere else in the world'. It was here in 1932 that he initiated the famous Christmas broadcasts. Like all good gardens Sandringham is intensely individual. You cannot help knowing that this is the garden of a royal home, for here are trees planted by Queen Victoria and Queen Mary, King George VI and King George V, and there is the small summer house known as The Nest presented to Queen Alexandra by General Sir Dighton Probyn, vc, who was Keeper of the Privy Purse. He was devoted to the widowed Queen and had this pretty retreat built for her. Against a wall near a sundial are the graves of some of Queen Alexandra's pet dogs, and beyond the terrace is the bronze statue plated in gold of the Buddhist divinity Kuvera presented to the Prince of Wales in 1869. The North Garden was created by King George VI. His rooms were at this end of the house and it was his wish to see a flower garden from his windows. There are long narrow beds surrounded by box hedges and divided by gravel and grass paths. The central path leads to a statue of Father Time bought by Queen Mary in 1950. The Norwich Gates of magnificent wrought iron, the work of Thomas

Jekyll of Norwich, were made for the Great Exhibition and
then given as a wedding present to the Prince and Princess
of Wales by the County of Norfolk and City of Norwich.
There is not a path about the place that does not have a
personal meaning for the Royal Family, and all lead to
pleasant places: the pergola walk in the flower garden, the
paths to the upper lake where you can see the red-brick
house set on a mound among trees, the path through beautiful open woodlands of birches and conifers to York Cottage,
for thirty-three years the home of George V and Queen
Mary, the Church Walk under an avenue of pines which is a
short cut to the church. It is all set in beautiful woodland
and grassland. The trees are magnificent and there is an
oak on the left of the path just past the lakes which is thought
to be eight hundred and fifty years old.

Somerleyton Hall

Zone Centre: Norwich, Route 2

Owners: Lord and Lady Somerleyton

Odd, you may think, that a house in Suffolk should have
connections with Nelson's Column. But Nelson was born in
the next-door county, and his famous monument was built in
1843 by the firm of Grissell and Peto whose partner, Sir
Morton Peto, bought Somerleyton the year after. Having a
great liking for things Italian Sir Morton reconstructed the

house in Italian style complete with campanile. W A Nesfield had recently made his name by planning the main avenues and vistas at Kew, and under his supervision the west front garden was made with balustrading to enclose a rose garden. He also constructed the famous yew maze which you approach under a pergola of roses and ornamental vines, alongside a herbaceous border. My Lady's Garden, yew-enclosed with a circular rose bed, has a charming Mercury, a bronze by Giovanni di Bologna, his foot poised on the head of a Zephyr as if in the act of springing into the air. On the lawn by the house is an Atalanta with her Golden Apples. Sir Morton added a Winter Garden designed by Sir Joseph Paxton, part of which is still a conservatory. Another part, unglassed, makes an attractive garden ornament. The clock you will see on a tower was made in 1847 by Vulliamy, the royal clockmaker, as a model for the new Houses of Parliament. But Big Ben won the competition. Incidentally, the new Parliament buildings were constructed by Sir Morton Peto. There are many beautiful trees at Somerleyton, including a davidia or Handkerchief Tree, and a fine wellingtonia about a hundred and forty years old.

Also open are :

MELFORD HALL **(Zone Centre: Cambridge, Route 3. Owner: The National Trust)** where you will find wonderful old walls and a beautiful garden house dating back to Tudor days, the only one of its kind in Britain. Its eight faces are crowned with pointed gables, and from the apex of each, and from eight corner-shafts, rise sixteen octagonal finials. There are lawns and splendid mature trees, among them a variegated Hedgehog Holly, a Tree of Heaven from China, a West Asian mulberry and a big Judas Tree glorious in May with rosy-lilac flowers. Fish ponds survive from ancient days.

TEWES (Zone Centre: Cambridge, Route 3. Owner: Mrs Gerald Millar) is a charming fifteenth-century timber-framed manor house in a delightful setting of mown grass and rose trees; in spring daffodils thickly planted in the orchard are followed by the blossom of the fruit trees. In the remaining part of the moat are wild duck. It is all amidst cornfields.

WELL VALE (Zone Centre: King's Lynn, Route 2. Owner: Mrs R Rawnsley) is in a picturesque and pretty setting, two acres surrounding the early Georgian house which stands on a small hill between the two lakes in its park. Lawns go down to them and to the roses growing in big borders against the walls of the old kitchen garden, all the sweet-smelling old-fashioned roses and hybrid musks. The rest of this garden is mostly shrubs. There is a wild garden where narcissi are a sight in April, followed by flowering cherries in the garden and in the park.

Open occasionally are:

GUN HILL PLACE. **(Zone Centre: Cambridge, Route 4. Owner: Miss Y Willsmore)** is set in the beautiful Constable country. There are good herbaceous borders and the long low house is clad with wistaria and creepers. Otherwise the thirty acres are mostly informal with flowering shrubs a speciality – rhododendrons, azaleas, camellias and many others. There is a small lake with ornamental ducks and geese. Peacocks and aviaries are an added attraction. The garden is about one hundred years old, though some of the trees, mainly oaks, cedars, beeches and Spanish chestnuts, are much older.

HILL PASTURE (Zone Centre: Cambridge, Route 3. Owner: Humphrey Waterfield, Esq) is a plantsman's garden of about four acres, beautifully laid out by its owner. From a countryside of rather bare fields you are suddenly among yew hedges, winding grass paths and a multitude of flowers. It is one surprise after another: coming round a corner to see the Temple, a delicate tracery of wrought iron on stone pillars; a pink lilac leaning over a large copper urn (these and lead troughs make decorative containers for splashes of colour); a little pergola rioting with such unusual clematis as *C chrysocoma* of downy foliage and soft pink flowers, side by side with Blue Wave hydrangeas and tree paeonies; a tapestry hedge which is a symphony of beech, box, yew, holly, hornbeam and copper beech with a sweet briar here and there to give the whole thing a scent. A beautiful Moon Gate reflects in a pool across stepping stones with a view over a gully. Mr Waterfield's rule – to plant anything that is both beautiful and uncommon. It has been called 'the best small garden in England'.

SHERINGHAM HALL (Zone Centre: Norwich, Route 1. Owner: H T S Upcher, Esq) is set in a celebrated Repton landscape, the work of Humphry and his son John who also jointly – in 1818 – designed the house. The approach is through renowned rhododendron woods. There is a small lake and distant views of the sea. In the five-acre garden round the house is a varied collection of flowering shrubs. Bulbs make a wonderful display in spring.

TALBOT MANOR (Zone Centre: King's Lynn, Route 1. Owner: L Maurice Mason, Esq) has probably the largest private collection in England of tender and hardy plants. There are nearly twenty thousand different species both outdoor and under glass. Mr. Mason travels to find new ones and has plant-hunted in all five continents – he has collected between two and three hundred species. You can see the hardy ones in his thirty-acre garden, which is a series of gardens opening one into the other, with beds of mixed plants trees and shrubs, a heather garden and a small lake. It was all planted by himself since 1945, except the two walnut trees already there. In his half-dozen heated glasshouses he has the largest private collection of orchids and ferns, with bromeliads and tropical and sub-tropical climbers. All are species.

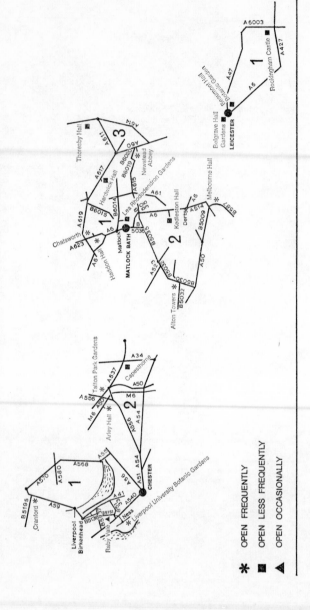

ZONE 7   In and around The Peak District

✱ OPEN FREQUENTLY

■ OPEN LESS FREQUENTLY

▲ OPEN OCCASIONALLY

ZONE 7

In and around the Peak District

ALTHOUGH YOUR JOURNEYS in this Zone will take you through parts of the Black Country (one of England's largest coal-mining areas) and the Potteries (home of beautiful Wedgwood ware and other porcelains), it is quite astonishing how little the countryside is scarred by industry. Two of the three Centres have been chosen not only for their axial value but for scenic beauty, and it is easy to get into the country quickly from Leicester.

Chester, the capital of Cheshire, is a delightful town, two thousand years old with picturesque timber-framed houses and unique shopping arcades, called rows, dating from the fourteenth century. It is the only city in England still possessing its walls intact in their entire circuit of two miles. The cathedral, dating from 1053, was a Benedictine abbey.

Matlock Bath, in Derbyshire, on the River Derwent in the beautiful valley of that name, is surrounded by mountain scenery. It has, as its name indicates, hot springs where invalids still 'take the waters' at the numerous hydropathic establishments. Nearby are the famous caves and petrifying wells.

The gardens again are varied. They include magnificent Chatsworth and romantic Haddon Hall, home of Dorothy Vernon. Another great garden is at Alton Towers, and there are two botanic gardens in the itinerary – Beaumont Hall, serving Leicester University, and the outstanding garden at Ness, attached to Liverpool University. Ness was a private garden made by Arthur Kilpin Bulley, the man who financed two of the greatest plant collectors of modern times, Frank Kingdon-Ward and George Forrest. Another much-loved garden is at Tatton Park.

Motoring along the country roads you will notice the many beautiful ash trees. They are a distinctive feature and you will see the word 'ash' incorporated in the names of villages and small towns. Nowhere else are such ash trees to be seen.

Alton Towers

Zone Centre: Matlock Bath, Route 2

Owners: Alton Towers Ltd

The former home of the Earls of Shrewsbury means two things – a vast amusement park with merry-go-rounds and all the fun of the fair, restaurants seating more than a thousand, and a twelve-thousand-car park. It also means the gardens, which the owners boast are the most magnificent in the British Isles. It could be called the unfinished horticultural symphony because, although the fifteenth Earl said 'Find me water and I will make the desert smile', part of his dream to create an earthly paradise was never quite realised. To me it seemed complete enough, with its seven lakes, Chinese Temple, fountains, rock garden, rose garden, dell and woodland walks, all in the glorious setting of an entire valley which looks to the Weaver Hills. The blast of the amusement park meets you as you enter, but don't be deterred; and before leaving the crowds behind you, take a trip in the aerial cable railway that soars over the Temple Lake and over the tops of trees. Gliding silently along, what is a better introduction than this bird's-eye view, looking down to discover a squirrel's dray in a tree and catching a glimpse of the Corkscrew Fountain which you will meet when you enter the valley? This is by way of the Rock Walk hewn through boulders lowering in primeval splendour and winding downwards. Pause for a moment to see far below the Pagoda or Bell Fountain on its island in a green pond. It was begun in 1831 and was to have contained a gasometer to light forty Chinese lamps suspended from the angles. Grotesque monsters were to have peered over the canopies, spouting water from their eyes, nostrils, fins, and tails. Fortunately this never happened. Instead, bells tassel the skirts of the three canopies, and I presume the alternative idea was that the eighty-foot-high plume of water was to have kept the bells a-ringing. Fortunately also this part of the symphony was left unplayed, for the bells have no clappers. On the rewarding walk down you pass the Corkscrew Fountain you saw from above. Then suddenly the thick ponticum hedges end, and the panorama of the valley is unrolled: the Bell Fountain on your left, and right at the other end the magnificent rock garden which climbs from the valley floor to the top, on the level where you will want to explore the conservatories and formal gardens. The rock garden is planted on gritstone and topped by big cedars, the stepped rocks broken by pencil junipers and coloured conifers. Even these in such a huge rock garden would not be enough to relieve the flatness of creeping alpines: there are dramatic clumps of *Yucca filamentosa*, umbrellas of red acers, a *Rhus cotinus* making a huddle of purple foliage beside a massive boulder. At the top is a waterfall with a bridge where you can watch the waters tumbling down into a canal that winds out of view. Director of the gardens is Mr C Rouse, and he intends to finish the symphony. He has just completed a new heath garden and is filling in horticultural gaps with new shrubs and unusual trees.

Arley Hall

Zone Centre: Chester, Route 2

Owners: Viscount and Viscountess Ashbrook

It is hardly believable that the charms of Arley's many gardens-within-a-garden could be squeezed into four acres and yet leave you with a feeling of spaciousness. As you enter by the seventeenth-century barn (the Ride where the family's horses were exercised in bad weather) you see the first two, a roses and lavender garden followed by one with fuchsias. From here a tall yew-hedged path leads to a rhododendron garden backed by ilex trees and *Taxodium distichum,* the Swamp Cypress whose feathery foliage you must stop to admire. The lawn, bordered with hardy hybrid rhododendrons – Loder's White, Professor Hugo de Vails,

Avalanche and Unique – looks out on a park, and between it and the gardens is the breathtaking Furlong Walk backed by huge clumps of pampas grass, brooms, buddleias and other large shrubs. The herbaceous garden has a surprise entrance between clipped yew hedges with topiary gateways. The borders are colourful with old favourites – blue anchusas and delphiniums, tall yellow mulleins with their velvet grey foliage, yuccas and salvias that mingle with phloxes and poppies, evening primroses and bergamots. At the end, a stone alcove invites you to rest and enjoy it all. Through a shrub garden planted with the attractive *Pieris forrestii*, viburnums and a fine *Magnolia sieboldii* is a little sunk garden charming in its simplicity of pale blue lobelias and silver santolina, with the fountain figure of a boy clasping a fish. In contrast beyond it are enormous columns of clipped ilex, twenty feet tall, an avenue of them, then huge island beds of shrub roses breathing clouds of scent from musk and briar. Do not miss the rose and hydrangea garden down from the Furlong Walk, where Erfurt roses and pink-flowered lace-caps are a joy. Down here, too, is a heath garden, with hostas, azaleas and primulas leading to the water garden. There is still more, and in the one-time kitchen garden is a plant that somehow characterises the Arley garden, the old English sweet pea, a purple mound of it, treasured for the rarity it is nowadays.

Beaumont Hall

Zone Centre: Leicester, Route 1

Owner: The University of Leicester

The name Botanic Garden, which Beaumont Hall is, sounds forbidding to those who imagine that science cannot possibly be pretty to look at. Here is a contradiction. True, there are Systematic Beds representing seventy botanical Orders, but personally I found them a source of happy ideas. Take the border where the Grasses are. I must, I decided, grow 'Squirrel's Tail' for the charm of its pale golden beard, *Stipa pennata* for its six-inch plume, and Lime Grass for its beautiful blue foliage. I put a memory-jogging asterisk against the Carline Thistle of the Alps for its decorative papery-white flowers; and against *Carlina acanthifolia,* single yellow sunbursts flat against the ground. The glasshouses here have beautifully arranged tropical displays – bananas in fruit, the crimson Wax Flower (*Hoya carnosa*), *Senecio citriformis* hanging like strings of green beads, and *Momordica charantia* of the yellow starfish fruits, to mention only a few. In the old garden of the house there are excellent herbaceous borders and a knot garden laid out on a medieval plan, a rose garden and a water garden, with a fine stone-pillared pergola. It is all done on a scientific planting plan, but to the ordinary visitor it is just a very pretty garden you are glad to be seeing.

Belgrave Hall Gardens

Zone Centre: Leicester, Route 1

Owner: The Leicester Corporation

The delightful Queen Anne house is a museum and its garden, too, has Systematic Beds. It is quite small but the whole place is a mass of colour, brilliant against dark yews. In the herbaceous borders at least five hundred different species were chosen to illustrate a wide range of plant families. Alpines are represented by two hundred species. The garden was laid out in 1709 and there are old mulberries of that date and a *Wistaria sinensis* over a century old.

Capesthorne

Zone Centre: Chester, Route 2

Owner: Col Sir Walter Bromley-Davenport, MP

Cheshire people who like to handle a rod know the Capes-thorne Gardens well. Their mecca is a lake where they can fish from sunrise to sunset, for a twenty-pound carp or twenty-three-pound pike, which weights have been landed. Other pools in the grounds are fished by angling clubs, but to the garden-lover these waters are mirrors reflecting the trees and flowers. Surrounding the big lake are the greenest and most beautifully kept lawns I ever saw, and coming down to the path by the water's edge are double herbaceous and shrub borders whose colours follow on across the lake. The lower ponds are in the woodlands which in spring are carpeted with daffodils and bluebells, with the white blossom of wild gean above. A charming feature in the garden is a rose tent, young as yet but promising a bower of red, pink and white in the summers to come. Brilliant kurume azaleas follow them, on the south side of the big lake. In autumn, their flowers gone, their leaves take on almost the colours the flowers had. It may have been the day I visited it, a perfect summer's afternoon, but I found Capesthorne utterly beautiful, a place of green and watery delights.

Chatsworth

Zone Centre: Matlock Bath, Route 1

Owner: The Duke of Devonshire

In describing Chatsworth one is inclined to run out of superlatives, for everything is on the scale of a Versailles, from the Emperor Fountain throwing its jet two hundred and ninety feet high, to fall in a massive plume where, with any glint of sunshine, there is always a rainbow, to the vista of the great house itself. Seen from the other end of the Canal Pond it seems to float upon it like a beautiful ship. The other tremendous feature of Chatsworth is the Cascade, built in 1699 and remaining unchanged. It falls from the summit of a long grass slope, down a wide flight of stone steps in cascade after cascade, and from the Temple at the top its splashing waters are like a carpet rolled out before you, a carpet of glittering diamonds. Beyond it is the house, and beyond the house the Derwent Valley and the rising slopes of the park. It was in the time of the Sixth Duke that Joseph Paxton was gardener here, he who built the Crystal Palace and took as his design for it the veins of an upturned leaf, a very unusual leaf, from a plant that roused the Victorian world to a state of great excitement. Paxton was the first to flower it in a hothouse at Chatsworth. It was dedicated to the Queen under the name *Victoria regia* – a water lily that was a vegetable wonder! Paxton stood his little daughter on a leaf in the pond, and she did not sink. The great Chatsworth conservatory was another wonder of the day. A coach and four could drive through it, approaching by way of a huge archway and leaving by its twin at the other end. These you can still see, though Paxton's conservatory has gone, but its site is now a garden with a maze in the heart of it, and it is bounded by part of the old walls which are now covered with roses. You can walk for miles at Chatsworth – to the Azalea Dell, which you must not miss if you come in spring, and to the Wellington Rock in a part of the gardens where Paxton had an army of labourers manhandling huge boulders, piling them here and siting them there to create on an immense scale the sort of grotto effect our Victorian ancestors so much admired. It is still a romantic place, of luxuriant vegetation and a path that leads you to the Ring Pond. You must not miss seeing a most unusual willow tree, all made of copper with water spurting in jets from its branches. And if you love to wander among trees there are the Pinetum and the Arboretum. Paxton and the Sixth Duke scoured the world for rare plants and trees to fill them, despatching expeditions to India and Nepal and North and South America. There is a wealth of statuary and a lovely rose garden where French and English roses grow together in happy *entente* – Papa Meilland, Lady Sylvia, Prima Ballerina, Queen of Hearts and many others. A serpentine hedge will intrigue you. It was eighteen inches high in 1953 and is now contained at ten feet (there's hope for you!) There is a Spanish chestnut with a trunk so beautiful that it might have been carved by an artist. There are the rhododendrons and the camellias and a thousand other things. You must see it all for yourself.

Cranford

Zone Centre: Chester, Route 1

Owner: T J C Taylor, Esq

A back strip of garden half an acre in size and side by side
with other gardens has been transformed into a little paradise.
Great use is made of hedging to divide the garden, making
odd corners and perspectives. Thus the straight lines of the
boundaries between Cranford and its neighbours are broken,
here by a hedge that juts inwards and then follows another
angle, and there by bushes and trees that blur the division.
There is a little bit of everything in this garden, yet because
the borders are generous in size nothing looks puny. You
enter by a grass path that could almost be called a lawn. It
widens to lead you to other paths, and narrows to let the
profile of an attractive shrub be seen against the grass; or
it goes round a corner where you find a blaze of red Cardinal
Flowers or another garden where there is a seat flanked by
two cypresses, with semi-circular steps leading up to it.
It seems to have no bounds, and when you open the wrought
iron gate far down the winding path, it is to discover yet
another part of the garden where roses grow ten feet tall and
where a flagged path leads to a secret place – a small curving
lawn surrounded by camellias and other flowering shrubs.
Trees have been chosen for their beauty of leaf and bark,
such as *Betula papyrifera* and *B costata*. Incidentally, to
keep his paper-bark birches clean of the Liverpool soot Mr

Taylor washes their boles with a well-known preparation
its makers recommend for keeping woollies soft! The planting has been done as skilfully as the planning, and decoration
has not been forgotten: you come upon the lead figure of a
child holding a bird's nest in his hands, and in the niche
of a circling yew hedge is a stone Madonna among berberis,
potentillas, paeonies. Surely never has so much been crowded
so beautifully into one small space.

Haddon Hall

Zone Centre: Matlock Bath, Route 1

Owner: The Duke of Rutland

It would be sad to find romantic Haddon Hall surrounded
by a garden that is not a perfect setting for the home of
Dorothy Vernon; but it is, and where best to explore it than
from Dorothy Vernon's Door and down the steps to the rose
garden? It is a terrace garden commanding a glorious view
of the River Wye and the wide Derbyshire countryside.
Spanning the water is the old packhorse bridge across which,
legend has it, Dorothy eloped with her lover. The terraces
are the charm of Haddon Hall, their balustrading crowded
with roses, as are the pale grey limestone walls and the flights
of steps leading from one to another. The Lower or Fountain
Terrace has a six-hundred-year-old lawn, and yet more roses
grow in surrounding borders, pink floribunda Nypel's

Perfection with leaves of an almost silvery sheen. Damask roses highlight the top of the steps here, and a riot of pink Albertine mingles with the beautiful blue clematis Mrs Cholmondeley. It seems all roses and clematis, though herbaceous plants make their own contribution and these have been chosen as far as possible as period pieces, strong blues, golds and crimsons complementing the grey walls of their background. The stout wall that supports the weight of the terraces, like an Atlas, has stepped buttresses carpeted with varicoloured aubrietias. Below, on ground level, the niches of the buttresses form shelters for tree paeonies, deep purple buddleias, Leverkusen roses and finally a glorious magnolia. We are now down by the river, by a pool haunted by rainbow trout, where in the spring the grass is yellow and white with daffodils and snowdrops. Looking up at the battlemented outline of the Hall with its rose-ribboned terraces, you wonder how Dorothy Vernon could possibly bear to leave it.

Hardwick Hall

Zone Centre: Matlock Bath, Route 3

Owner: The National Trust

It is around Bess of Hardwick that the story of Hardwick Hall revolves. She was four times married (the first time in 1520 when she was twelve), and with each marriage grew richer and more powerful. She built Hardwick Hall and she laid out its garden, which could not have been anything but a formal one to accord with the rectangular house with its tower-like blocks. But behind a high wall spiked with decorative finials are long herbaceous borders on three sides of the lawn filled with sun-loving and shade-loving plants. The best of the garden is a collection of herbs, both culinary and medicinal as used by the herbalists and apothecaries of the sixteenth century. Some are so pretty, in fact few are not. How blue is the borage, how misty-foliaged the fennel, which begs the question – why don't we plant herbs among our border flowers? Some gardeners do, but they are few. In the orchard are old shrub roses, which nowadays more and more people are growing. By and large they take care of themselves and their scent is incomparable: Madame Pierre Oger, Isle de France, Gloire de France, the crimson gallica Charles de Mills, Surpasse Tout, and, added the gardener: 'A lot nobody knows.' Perhaps Bess of Hardwick did.

Kedleston Hall

Zone Centre: Matlock Bath, Route 2

Owner: The Viscount Scarsdale

In front of the Palladian house and to the right of it stretch eight acres of lawn, sweeping round in splendour and separated from the eight-hundred-and-fifty-year-old deer park by a ha-ha. The north front of the house is by James Paine, the south front with its twin stair by Robert Adam and it was he who designed the balustraded bridge with its three arches spanning Cutler Brook which widens into thirty acres of lake. He also designed the boathouse there. Nor could any other hand than his have devised the graceful Orangery on the lawn. Some distance behind is the Long Walk, all daffodils in spring. You come back to the lawn through mounds of rhododendrons and island borders of azaleas, and to the heart-shaped rose garden which was the creation of Sir Edwin Lutyens in 1925. It has two thousand roses and at the apex of the heart is a charming stone pavilion. Across the lawn from it is the old Adam aviary, now used as a summer-house. It looks on to a swimming pool, the centrepiece of rose pergolas on each side. Nearby is a curious fountain whose octagonal base has eight crowns. It is really the top of a pillar and it came from the House of Lords.

Lea Rhododendron Gardens

Zone Centre: Matlock Bath, Route 1

Owners: Mr and Mrs E S Tye and Miss J Colyer

Surprising to find a rhododendron garden in the middle of the Derbyshire limestone hills. Not so surprising when one learns the history of this lovely place and the man who made it. He was the late J B Marsden-Smedley, a Matlock business man who as a little boy was laughed at because he loved flowers. It was a good thing he did, for at the age of four he inherited an eight-hundred-acre estate. Orchids were his first love, then bulbs. Finally he turned to shrubs and rhododendrons. At sixty-eight he decided to devote the remaining years of his life to them. There was an old quarry. He carted earth from the neighbouring moors, so that in an artificial geological way its soil was right for them, and in the next twenty-four years he created a home for them which today is one of the loveliest rhododendron gardens I have seen. The slopes of the one-time quarry are massed with spectacular washes of bloom, and the screen of trees – silver birch and conifers – gives just the right amount of shade. Now three of his friends are carrying on his work, extending the plantings and with them the paths that wind down and around. They were lucky in finding a local stonemason who was an artist at building retaining walls that are as natural looking as the plants. He now builds wonderful gateways and has become one of the foremost stonemasons in Derby-

226

shire. The Lea Rhododendrons – there are about four hundred different kinds, both species and hybrid – have won many prizes at RHS shows. For those who like trough gardens there is a charming side-show of them, all sizes, alone worth a visit.

Liverpool University Botanic Gardens, Ness, Wirral

Zone Centre: Chester, Route 1

Owner: Liverpool University

The gardens were started at the turn of the century by Arthur Kilpin Bulley, the man who financed the two most prolific plant collectors of modern times, Frank Kingdon-Ward and George Forrest. The place was a scrubland of gorse, broom and bramble, the home of rabbits and badgers. There were no trees beyond an occasional ash; and the future rock garden, a worked-out quarry, was a bare crater. He cleared and planted and in 1919 opened the garden to the public who could now come and see plants nowhere else to be seen. In 1942 Bulley died and six years later his gardens were given to the University by his daughter, 'as a practical and fitting tribute to his memory'. Since then the University has developed them, adding greatly to their botanical worth and interest. The heather garden, claimed as the best in Britain (and I have seen none finer) carpets a sloping site which

227

shows it to the best advantage. A fascinating feature is the Rose Section with demonstration beds (of sheer loveliness) showing how this first favourite of all flowers developed from its antecedent Chinese roses, Austrian damasks and Bourbons, down a long line, to produce our modern hybrids. A board explains all this in simplified genealogy, and it is very popular even with those who have but a few roses in a small back garden. I must mention the charm of the many flagged paths. The Director of the Gardens, J K Hulme, NDH, is a man of uncommon ingenuity not only with plants but in rushing off to buy up old stone. A wall at Ness built in 1965 once paved part of Jubilee Drive, Liverpool! A redundant railway station and part of Liverpool Docks built paths and other walls. You must follow some of these paths, for they lead into and around forty-three enchanting acres.

Melbourne Hall

Zone Centre: Matlock Bath, Route 2

Owner: The Marquess of Lothian

This is one of the famous formal gardens of Britain, considered by some to be the finest. Certainly it is a lovely place and the best remaining example of a Le Nôtre-style garden, its six acres not, of course, on the scale of Versailles, though that was how its seventeenth-century owner wanted it to look. In 1696 he engaged Henry Wise whose partner

George London had been taken round some of the great French gardens by Le Nôtre himself. He brought back with him some Le Nôtre plans, so what you see at Melbourne is a beautiful garden touched by the hand of a Master. Time has softened its edges and succeeding owners have changed it here and there, much of the ornamentation has disappeared, but standing on the terrace in front of the house you are still seeing the prospect Henry Wise planned; and as you wander along paths or alleys you can still see his vistas, each of which ends in a vase or fountain or statue. The most beautiful ornament in the garden, however, has nothing to do with Henry Wise or Le Nôtre. It is the exquisite wrought iron pergola by Thomas Bakewell, the famous eighteenth-century ironsmith, looking so much like a bird cage with its ornamental railings and double-domed roof that this is what it is called. With its black paint and fresh gilding it is quite enchanting. There is a sense of humour, too, in the garden, in the adorable lead cupids one finds tucked away in corners, loving or fighting, stringing their bows or robbing the nests of wild bees, with unhappy results. In the centre of four converging lime avenues is the mighty Four Seasons monument, the work of Dutchman Jan van Noss and the gift of Queen Anne. A swan on the lilied lake and some sooty-black ducks were obviously enjoying life at Melbourne as much as you will enjoy your visit there.

Newstead Abbey

Zone Centre: Matlock Bath, Route 3

Owner: The Nottingham Corporation

Before you pass through Newstead's gates, have a look at the enormous tree just outside. It is known as the Pilgrim or Gospel Oak because it was preached under by the monks who had the Abbey in *c* 1160. The oak is one thousand years old which is proof enough of the antiquity of Newstead, and it is to the monks we owe much of the garden's present-day beauty. It was they who made the lake (it is known that they built a dam on the west side of the Priory), and today their old stewponds are still used for breeding fish, the carp which stock angling clubs in the district. The whole garden breathes history and romance. This was the home of the poet Byron and you can see on the lawn by the house the touching memorial to his beloved Newfoundland dog Bo'sun. You can also see the Byron Oak, or rather the last of its stump, which the poet planted. Newstead has many pleasant gardens. You will probably first go and see the rock garden, mainly planted with winter-flowering heathers, red-berried skimmias and other plants cheerful in the dull days. The Japanese Garden is reached by a path leading down from the lake, at a weir. A grotto tunnel, green with mosses and ferns, makes the entrance to the scene of the 'Willow Pattern' with its bridge, tea house and willow. Strikingly coloured conifers stand out against the other greens.

Very magnificent is the Eagle Pond and its surrounding garden with its long herbaceous border on a terrace, terraced lawns and formal beds, all on an immense scale. It is said that treasure is buried in the lake. When the monks fled at the time of the Dissolution they threw all their valuables into it. Two brass candlesticks and their eagle lectern were recovered but two chests of treasure remain unsalvaged. I should add that many attempts to find them have been in vain, and that the lake is very deep and muddy at the bottom. You can spend all day at Newstead finding other treasures, in flower and tree and statue in all its many gardens, and these after all are the best sorts of treasure.

Rockingham Castle

Zone Centre: Leicester, Route 1

Owners: Sir Michael and Lady Faith Culme-Seymour

To me, Rockingham is a garden like *Alice*. Where else will you find an avenue of tall standard roses? I expected to see the Queen come rampaging along at any minute, ordering everyone in sight to be beheaded. The roses at Rockingham are its loveliest feature, with a garden of them enclosed by jumbly yews (surely once strict topiary), rose-bed islands in grass, cut in circles, square-ended cresents and rectangles, with a lead boy in the centre regarding it all.

231

Relics of the most ancient parts of the castle have been skilfully used to create a rock garden, and beyond the ramparts by which you enter is an unforgettable view across the Welland Valley. On these battlements paced the guardians of the castle from the time of William the Conqueror, and you can look down from here to see the grassy terraces of the old tilting yard where they trained for battle. Ascending a flight of steps to a high terrace, where the wind on most days is your companion, you can easily imagine yourself centuries back in time when Rockingham was a fortress, and from there you have a perfect view of the garden below, roses and lavender in the form of a huge cross, with clipped golden yews to add a sunny note. Nine arching and turreted yews lead to a wide circular grass walk which follows the curving wall, part stone and part brick, which was the site of the old Keep. There is a little gate leading down into a woodland now being planted with colourful shrubs. It is a pleasant walk by the riverside.

Tatton Park Gardens

Zone Centre: Chester, Route 2

Owner: Leased by the Cheshire County
Council from The National Trust

It is advertised as the show-place of the north-west, and
certainly it would be difficult to disagree with this statement,
for Tatton Park has everything, not only a series of delightful
gardens but so excellently planted that each is of horticultural interest. Developed through successive generations of
the Egerton family Tatton Park was landscaped by Humphry
Repton in 1791 (his 'Red Book' of plans for it can be seen
in the Library), and since then the gardens have increased
in number and beauty. The Third Baron was responsible for
the Japanese Garden and the Shinto Temple. The Fourth
Baron added the huge collection of rhododendrons and
azaleas – more than six hundred kinds, species and hybrid.
So many things at Tatton Park are satisfying, such as the
Lewis Wyatt orangery which, unlike those of most English
country houses, really does have oranges growing in it, with
lemons, pawpaws and a banana palm, and a plumbago that is
a cloud of blue to the roof. Along by the Orangery is a border
with a remarkable and successful mixture of roses, shrubs
and herbaceous plants. Climbing honeysuckles and clematis
are grown in the border in mounds. The background is a
high wall again covered with climbers. At the end is a
magnificent eucryphia tree beloved by bees when it is

mantled with white flowers. On the lawn in front are a group of magnolias and specimen trees including a *Picea breweriana* with its soft flounced skirts. As you walk around you will discover all sorts of interesting things: the thatched African hut and the old Sheepwatcher's Tower which stands in a dear little garden of fuchsias and potentillas where small stone lions guard the boy fountain. In the woodlands I hope you will find the Japanese Snowdrop Tree in flower, and you must find the glade of Fossil Trees (*Metasequoia glyptostroboides*), so-called because until quite recently they had been found only in fossil form and thought to be extinct. Their light green feathery foliage is beautiful. The Broad Walk leads to the Grecian Choragic monument, but before reaching it you must spend some time in the Japanese Garden which is exquisite, and authentic. It was made about 1910 by labour specially brought from Japan, whence came the nearby Shinto Temple. Every Japanese garden must have a story, and the design of this one shows scenes typical of the garden of a wealthy Lord, on which he has implanted his character, and where he has his Tea House as a central feature and his Island. Four-fifths of a Japanese Garden should be foliage, and here it is, with a thousand different greens in moss, leaf, pine foliage and fern, among which lead herons fish. There are shrine lanterns, a pagoda, a hill cascade, a Yukioseki (Stone of Amusement) and a Flying Goose Bridge. A summit stone on which to sit in tranquil contemplation completes the picture. As you come back from the Monument the Japanese garden is seen to your left in panorama. It was my last glimpse of beautiful Tatton Park, and a dove had come down from the high trees to perch and coo his evening notes on the Shinto archway. It was nearing closing time and the last of the visitors were making their way back to the world outside.

Thoresby Hall

Zone Centre: Matlock Bath, Route 3

Owner: The Countess Manvers

Stately formal gardens surround the Hall, in keeping with the magnificence of Thoresby which is the home of the Pierrepont family. It looks as if it had been there for centuries but was in fact built in the reign of Queen Victoria. Anthony Salvin, then the greatest authority on medieval architecture, designed both house and garden. The borders, all in perfect symmetry, are examples of Victorian carpet-bedding, and very gay they look, varied each year with different subjects and trimmed with neat little plants. They are to be seen in the West Front Garden and from the South Terrace which overlooks Thoresby Lake. Inevitably great stone lions *couchant* guard the precincts. There is a delightful Victorian gazebo, and surrounding the gardens are woodlands to remind us that we are in the heart of Robin Hood country. Indeed, you pass through Sherwood Forest on your way here. In the forecourt of the Hall is a statue of Robin Hood himself.

Open only occasionally is

RABY VALE **(Zone Centre: Chester, Route 1. Owner: C F J Beausire, Esq)** The three acres of this garden are a perfect combination of pool garden, bog garden, woodland rock garden, and rose garden on whose low retaining walls Europeana and Orange Sensation grow in clusters of one hundred roses on each head. This is typical of Raby Vale where flowers are grown to perfection. There are glorious herbaceous and shrub borders; and a garden theatre done in clipped yew, wings and all, looks over a perfect lawn.

ZONE 8 The Yorkshire Dales and The Lake District.

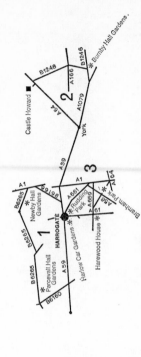

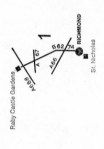

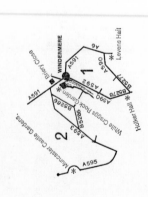

* OPEN FREQUENTLY

■ OPEN LESS FREQUENTLY

▲ OPEN OCCASIONALLY

ZONE 8

The Yorkshire Dales and the Lake District

AT MERE MENTION that you are going to the Lake District you will be envied, for it is unquestionably the most picturesque part of England, seven hundred square miles of such lovely lakes as Windermere – the largest, ten and a half miles long and a mile wide – Grasmere, Ullswater and Derwentwater – considered the most beautiful of all. They are embraced by the mountains of the Scafell range, Scafell Pike being the highest summit in England (3210 feet); Helvellyn, Skiddaw and Great Gable rising almost as high.

The lakes had their poet in Wordsworth who wrote of the daffodils stretching 'in never-ending line along the margin of a bay', 'tossing their heads in sprightly dance'. These wild daffodils still grow by the thousand along the lakesides.

County-wise the Lake District lies in Cumberland, Westmorland and Lancashire, and you will constantly find yourself popping in and out of these counties as you go along.

Then there are the Dales. What pleasing sounds they make: Wensleydale, Ribblesdale, Lunedale and Edendale;

and what pleasing countryside, steep and rolling green hills cheerful with the music of rivulets cascading down to join the rivers watering the valleys below. You climb up and climb down, rewarded at every turn of the road by another splendid view. The houses are all built of stone, domestic strongholds against the reiving Scots who before their Stuart king sat on the English throne came across the Solway Sands to drive away cattle and burn and loot.

There are some fascinating gardens in this Zone: Muncaster famed for rhododendrons, White Craggs on Ambleside with a spectacular rock garden climbing up a hillside (but an easy walk), Levens Hall with ancient topiary, St Nicholas, a picture in summer with its roses and long herbaceous borders, and Harlow Car, the 'Wisley of the North', owned by the Northern Horticultural Society and a garden of unending interest.

Bramham Park

Zone Centre: Harrogate, Route 3

Owners: Col and the Hon Mrs F Lane Fox

The garden is in process of restoration to its original glories of T-shaped canal, cascade, basins and ornamental stone ponds. It was designed as a French garden on the lines of Versailles and Vaux-le-Vicomte. Le Nôtre, it is claimed, had a hand in it, but it was laid out between 1710 and 1713 by Robert Benson, Lord Chamberlain to Queen Anne and

British Ambassador to Spain, who became Lord Bingley. Queen Anne was a frequent visitor. Part of the design were great avenues of clipped beeches forming long vistas leading to a temple or a fountain. One, the Broad Walk, extends southward to the elaborate water gardens. Along it on the left is a border of herbaceous plants and shrub roses inter-planted with sweet-smelling stocks, its centre broken by an enclave where a fish fountain plays into a pool with crimson water lilies. On the West Front of the house a large formal garden cuts into the slope of an extensive lawn. The retaining wall at the back is niched and decorated with stone vases. Conical yews form a pleasing pattern among the roses, and at the far end of the lawn are symmetrical beds of shrubs. Beyond, a background of trees is broken in the centre to form yet another long vista. You see the formal garden as you enter, and you must pick your way across the flagstones leading on to the walk: its pockets of low-growing plants are as thick as chessmen on a board, a delightful feature.

Briery Close

Zone Centre: Windermere, Route 2

Owners: Major and Mrs T W I Hedley

What a lovely garden! It steals your heart, and where will you find at the same time a more beautiful panorama of Lake Windermere? The viewpoint is the end of the lawn in front of the house, where an exquisitely cut box hedge is angled and then widens out in a semi-circle like a big bow window. Another charm of the garden is the undulating lawn to the left of the house sloping down to a pool ringed with moisture-loving plants that reflect in the water, with acers and azaleas behind and a green touch of low-growing juniper to set off their colours. The pond is fed by a small stream ribboned with colourful bog plants, coming from rising ground where pine trees break the skyline. This marks the beginning of a woodland which you can enter from various gates along the drive, to climb up among the trees with their rhododendrons and other flowering shrubs, and where in spring wood anemones bloom like drifts of snow.

Burnby Hall Gardens

Zone Centre: Harrogate, Route 2

Owner: The Trustees of Stewart's Burnby
Hall Gardens and Museum

When a hunting-shooting-and-fishing Major, famed for his
exploits in all parts of the world (round which he has travelled eight times), after tarpon in Mexico, sharks in Australia,
Blue Morpho butterflies in Brazil, lions in Africa and
buffaloes in the grassy damboes of India – when a man like
this returns to the quietude of the Yorkshire countryside,
something is bound to come of it. He must hanker after fish
to fish. His rods must beckon him from their racks. So,
having bought Burnby Hall and its eleven acres consisting
of a few bare fields, Major Percy Marlborough Stewart
decided to provide himself with his own private stretch of
trout fishing. The ground was excavated and the entire lake
bed lined with concrete. That was in 1904. In 1910 he
constructed the Lower Water. In 1920 he doubled the size
of the Upper Water to an acre and a half. Between the two
ran a stream with ten miniature waterfalls. He was now able
to cast away to his heart's content. He had meanwhile, on
home leaves from the army, managed to plant a nice garden
round the lakes, shelter belts of trees round about, a rose
garden, and build a huge conservatory. Then something quite
unexpected happened to him: he fell in love with water
lilies. Today the collection he started is the finest in Europe.

I

Over 3,000 of their flowers open to the sun every day between noon and 4 pm in July, 2,000 in August, 1,000 in June and September and 500 in October. Among them are Gladstonia (white), Escarboucle (red), Mrs Richmond (with dark red leaf and dark pink flower), the rare Pigmy Helvola with its tiny red leaf and tiny yellow flower; Firecrest, a beauty with its pink flower and red under-leaf, and many many more; the striped white and pink Sioux, William Faulkner of rich wine colour, the bright yellow Noofa Lotus and the pink spiky-petalled René Gérard. Percy Marlborough Stewart was a descendant of the Earls of Galloway and godson of the Duke of Marlborough from whom he took his middle name. When he died he left over sixty thousand pounds to endow the gardens and build a museum. In it are just some of the Major's hunting trophies, including his Blue Morpho butterflies whose iridescent wings we often see mounted in brooches. The Museum illustrates the story of his life in photographs and exhibits of all kinds such as his tracking-diagrams and native objects from the many countries he visited. Outside is the last facet of his life, his water lilies, and these – the Nymphaeas in all their lovely colours – will go on telling his story.

Castle Howard

Zone Centre: Harrogate, Route 2

Owners: Mr George and Lady Cecilia Howard

The garden was planned by George London on a magnificent scale, suitable for a house which was John Vanbrugh's first attempt at a building of any kind, though without the help of Nicholas Hawksmoor he could not have built either Castle Howard or beautiful Blenheim. Hawksmoor was responsible for the great Mausoleum beyond the bridge over the New River. Crowning the summit of a rise it dominates the landscape and is his finest work. He did not live to finish it, and the vast platform on which it rests – described as 'rolling along like a parade of chariots' – was built by Garrett. Temples, statues, lawns and trees were what the eighteenth century demanded of grounds surrounding a great house. Flowers were *de trop*. Castle Howard's grounds remain almost as they were in those days. There is however the Colonnade border to the east of the house, and the shrub-rose walk – called the Victoria Walk – on the site of the old road to Henderskelfe Castle where Castle Howard now stands. At the south end of this walk, away from the house, is the Temple of the Four Winds, where indeed they all do blow. Again it is perched on a hill. It is a gem of garden architecture and was Vanbrugh's last work. On the south side of the castle is the great fountain whose figures were on view at the Great Exhibition of 1851, four Tritons blowing water through their wreathed horns and looking towards a central figure, Atlas supporting the globe. It stands there on a parterre of restful lawns and hedges. If you would see flowers in profusion at Castle Howard, come in the spring when millions of daffodils and narcissi are out along all the great walks, sixty or seventy different species. A new woodland garden has been planned to house a famous collection of rhododendrons, including new Exbury hybrids.

Harewood House

Zone Centre: Harrogate, Route 3

Owner: The Earl of Harewood

Lancelot 'Capability' Brown laid out the garden in 1780. It has a great terrace overlooking his parkland where inevitably there is a lake, a large and very beautiful one. It wanders off into the distance to the right. The terrace is a grand Italianate affair, designed by Sir Charles Barry, architect of the Houses of Parliament, its symmetrical beds filled with dahlias when I saw them. The beds are large, with an ornamental vase in the centre of each. They surround a fountain and are themselves surrounded by grass borders where more pedestal vases stand. At each end of the terrace are immense rose borders. Leading down to it is a stair flanked on each side with beautiful herbaceous borders. The balustrading of the walk above, at house level, is garlanded with virginia creeper. A wander round the lake is rewarding for its beautiful plantings of acers and larger maple trees, willows dipping into the water, flowering shrubs – among them plenty of rhododendrons – among fine old beeches, elms and oaks. Near the end of the lake you come to a bridge spanning a waterfall, and look down into a dell gay in early summer with candelabra primulas. The opposite side of the lake holds a surprise, for you push open an iron gate and suddenly find yourself in a rose garden. It is filled with so many roses that it quite takes your breath away, hundreds of thousands of them. I saw them on a June evening when the sun was flooding over them, touching reds and pinks and whites with an overlay of gold, and lighting up the yellow roses as if they were lanterns. I walked back to the weir where fantails were flying in a white flutter across the water.

Harlow Car Gardens

Zone Centre: Harrogate, Route 1

Owner: The Northern Horticultural Society

Under an imaginative committee and a knowledgeable and enthusiastic young director Harlow Car is already well known, though it deserves an even wider public. Its forty acres were taken over in 1948 by the Northern Horticultural Society with the idea of making it a 'Northern Wisley', and it is shaping that way. Ever developing and expanding, a

247

further twenty-three acres were recently added. It is intended to be a 'gardener's garden' stocked with plants of each genus which are of greatest garden value. Unlike a botanic garden, plants of the same family are not grown side by side but worked into a general ornamental scheme; and a most attractive scheme it is, both as to planning and planting. Garden follows garden in a natural-seeming sequence, heath garden melting into the sandstone rock garden with, first, its Alpine lawn followed by the main rockery and scree. The lie of the land is south-west. It slopes to a stream where of course moisture-loving plants of all kinds are at home. Between it and the rock garden are peat beds, all as nature would have contrived it herself. Behind the stream are the original woodlands, part of the remains of the famous Forest of Knaresborough. Here thinning and clearing has been done carefully to leave a birch wood and oak wood for rhododendrons and other shade-loving shrubs, already making wonderful displays of colour in spring and early summer. The Society hopes that these woodlands will one day be of outstanding value to gardeners in the whole of the north of England. Already growing there are more than two hundred species rhododendrons and over two hundred and fifty named hybrids. There are other collections, always increasing. The Society follows the policy of staking an interest in plant-collecting expeditions. Thus new plants, including many cyclamens, have come from the Bowles Memorial Scholarship Expedition to Iran, the 1965 Mathew and Tomlinson expedition to Yugoslavia and Turkey, and from some of Admiral Furse's expeditions, and others. The visitor to Harlow Car finds unending interest, not only in the ornamental beauty of each garden and the plants they contain but in the Trial Beds area where trade members of the horticultural world can submit seeds or plants for trial and demonstration under northern conditions. Here the Society's aim is to show northerners what they can grow in their own gardens. Included are new roses, the gift each year from

248

the Royal National Rose Society's Trial Grounds, of those which have gained a certificate or higher award in the previous summer. There are also special displays of particular plants the public show an interest in: for instance, when scent began to be bred out of hybrid roses gardeners turned to the old shrub roses which had plenty. Thus Harlow Car has two long wonderful borders of them. And when flower arrangers began to look for unusual textured leaves, the Society planted a Foliage Garden. At Harlow Car there is so much to enjoy, and much to inspire.

Holker Hall

Zone Centre: Windermere: Route 1

Owner: Richard Cavendish, Esq

It is pronounced 'Hooker' and is Lancashire's Stately Home between the Lakeland mountains and Morecambe Bay. The twenty-two-acre garden is at its best in spring and early summer when ancient trees throw blue shadows of wild hyacinths, and banks of daffodils and narcissi are followed by magnolias, cherries, azaleas and magnificent rhododendrons in colourful mounds at the end of the lawn. But summer is hardly less beautiful with its species roses, such as the old French gallica, the exquisite white Noisette, and Provence, the oldest garden rose known. Growing on the house is a Banksian rose which becomes covered with little yellow buttons, and there is a paved rose garden with a seat flanked by lead figures where as you sit a stone at your feet records that 'Here shall ye see no enemy but winter and rough weather'. In summer, too, the eucryphia trees are snowy with their scented blossom, embothriums fiery scarlet, the davidias wave their white handkerchiefs and the May-flowering paulownia throws out its hyacinthine flowers which are somewhat like foxgloves. You can easily distinguish this tree by its handsome leaves, sometimes ten inches long, which give it a tropical appearance. At Holker too you can see the oldest Monkey Puzzle in the country. It was planted by Paxton in the last century, and when a storm blew it down some years ago eight Shire horses were brought to pull it upright again, and its base was bedded down with stones and concrete. Today it looks none the worse for its alarming adventure.

Levens Hall

Zone Centre: Windermere, Route 1

Owner: O R Bagot, Esq

This is a famous topiary garden where box and yew are trimmed in fantastical shapes of birds and animals, spirals and tiers (piled muffin-wise), bells and balls, crowns, arbours and umbrellas. Some are like chessmen. It is all rather like an interrupted game of chess on a giant scale, especially as the pieces stand about on a square parterre that might be the chessboard. Not that they appear wooden; they seem quietly still as if temporarily spellbound, and, as the garden is said to be haunted, I am quite ready to believe that on moonlight nights when no visitors are about they move to and fro in a slow topiary pavane! A great deal of clipping goes on at Levens Hall. Vast beech hedges, twenty feet high, vie in trim precision with the yew and box. There is a charming beech circle of them enclosing a carpet of grass with four paths leading out of it. From here you can visit the old orchard where there are square borders always gay with bedding-out plants, or, forsaking the hedges, wander along a grass walk between lovely herbaceous borders. But of course the Topiary Garden will claim your first interest, and before you go you may want to slip back and see it again, this time to notice how prettily the knot beds are planted. When I saw them the sky was blue and the topiary figures were standing in what seemed a piece of it, a carpet of blue forget-me-nots. The topiary is very old. The gardens were laid out all but three hundred years ago by a Monsieur Beaumont who was a pupil of the great Le Nôtre. Since then his plan and the original shapes of the beds have remained unchanged. His correspondence and original plans are in the possession of the Bagot family.

Muncaster Castle

Zone Centre: Windermere, Route 2

Owner: Sir William Pennington-Ramsden, Bt

The garden contains one of the finest collections of rhododendrons in Europe, 300 acres of them. There are grand
specimens of the big-leaved *sinogrande* and *macabeanum,* Sir
Joseph Hooker's Himalayan *falconeri* which he named after
his friend Hugh Falconer, superintendent of Calcutta's
botanic garden, the tree-rhododendron *arboreum* loaded with
scarlet flowers, *mollyanum* – a rare cousin of *sinogrande* – with
its clusters of clear rose-pink, and hundreds more. Stand on
the castle terrace that faces across a sharp deep valley, and
you can hardly believe what you see – not just bushes of
them, not just exceedingly well-grown shrubs, but mountainous mounds and so crowded with blossom that hardly a leaf
can be seen. Never did any plant make such an impact on the
gardening world as the rhododendron, and at Muncaster the
terrain is ideal, a series of valleys whose walls make palettes
for the colours they splash upon them. There is another
terrace from which to view them, a mile-long stretch walled
in front with a box hedge battlemented with yew. The background is of shrubs and trees making colour all the year
round. Stand on this terrace where the ground drops steeply
away. You are looking at the width of the Esk Valley, with the
sable Muncaster Fells to the left. Now look across to a
hillside slightly to your right, and there you will see more

rhododendrons, this time planted with a sense of humour – in Sir John Ramsden's racing colours! It was due to him that Muncaster became famous for rhododendrons. He succeeded to the baronetcy in 1914 when he was living at Gerrards Cross, where his garden was known for its rhododendrons and was a mecca on Empire Day for those who enjoyed seeing them. When he moved to Muncaster he brought them with him, and there he proceeded to plant the Muncaster we see today. There are 'Muncaster Rhododendrons', hybrids which Sir John crossed and raised: Blue Haze, Ember Glow, Muncaster Bells, Muncaster Trumpet and others, his contribution to the genus of plants he loved so much.

Newby Hall

Zone Centre: Harrogate, Route 1

Owner: The Newby Hall Estate Co

When people go round Newby they start off by chattering in excitement at the prospect of seeing it all, for Newby is classed as one of the great gardens of our country. But as they progress – from terrace to terrace, from the Blue and Yellow Garden to the Rock Garden, the chatter becomes a murmur of 'Oh, look at that . . . how lovely!' or 'It's just like a dream. . . .' It was the dream of Major Edward Compton who inherited Newby Hall in 1925 when the garden was little more than 'bare fields and some trees'. True, there was a period-piece rock garden designed by the famous Miss Ellen Willmott, and Victorian parterres on the south front and the west. Otherwise a number of paths wandered pointlessly through rough grass. Major Compton decided to create a garden worthy of his beautiful Queen Anne house. This he has certainly achieved. He planned it on a central axis sloping down from the house to the River Ure, extending the existing short double borders so that they ran the whole distance. And what borders they are, full of old plants and new perfectly blended in colour, levels and texture. The rest of the garden he built round this axis and the few existing trees. Each part was to represent a certain picture at a certain time of year. Thus the Autumn Garden came into being, the July Garden, and so on. You think, as you come into one, you would be utterly content to have it as your own, and then you discover another even more lovely. There is a very green place I remember, a sort of amphitheatre at the bottom of the garden. It was lit with gold from the evening sun, the right place to sit and remember all I had seen: Sylvia's Garden where Major Compton's late wife grew her favourite flowers, such simple flowers but with sudden dramatic clumps of Regal lilies. I remembered the archway, a plank laid across two brick pillars with a big yellow rose growing up one and a red rose the other, framing against the greens of distant trees the burning bush of a *Rhus cotinus*; and the beauty of the ligtu hybrids of alstroemeria, the Herb Lilies, pink through coral, salmon to orange; the way Major Compton used red-leaved malus for backgrounds, and the red foliage of *Prunus pissardii* in the Statue Walk; and that never-to-be-forgotten grass walk to the river between those herbaceous borders.

Parcevall Hall Gardens

Zone Centre: Harrogate, Route 1

Owner: Walsingham College Yorkshire Properties Ltd

Four terrace gardens eight hundred feet above Wharfedale and looking over to Simon's Seat rising another two hundred feet, is a beautiful enough setting for any garden, and when the terraces are as pretty as a picture and there is a cliff garden as well with a view of lonely hills, no wonder those who come here seeking peace find it. It is the garden of the Bradford Diocesan Retreat House, eight cultivated acres surrounding a house of millstone grit whose walls with those of the four terraces form backgrounds for all sorts of climbers and shrubs. Each terrace has its lawn but each a quietly individual character, one distinguished by the crimson of a Hugh Dickson rose against a grey wall ('And never a scent like it,' said the gardener), another by its herbaceous border and yew hedges. There were the shrubs, a carpentaria that later in the summer opens a fresh batch of flowers each day, so hurriedly unrolling their petals that they are like crushed tissue-paper; a clerodendron with its heart-shaped leaves – 'A miracle to grow so high here,' said Alec Dalgano – and lace-cap hydrangeas and lily ponds, a double pink cherry in a corner; old-fashioned roses, sweet of scent. Alec showed me with pride the well-grown camellias he had raised from leaf cuttings, growing against the high side wall retaining the terraces. The path here leads to the private chapel in the rock garden – with hardly a rock to be seen, they are so covered with flowers. A path climbs up to the Cliff Garden through rhododendrons and by a pool fringed with the sulphur flowers of *Primula florindae*. You come unexpectedly on a pink cloud of Farrer's Threepenny-Bit rose from Tibet, in a sunlit glade. At the top you look from a grassy precipice across to green hills scarred with grey rock. That is all, and you wonder where the garden is. It was meant to be a rock garden on a vast scale, that bare hill over there, but was never completed. I hope it never will be, for there is something up there which completes this Retreat, as I think you will find.

Raby Castle Gardens

Zone Centre: Richmond, Route 1

Owner: Lord Barnard

A grey battlemented castle is a fine background for any garden, rising above yew hedges, mirrored in a lake. In this case it is a series of lawns and gardens side by side and sloping down to parkland. Raby Castle is famous for its sweet peas, and I hope you will see them in their full glory, rows and rows and rows of them melting into a rainbow-coloured cloud. It is also famous for its White Ischia fig tree which is nearly two hundred years old, and for its Regal lilies. Colour is not spared at Raby but painted on with a lavish horticultural brush – in huge long beds of Sweet Williams, beds of blue annual echiums, penstemons and clary. Not all are massed. I came on one corner where a paeony grew among some irises. It was so rightly called Globe of Light, a pink-petalled basinful of yellow that somehow seemed to epitomise the good gardening that goes on at Raby Castle.

Rudding Park

Zone Centre: Harrogate, Route 3

Owner: Capt Everard Radcliffe, MC

A peacock walking along the top of a yew hedge. A peacock perched on a garden temple with a flurry of white fantails round him. A most friendly peacock walking determinedly but with stately tread across a cedared lawn to demand a piece of biscuit. Crested heads on metallic blue, the spread of green-eyed tail feathers shining with bronze. Where else can you find such peacocks? It is a large garden whose focal point is called The Vase. It is ten feet high and from it radiate paths, every sort of path leading to every sort of garden. Two tall feathery walls of roses lead to the rose garden where hybrid musks and floribundas mingle with old-fashioned shrub roses. Rudding Park boasts one of the finest collections of old roses in the north of England. A wrought iron gate leads to vast herbaceous borders a hundred and twenty yards long by thirteen feet wide, with an old orangery at the top. It is all set in woodland glades in which there are azaleas and fine species rhododendrons companioned by those attractive lace-cap hydrangeas which everyone with a suitable garden soil should grow.

St Nicholas

Zone Centre: Richmond, Route 1

Owner: Lady Serena James

I cannot think there is any garden quite like St Nicholas. You come to it off a steep road, and all you can see at first is a house with a terrace in front and some very nice shrubs (such as a magnificent green-tasselled *Garrya elliptica* against the thirteenth-century walls), with a view of Easby, a pleasant prospect of miles of fields framed in a topiary hedge. You are quite unprepared for what happens when Lady Serena James says she will show you around. First, though, she will take you to see the hybrid *Laburnum adamii*. It has yellow, pink and purple flowers all on the same tree. The garden, laid out by her late husband, the Hon Robert James, was 'made from a seed pan'. There are rhododendrons from the Western Himalayan expeditions of Forrest and Kingdon-Ward, and plants from other expeditions to which Robert James subscribed. Some are at the bottom of the

258

garden in a glen; others make backgrounds elsewhere. On the right of the terrace a pinnacled and battlemented yew hedge leads upwards in a series of lawns with island beds of shrub roses. And this, again you think, is all the garden. You have hardly begun, for garden leads to garden, on and on bewilderingly. It is all 'a plantsman's garden', with such unusual things as the white daisy *Chilotrichium rosmarifolium,* the meconopsis *cheladefolia* with its tiny little yellow flowers like a buttercup; the white starry flowerets of St Bernard's Lily (*Anthericum ramosum*), and *Lonicera syringantha* with its hyacinth-scented rosy pink flowers. One would have to spend days in this place, getting to know it. There is the border where cottage-garden flowers grow – Hen-and-Chicken daisies, pansies. . . . There are roses galore, a vegetable garden in the French style divided by red currant and gooseberry hedges, and long borders of cool colours looking to the Hambledon and Cleveland Hills. I hope when you visit St Nicholas you will be able to see and smell the wonderful Malmaison carnations, big frilled rosettes with a scent of the past, and that the two tender rhododendrons, Lady Alice Fitzwilliam and *lindleyi,* will be in sweet-smelling bloom to greet you. For, as another Alice might have said, what is the use of a flower without fragrance?

White Craggs

Zone Centre: Windermere, Route 2

Owners: Miss D Hough and Mrs G Aitchison

You see it from afar, a colourful patchwork quilt on a hillside, the famous rock garden overlooking Lake Windermere with Lough Rigg Fell behind. It has some of the finest shrubs, alpines and conifers to be found in the north of England, and worth seeing at all times of the year, though at its best in May. You must be prepared for a climb, but the paths if narrow wind up in easy gradients, and there are steps to help you and seats on which to rest and enjoy the plants growing around you. There are many rare ones, for it was Reginald Farrer, the famous plant-hunter, who helped plan this garden, and here he grew many of his discoveries. Incidentally White Craggs is not only a rock garden but one of the Loca Sancta of the diocese of Carlisle, where at the little shrine almost at the summit, with its Oberammergau crucifix and Easter garden, an annual service is held at Ascensiontide. It draws a congregation of between two and three thousand people, and year after year the procession winds up the path among the gorgeously coloured and scented azaleas which are in flower at that time.

ZONE 9 Wales and The Welsh Border Country.

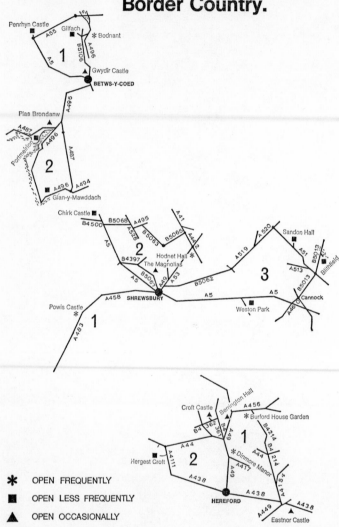

* OPEN FREQUENTLY

■ OPEN LESS FREQUENTLY

▲ OPEN OCCASIONALLY

ZONE 9

Wales and the Welsh Border Country

THE APPROACH TO Wales cannot fail to stir you: a line of blue hills that seems to beckon you all along the road. There is no distinguishable boundary, though you can still see Offa's Dyke, in some places twenty feet high. The names, though, are distinctly Welsh, and for all the bloodshed in the old days you will find a Welsh welcome awaiting you. The people are most friendly, going out of their way to be helpful. They have some lovely gardens to show you, among them famous Bodnant at Tal-y-Cafn, generally acknowledged to be not only the greatest garden in Wales but the best and most beautiful in Britain. It combines a classic design with plantsmanship of the highest degree, and both formal and informal types of garden – the superb terrace gardens that gaze across to Snowdon, and the woodland where shade-loving plants are at home among splendid trees. So you have the best of both garden worlds.

Shropshire, one of the border counties, is sheer beauty, with tremendous views of a patchwork of fields and woods stretching mile after mile to the horizon: an uplifting landscape.

In Denbighshire you will visit the gardens of Chirk

Castle and see from the ramparts another amazing panorama, for this was one of the strongholds built by Edward I. But where soldiers once paced are now rose gardens.

Portmeirion in Merioneth is a piece of Italy, a complete Italian village built by the famous architect Clough Williams-Ellis whose private garden four miles away is also in the Italianate style and very beautiful.

Parts of seven counties are included in this Zone, with gardens as varied in character as the counties themselves. If you like trees and know something about them, Hergest Croft has a garden and woodland full of rare and interesting specimens, and a glorious collection of rhododendrons and azaleas. If an intimate and unusual small garden appeals to you, lovely Dinmore Manor is a delight you will long remember.

Blithfield

Zone Centre: Shrewsbury, Route 3

Owner: Nancy, Lady Bagot

For one reason alone you should visit Blithfield – to see the Bagot Oaks, once the finest in the country and still two or three left, one reputed to be one thousand years old. There are some very nice lime trees, green to the bottom as good limes should be, these by the Archery Ground from where – at the end of a long ride – is a vista looking to Cannock

264

Chase. The Orangery faces south and was built by the Staffordshire architect Samuel Wyatt from the design of Athenian Stuart and under his direction. Its pillared front looks on to a formal rose garden where good modern hybrids are grown. A little octagonal building on the right has been happily converted from a game larder to a dovecote. White and coloured peacocks add a stately note. Camellias, fuchsias and magnolias grow, too, in this peaceful place, and a wistaria clambering up the pillars of the now open-fronted orangery.

Bodnant

Zone Centre: Betws-y-Coed, Route 1

Owner: The National Trust

Every garden-lover, every gardener amateur and professional, must visit Bodnant eventually. It is the perfect garden – in the grandeur of its situation, looking south-west across the Conway Valley to the mountains of Snowdon; in its background of native trees, and of course in the way it is planned and planted, the culmination of four generations of the family's love for it. It all began in 1875 when Henry Pochin bought the house and estate. There was a dell. He planted it with the conifers you now see soaring up from its floor 100 and more feet high. His daughter, the first Lady Aberconway, wanted to see flowers about the place: she added herbaceous borders, masses of bulbs in the natural woodlands and hundreds and hundreds of flowering shrubs, and when her son, the late Lord Aberconway, was still a young man she handed the garden over to him. Under his care for fifty years it became the great Bodnant we know today. They say it takes an hour and a half to go round Bodnant, but if you can tear yourself away from it in that time, which I doubt, you will certainly wish to come back again – in spring when the Dell is carpeted with daffodils and bluebells and the rhododendrons are in flower; in summer when the herbaceous borders, roses and flowering trees are at their best – and what more lovely sight than the eucryphia trees mantled with their snowy single-rose blossoms, or the embothriums standing like torches of fiery scarlet. If you make a pilgrimage in springtime to see the rhododendrons – sheets of colour cascading down the woodland slopes, famous rhododendrons that came as seeds from the great plant-hunting expeditions of 1900 onwards – you will want to join the thousands who come to see Bodnant in the autumn, when it is lit from end to end with flames of golds and reds and scarlets mingling among indescribable greens, when the shrubs that gave such joy in their flowering period are bunched with berries. An hour and a half to walk round Bodnant, when you can stand for minutes looking at a single tree, a cercidiphyllum with its gold coins running up the bare boughs, or the painted beauty of even the bark of a tree, a birch which has donned a green and silver snakeskin! You will want to know something of its lay-out. There are four terraces stepping down from the house, not great and grand as at Powerscourt or Blenheim, all Italianate formality, for although stone balustrading divides each and there are decorative vases and a statue of Priapus, the god of garden fertility, even the long rectangular canal at the bottom sits greenly in a lawn instead of stiff paving. Here it is the splendour of plants that matters, the wealth of bloom, the choice of the best species, the skill with which they are grouped and grown. What better way to see magnolias than from

above, so that you can look down into the pure white cups of
Magnolia denudata and the enormous pink flowers of *Magnolia robusta*. What better introduction to the main shrub
borders than the bank of varicoloured brooms leading to
them. To the right of the terraces are smaller gardens. The
first terrace is filled with roses, at one end of which is an
Arbutus andrachnoides, a Strawberry Tree with graceful
curved stems and upstanding foliage. How many people
caress its beautiful shining red bark as they pass! You
descend to the Croquet Terrace by steps dividing on either
side of a small baroque French fountain. An arras of white
wistaria hangs on the wall and down to where its stone
scallop pours a cascade over a mossy rock into a basin. On
the next terrace is a pool islanded with all kinds and colours
of water lilies, and to the right and left of it are two cedars,
a single splendid specimen of the glaucus *Cedrus atlantica*
with silvery skirts sweeping the ground, and balancing it
on the other side a mighty Cedar of Lebanon. Down at the
bottom the Canal Terrace reflects the colours of the terraces
above, and the quaint Pin Mill at one end is made all the
more interesting inside with tapestries woven at Fontainebleu
in 1565. At the other end of the canal is an open-air theatre
in clipped yew. Lilies grow against its convex apron-stage,
and vivid blue hydrangeas at each end. You must see the
little North Garden, reached either from the Rose Terrace
or the Croquet Terrace, where grow all sorts of interesting
plants – the Dieramas or Wand Flowers with pink and carmine bells bending down their long stems; that favourite of
flower arrangers *Phlomis fruticosa*, grey-leaved with yellow-
lipped flowers; big groups of blue agapanthus, and many
more. You follow on into a shrub garden of azaleas and
rhododendrons backed by magnolias and eucryphias against a
background of beeches, cedars and Irish yews. On the other
side of the terraces lies the Dell, where you will want to
wander and linger. When the rhododendrons are past, the
wonderful trees come into their own. Larches hang their new

green curtains like veils, and almost the only flowers to be seen are the groups of hydrangeas that here and there follow the course of the Hiraethlyn, a blue as intense as the sudden dart of a kingfisher, so blue that the water itself seems to flow blue through the varying greens of ferns and hanging boughs. You are never out of the sound of water in the Dell, with streams and rivulets trickling down and the mill-race making a thunderous bass. Stand on the bridge that spans it to see some of the giants of the forest, greatest of them the *Abies grandis* planted in 1887, one hundred and fifty feet high and the tallest tree at Bodnant. From the bridge, too, you can see all the beauty you have passed through, tree after splendid tree in a maze of greens, climbing up and up on both sides till their tops reach the skyline. As you wind your way out of the Dell you will come to what is called The Poem, a mausoleum where there is a memorial to Henry Duncan, the late Lord Aberconway who died in 1953 and gave his garden to The National Trust so that it should 'always remain a joy and inspiration to garden lovers'.

Visitors to Bodnant usually run out of superlatives – as you will, I think, if you are there in late spring and walk under the laburnum pergola, dazzling curtains of 'golden rain', on and on. Two American visitors did: they fell silent, till finally one turned to the other with the awed whisper: 'Num . . . NUM!'

Burford House Gardens

Zone Centre: Hereford, Route 1

Owner: John Treasure, Esq

It was a cold miserable day in 1953 when John Treasure saw it. The house was far too big. The garden was a wilderness. But he thought he could make something of it. His builder brother pulled down the two big wings encumbering its original good square Georgian shape. John Treasure paced the four neglected acres and for six months sat down putting it all on paper. He is an architect by profession and by nature an artist. The result is a garden you envy, for the charm of its lay-out and for the excellence of the plants growing in it. Not for him any ordinary species of spindle, however pretty the little pink hearts in autumn – he planted *Euonymus oxyphyllus* whose fruits are arrestingly bright; and who else would have thought of the decorative qualities of the common red cabbage with its blue leaves frilled with crimson? He has an eye for ornamental grasses, missing in quite three-quarters of the gardens I have seen, but here they are, graceful clumps of *Festuca ovalis glauca* of compact form fringing a border with candidum lilies behind and the glowing pokers of kniphofias; and, in the big border where misty-foliaged fennel grows against a wall – *Pennisetum setosum* with its bristly plumes; and the striped grass he uses with such effect as a foil for softer-leaved plants around. The garden is a series of lawns and island borders, but until

I saw Burford I tended to see these as things stuck on like postage stamps. How unlike they are in this imaginative garden, for the lawns flow round them like green rivers and they do really appear like islands. At the front are low-growing plants rising irregularly in different levels of other plants and with a tree here and there, so that the silver bark of a birch shows against first one splash of colour and then another, all up its stem. There are quite a dozen islands, each different, each a careful study of colour, texture and levels. You feel you ought to go by some fairy boat to visit them. It is not the first time one has seen clematis draping trees and shrubs, but here it is also used as a ground-cover plant. And I liked the absence of 'pencil' trees dotting the landscape meaninglessly. Mr Treasure uses them in groups and as gateposts of hedges: they seem much better that way. It is all quite simple when you see it, but it is the simplicity of a well-cut gown.

Chirk Castle

Zone Centre: Shrewsbury, Route 2

Owners: Lt-Col Ririd and Lady Margaret
Myddelton

If you have to wait for opening time you will not be bored, for the eighteenth-century entrance gates are exquisite and a rewarding study. They are now in the guardianship of the Ministry of Works under the Ancient Monuments Acts. They lead up to a stark fortress protected by a regiment of topiary. More topiary, buttressed and battlemented, is used to enclose the croquet lawn and to make a crown-topped arbour for a seat, with other buttressed yew hedges fifteen feet high. You will want to see the magnificent view of the Cheshire countryside and the Pennines. Follow the grass path from the croquet lawn. You will find a charming thatched sun house covered with ornamental vines above a rock garden. Behind is a woodland with rhododendrons. The view is straight ahead. Opposite the sun house is a shrub garden with a delightful mixture of things – magnolias, lace-cap hydrangeas, cherry trees and eucryphias, shrub roses and camellias, with ligularia making bold patches of yellow. There is a rose garden with a sundial and steps flanked by clipped yew pyramids leading to a wide herbaceous border. A mixed shrub border makes gay the foot of the old castle wall.

Dinmore Manor

Zone Centre: Hereford, Route 2

Owner: C Ian Murray, Esq

You will never get a better shilling's worth than at Dinmore Manor, this being the modest token fee, part of which goes to help upkeep the twelfth-century chapel in the garden. Yew trees here are one thousand years old. The place is steeped in history. It was a hospital for the knights of the Crusades, and today the little chapel is still the Commandery of the Knights Hospitallers of St John of Jerusalem. The property was bought in 1927 by Richard Hollins Murray who rebuilt the cloisters, and it is like walking through a rainbow when the sun is setting behind their stained-glass windows on the closed west side. The colours spill in pools on the paved floor, and at the end is the vista of another stained-glass window which is all by itself in a grotto. It depicts a Jerusalem scene of palm trees and hills, and again the colours are twice seen, this time reflected in a ferned pool. The garden, though not half a century old, is in perfect keeping with the cloistered Hospital. A music room was also built by Richard Hollins Murray, and it is through this you climb by an oak staircase to gain the parapet where you can walk above the garden to see it spread below: the chapel in a green expanse of lawn with trough-like borders gay with small flowers surrounding it; the rock garden lapping the foot of a tower, with its stone bridge spanning a lilied pool, a garden which may not be filled with the rarest of plants, but there are some and it is full of colour. Dwarf conifers and acers tucked among the boulders break the background of the cloisters whose pillars are hung with virginia creeper, and beyond the green lawns the open countryside ends in the haze of the Malvern Hills. There are tender touches at Dinmore, like the flowery baskets hanging from the ingles of the roof, and the motto in one of the cloister windows which bears the wondering thought: 'Little flower, if I could understand what you are root and all and all-in-all, I should know what God and man is.'

Gilfach

Zone Centre: Betws-y-Coed, Route 1

Owner: Miss Iwline Gee

'The function of my garden,' its owner told me, 'is to cheer people up when they have been overwhelmed by the glories of Bodnant! It makes them realise that even an elderly amateur can have a lot of fun in a small way.' The acre-sized garden is set among the hills of Conway. On a fairly steep slope it is the butt of all the winds that blow, so Miss Gee has chosen her plants for their wind-resisting qualities, though tender things grow here. The winter pieris is in flower in February and sometimes the month before. Fuchsias flower out of doors all winter long, as do many potentillas, and this in a garden where twice the summer house has been wind-borne and tossed over the wall. There is not, however, much frost, as the River Conway in the valley below is tidal. The lay-out is a series of winding grass paths and semi-lawn, hidden by hedges that bring vistas into view, or by mounds of such shrubs as tree heathers. Miss Gee never stakes any plant. Either they support themselves or each other or she grows something else, a labour-saving policy that fits climatically with Gilfach: Nature herself would do the same thing. Among other out-of-the-ordinary plants, look for the montbretia with pink flowers instead of orange, a pretty flower that should be better known. In a garden so small everything matters and everything can be appreciated.

Glan-y-Mawddach

Zone Centre: Betws-y-Coed, Route 2

Owner: Lady Russon

It could be called a Hanging Garden, for it is made of terraces carved out of the mountainside. The house terrace has an uninterrupted view of the most beautiful estuary in Wales, Mawddach, with a panorama behind of Cader Idris and his mountain brethren. There are twelve acres of gardens with winding walks to reach them through woodlands richly planted with rhododendrons and azaleas, and there is an established pinetum with a blue spruce claimed as the largest specimen in Wales, and white pines one hundred feet high. But it is the terraces that are the wonder of this garden, shelving up and up, and although each has its pool (of crystal-clear water) each is completely different. A fantastic arcade leads into one of them, and at the highest point is a rock garden created by baring the natural mountain stone. Glan-y-Mawddach was the home of the late Sir Clayton Russon for thirty years. He was the head of the largest seed distributing combine in the world, and you could say it is no wonder his garden is so well planted and so colourful. But this would be only half the story.

Hergest Croft Garden and Park Wood

Zone Centre: Hereford, Route 2

Owners: W L Banks, Esq, and R A Banks, Esq

To those who love trees – come this way. But you must know something about trees to appreciate those at Hergest Croft and its Park Wood, for garden and woodlands between them make up one of three supremely important private collections. It is not on every lawn you can stand, looking left to a belt of sheltering trees, and know that among them there are not two of the same species. Indeed, walking round Hergest Croft is one discovery after another, of trees you have never seen before: something similar, perhaps, like the variegated holly;

K

but whereas the ones you commonly see have leaves edged with yellow, here is one with white-splashed leaves edged with green. The difference is remarkable. From a little distance each leaf seems to hold a shining pinch of snow. There is a rock garden at Hergest Croft where you will find attractive shrubs among the smaller plants, *Kirengeshoma palmata* with its clusters of yellow bell-like flowers in September, on purple stems; and again things you may see elsewhere but unusual varieties of them – the currant-leaved *Acer palmatum,* the feathery-foliaged *Cupressus obtusa,* the camellia-leaved *Prunus laurocerasus,* and many another. But it is the trees which are the important feature. They begin at the end of the lawn and become woodland. I liked the red-leaved form of chestnut with the unfortunate name of *Aesculus neglecta erythroblasta,* and *Prunus maackii* of gold satiny bark. Mr Banks senior has made a collection of birches, among them the rare white form of *Betula utilis* The soft white skin of the branches goes right up to the topmost twig, and the sight of three of them in a group is exquisite. There is also a rare lime (*Tilia maximowicziana*) which is spectacular with its seed-wings in clusters. There is a *Torreya nucifera* with fruits like large green olives. Even the dendrologists, those expert men of the trees, have to see it before they believe it can fruit in this country. Its home is Japan. But a mere list of these rare and beautiful trees means nothing: you must see for yourself that satin-barked prunus and the unusual *Taxodium ascendens* with its lovely misty foliage. In rhododendron time you must head for Park Wood, with its pool in the middle and valley whose steep slopes are a spectacle with species and hybrid rhododendrons one sheet of colour. Having had your fill of them wander on to enjoy the conifers, and don't be tempted to touch the purple cones of the crisp-foliaged *Abies delavayi* – it took me a day to get rid of the resin! There is a collection of maples in Park Wood, at their best of course in autumn, and these if you have come in spring you must come back again to see.

Hodnet Hall

Zone Centre: Shrewsbury, Route 2

Owner: A E H Heber Percy, Esq

It does not matter when you visit Hodnet Hall: from
Christmas onwards there is a sequence of bloom. Make it
spring for the millions of bulbs, a spectacular show, late
May for the azaleas and rhododendrons, magnolias and
flowering cherries, June and early July to enjoy the species
roses and clematis, and at the end of July the astilbes and
great blue masses of Himalayan meconopsis in the pretty
water garden. Hodnet Hall is real landscaping where advantage has been taken of everything nature offered – contours
to vary the scene and where to lay undulating carpets of
daffodils, springs to turn into lakes and streams, rocks to
make a natural rock garden. Lake after lake fills the valley, a
chain of them several miles long making ideal homes for the
moisture-loving plants that fringe them, and mirrors to
reflect their colours. The gardens themselves cover sixty
acres and the view from the terrace by the house looks south
to Caradoc and the Stretton Hills, with the Long Mynd on
the Welsh border, the Wrekin on the south-east. This was
one of the Armada beacon hills which at the east end
encloses the Shropshire plain. It is, as you will see, a lovely
prospect from which to explore the gardens. First, the top
rose garden with its clipped yew hedging and yew gateposts,
Hidcote lavender of compact growth and deep purple spikes

trimming the four big beds, the roses graded white through pinks to purples and dark reds. An old sundial is in the centre. Below is the main lake. Reach it direct by the flight of steps leading straight down between huge banks massed with ericas and shrubs, shrub roses and such beautiful things as *Yucca filamentosa* in big dramatic clumps; but preferably go via Mother's Garden, to the left, where camellias are interplanted with lilies, dwarf rhododendrons and heathers, where forsythia makes golden patches in spring followed by the snowy bloom of eucryphias. Hodnet has some lovely surprises, and from here you look down to the lower rose garden laid out in the form of a cross, with azaleas and paeonies white to darkest red circling the roses. In the centre Old Father Time stands in the thick of massed hydrangeas, the deep cream *paniculata grandiflora*. Having crossed the bridge at the end of the lake you will find an odd stone sitting by itself on the grass. It is a huge glacial boulder which was fished out of the Horse Pond. Interesting, too, is the beech avenue where Bishop Heber composed 'Greenland's Icy Mountains'. The gardens were planted by their late owner, Brigadier A G W Heber Percy, mostly on home leaves from the war, and now the estate which has been in the family since the Norman Conquest is being carried on by his son who has inherited his love for them.

Penrhyn Castle

Zone Centre: Betws-y-Coed, Route 1

Owner: The National Trust

There are two acres of formal garden in forty-seven acres of parkland surrounding the castle with its mountain views looking to the Menai Straits. Follow down from the lawns to find this walled garden with its cosmopolitan collection of unusual trees and shrubs. Here is the red-leaved dogwood from Florida, of which there are few in Europe, two Umbrella Pines from Japan, a Fire Bush from Chile and a Chilean Lantern Tree, a Brazilian feijoa, Japanese maples and a Japanese stewartia – what a wealth of beautiful plants come from Japan! With an Indian Bean Tree we are only half-way round the world: other shrubs and trees growing here come from the eastern United States, from Asia Minor, from the Mediterranean, Australia and Tasmania. Chusan palms, with their huge creamy flower-clusters, add a final exotic note. Above the shrubs and trees is a paved terrace with twin fountains and knot beds. The high wall behind provides space and shelter for a whole array of climbers and tall shrubs needing protection, and in the centre of the wall is a loggia bowered in the pink-flowered *Clematis montana*. Beyond the garden is a rhododendron plantation. To greet you as you open the white door leading to it is a mimosa. The lawns round the noble and beautiful castle are studded with magnificent beeches.

279

Portmeirion

Zone Centre: Betws-y-Coed, Route 2

Owner: The Portmeirion Trustees

The whole thing came into being on the inspiration of
Clough Williams-Ellis, the famous Welsh architect, who had
the idea of creating on a sea-girt peninsula in Merioneth a
complete Italian village. The notion was laughed at, but few
could help admiring it when they came to see it, and here it
is today with its soaring campanile, its baroque archway by
which you enter, its pretty wrought iron balconies, its
colonnade, and shutter-windowed and pantile-roofed houses
with a real street winding in and out among them and round
a village square. Visiting it you are transported to Italy, but
if you have come to see a garden you will find it in spring,
in the woodland behind where there are magnificent rhododendrons from the Kingdon-Ward expeditions, up to forty
feet tall. Apart from these, much more interesting to garden-
lovers is Mr Williams-Ellis's private garden at **Plas Brondanw** four miles away, seldom open but worth waiting for,
wherein again his love of Italy is expressed. We find pencil
junipers and tall conical yews punctuating the scene. A
delightful flagged terrace runs the length of the house and
beyond. The whole garden is planned for vistas – a view of
Cnicht, the Welsh Matterhorn (which he owns), and breaks
in yew hedges to command a view of Snowdon rising above
the trees. It is a very lovely garden, and in it you can see

the famous little Fire Boy with his helmet and hose, which
he designed.

Powis Castle Gardens

Zone Centre: Shrewsbury, Route 1

Owner: The National Trust

What a romantic place is Powis, its castle set on a lofty
ridge, its gardens cascading down in terraces to acres of
green lawn. How excellently and colourfully are its gardens
planted. Looking from the Wilderness on the opposite side,
glorious in spring with its species and hybrid rhododendrons
and at all times for its interesting trees, you see it in all its
splendour, the unbelievable terraces rising up and up to
the castle with its walls of glowing pink sandstone aflame
with virginia creeper. Dividing the castle from the terraces
is a line of bonnet-shaped yews. They are somehow Powis.
How can I describe this wonderful garden? It is fifty acres of
sheer delight which I hope you will not rush round like the
tourist who took one sweeping look from the top terrace and
came out saying: 'Most beautiful garden I ever saw.' Powis
deserves hours. It is full of interesting plants beautifully
displayed. On the first terrace you will find a lovely border
of floribunda roses with a fuchsia hedge above them. There
are mixed borders with such delights as *Yucca recurvifolia*
with its bent-back sabres and single spire of white bells.

Magnolias grow against the high retaining wall, and at the eastern end you will see the magnificent statue of Hercules slaying the many-headed dragon. When you go down to the second or Aviary Terrace, note the rare *Helichrysum rosmarinifolium* against the wall. Its bunches of creamy flowers are beloved by the Humming-Bird Hawk Moth. In the old aviary tender rhododendrons are grown in a raised border, all chosen for their sweet scent, and outside are stone troughs filled with the charming blue daisy, *Aster pappiae*. Along the balustrading stand delightful shepherds and shepherdesses. The wall at the back is important for its wealth of climbers and wall shrubs including the attractive *Clerodendron bungei* from China with its starry pink flowers. The third or main terrace has as its centrepiece the old Orangery, and on the balustrade here are terracotta vases filled with silver helichrysum and dusty-coral geraniums of exactly the same colour as the castle walls, a touch of Powis artistry. Along this terrace are herbaceous borders gorgeous with colour – the scarlet of Cardinal Flowers, the gold plate of achilleas, brilliant puce phloxes, bronze heleniums, pyramids of sweet peas, golden dahlias and montbretias, malvas, penstemons. . . . The steps leading to the Apple Slope are roses all the way, and to the right is a walk of well-grown acers and such colourful things as Japanese spindles with their brilliant scarlet hearts. To the left is an English border dominated by hollyhocks. At ground level are various enclosed gardens, quietudes with lawns and fountains and sundials, clipped yew hedges, pyramid apple trees and a border massed with vivid purple phloxes. It is here you must turn to see again the rosy-stoned castle against the skyline with the fantastic thirty-four-foot-tall yew hedges sheltering it from the cutting east wind. Powis Castle and its gardens you will long remember.

Sandon Hall

Zone Centre: Shrewsbury, Route 3

Owner: The Earl of Harrowby

It is a family garden full of memories, and perhaps as Lord Harrowby says you may catch a glimpse of some Shade gliding among the trees. But I am sure they are happy ones, for it is a pleasant place with its restful woodlands and formal and informal gardens. There are some outstanding features, such as the Amphitheatre, an impressive circular garden mainly devoted to roses but surrounded on one side with a towering bank of rhododendrons with ash and beech trees behind. To the left, over an attractive cornus hedge, is an open view of splendid mixed conifers. A fountain plays among the roses, and golden-privet balls are used as a formal decoration. Quite different is the Rose Walk with its broad flagged path between beds patterned in inter-locking L-shapes. Each bed holds a different rose and the colours are carefully grouped. At one end is an orangery and at the other is the Temple Garden reached by a pergola all roses and vines. Two huge Chinese lions guard the entrance to a small ante-room garden where all the roses are red. The Temple Garden is circular, with a grass cross dividing the rose beds. Deep in the woodland you will find a Tree Garden of Remembrance. On a Sunday evening, 17th May 1936, ex-servicemen of all the combatant countries of the Great War met here to plant ornamental trees in a gesture of friendship.

The trees were then linked with ribbons of each country's national colours. But the part of the garden you may like best is the lawn at the back of the house surrounded by curving beds of rhododendrons, acers, berberis, roses, with fine clumps of trees breaking the skyline. Atlas cedars, weeping beech, conifers, sorbus, birches and willows, all are perfectly positioned, each tree complementary to its neighbours, each seen in its individual beauty. The planting is skilful. No heavy hand but lightness and airiness without sacrificing any sense of shelter.

Weston Park

Zone Centre: Shrewsbury, Route 3

Owner: The Earl of Bradford

There are some nice things to be found in the fifty acres of this garden and woodland, with a 'Capability' Brown lake in the parkland and some truly wonderful trees including three massive sweet chestnuts growing side by side, and a quite enormous oriental plane with spreading branches that lean on the ground and grow up again like a forest. It is reputed to be as old as the house, which dates back to 1671. In the formal gardens in front of the house are charming lead figures of children, and on the far side of the lawn a tunnel leads to a Temple of Diana which has an exquisite plaster ceiling and Doric pillars, the work of James Paine.

You reach it by a woodland walk among rhododendrons growing in the shade of beech trees, sweet chestnuts and planes. Then comes the Temple Pool with its delightful Paine Bridge. Cross it to see the cherry avenue and the Pink Cottage. From the house in the opposite direction you must visit Pendrill's Cave, dwelling place of a famous tramp. You can read a long poem about him at the entrance to the Orangery. Above the cave is a long rose walk curving round almost in a complete circle back to the house.

Also open are:

BERRINGTON HALL **(Zone Centre: Hereford, Route 1. Owner: The National Trust)** with a 'Capability' Brown landscape and herbaceous borders.

CROFT CASTLE **(Zone Centre: Hereford, Route 2. Owner: The National Trust)** which has an enclosed herb garden and whose grounds contain the best Sweet Chestnut avenue in Britain.

EASTNOR CASTLE **(Zone Centre: Hereford, Route 1. Owner: The Hon Mrs Hervey Bathurst)** where there are fine specimen trees in an arboretum.

GWYDIR CASTLE **(Zone Centre: Betws-y-Coed, Route 1. Owner: Richard Clegg, Esq)** with a courtyard garden, peacocks and four vast cedars remaining from twelve planted to commemorate the wedding of Charles I.

There is also Percy Thrower's garden, THE MAGNO-LIAS **(Shrewsbury, Route 2)**, open seldom but worth seeing. It was started in 1963 and looks long established: real life this time, not television. An inspiration to others who have a new garden and wonder what to grow in it. Here in one and a half acres is a bit of everything – rock garden, island beds and mixed borders, with a labour-saving policy of permanent planting.

ZONE 10 The South-West Lowlands and The West Highlands.

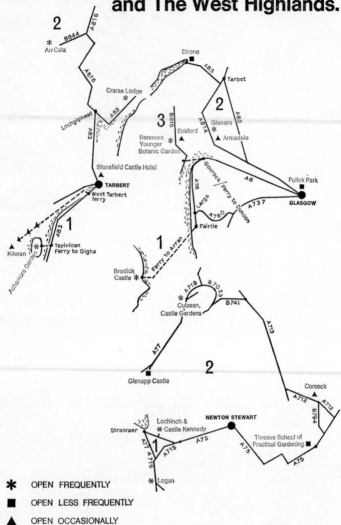

2
* An Cala
B844
A816
A816

Strone
A83
Tarbet
Crarae Lodge *
A83
2
Glenarn
A82
* Glenarn
Armadale

Lochgilphead
A83

3
B815
Eckford ▲
A814
Benmore Younger Botanic Garden *
A83

Stonefield Castle Hotel
A83

● TARBERT
West Tarbert ferry

Gourock / Ferry to Dunoon
A8
Pollok Park

A78
Largs
A737
GLASGOW ●

A760
1
Tayinloan Ferry to Gigha
A83
Ferry to Arran
Fairlie

▲ Kiloran
* Achamore Garden

Brodick Castle *
1

A719
B7023
* Culzean, Castle Gardens
B741

A77
A713

2

■ Glenapp Castle

Corsock ▲
A712
B794
A712

Lochinch & * Castle Kennedy
NEWTON STEWART ●
Stranraer
A77 A716
1
A715
A75
A75
Threave School of Practical Gardening ■
A75
A75

* Logan

✱ OPEN FREQUENTLY

■ OPEN LESS FREQUENTLY

▲ OPEN OCCASIONALLY

ZONE 10

The South-west Lowlands and the West Highlands of Scotland

THE SCENES OF this Zone are set in two very different parts of Scotland, each with an entirely different historical background. The countryside around Newton Stewart is gently hilly, and it was in these green folds that the Covenanters held their prayer meetings and were routed. You can see in the churchyard at New Galloway and all around the graves of the martyrs who died for their faith. Others, more fortunate, were sent to the plantations in America. The struggle ended at last in 1688.

Just north of Glasgow begins the romance and grandeur of the West Highlands. Our gardens tour takes you to three of the islands – to Gigha (pronounced Gee-a with a hard G), where Sir James Horlick has one of the greatest rhododendron gardens in Britain; Islay (pronounced Isle-a), home of Lord Strathcona and Mount Royal (the same Mount Royal as at Montreal, Canada); and Arran, Glasgow's wonderful holiday island. Your journey from Glasgow, if you come that way, is an unending panorama of magnificent bens and glens, with lochs and sea lochs from Balloch onwards. Lovely islanded Loch Lomond, the largest in Scotland, stretches for twenty-three miles and ends in the mighty Ben of that name, 3,192 feet high. From Glasgow to Inveraray is with hardly a doubt the most beautiful motor run in the whole of Scotland, and it is not hard to people the heathered hills with the kilted supporters of Bonnie Prince Charlie, for thousands of them marched this way. Once on Loch Fyne you are in Campbell country, and approaching Inveraray you will see the picturesque castle home of the Duke of Argyll. Now you are well and truly in the Highlands.

Many of the gardens are at their best in rhododendron time. It is a long season, starting from early spring and going right into the summer, when other flowering shrubs and formal gardens come into their own. At Logan you have the complete contrast of a sub-tropical garden with palm trees and exotic plants from warm climes all over the world.

Achamore Garden, Isle of Gigha

Zone Centre: Tarbert, Route 1

Owner: Lt-Col Sir James Horlick, Bt, OBE, MC, VMH

This is a pilgrimage garden which comes into the fabulous class. If you have never appreciated the really astonishing and varied beauty of rhododendrons, you will do so here. For who could help it? There are sixty acres filled with them, and the lay-out is a design around the plants rather than borders of plants as a decoration to a landscape. There are massed displays in the woodlands and there are 'rooms' of them there. When Sir James Horlick has any special rhododendron he wants to surprise you with he plants walls around it, a living green background of cupressus. He makes you approach it by a winding path, so that you come upon it suddenly, and there it is, a single breathtaking specimen you must stop to admire – a magnificent *sinogrande* with its elephant leaves and enormous creamy-white trusses of flowers; in another, *calophytum*, pale pink with a crimson throat. In the East Spring Garden are the tender rhododendrons, *fragrantissima* for one. Down south you have to grow it in a greenhouse. In another part are the dwarf rhododendrons like little Songbird of dark purple flowers, Sir James's outstanding contribution to the rhododendron world, and his Songster and the Titness series he has produced – Titness Beauty, Titness Pink, and Titness Park which blooms very early in March and has won him a Royal Horticultural Society Award of Merit. Not that Achamore is all rhododendrons. There are more formal places such as the walled garden – 'the windiest garden', as Sir James described it, but even here he grows Queen Elizabeth roses ten feet tall, and the rare *Rubus* 'Tridel' with its white butterfly petals, the fascinating Lobster Claw and a white form of it which is the biggest in the country. The Mexican Pine is supposed to be rather a delicate tree: Sir James has a fine specimen of it here and admits justifiably: 'I'm proud of that.' There is a natural bog garden where grows the single white marsh marigold and where drifts of candelabra primulas find a happy home, orange, coral, white, where mecanopsis, the Himalayan poppy, opens its bright blue cups and the ten-foot-tall *Lilium cardiocrinum* makes magnificent bursts of white. From the moment you enter the gates of Achamore you know you are entering somewhere special. I deplore any drive that is neglected: you are still worrying about it even while admiring a good garden at the end of it. The drive up to Achamore is spectacular with azaleas in exquisite combinations of apricot and peach, apricot and cream. They are in winding beds on a carpet of wide and perfectly kept grass verge, all against a background of solid green. Achamore is all like that. Sudden perfect groups of flowers. But of course it is the rhododendrons that hold you spellbound, garden after garden of them in the woodlands: the Leo Garden a magnificent blaze of scarlet among tree ferns, where also grow the sweet fresh pink Flamingo and Nasturtium, both bred by Sir James; the Loderi Garden, the Outer and Inner Circles, the Chestnut Grove, and the Wee Walk on the way back to the house where you will find Brocade and Brocade Plus – one of Sir James's favourites and 'one of the best in the garden'. He started making Achamore's garden in 1945 when he purchased the Island of Gigha. It was a jungle of ponticum, the old common rhododendron that has become a pest. What he has done with it you must see for yourself. Soon that fine garden at Brodick, owned by the National Trust for Scotland, will be a 'home from home' for his collection. Gigha will still go on, the parent plants will still be there; but in order to ensure that his collection will not be scattered, he has 'left his plants' to the Trust.

An Cala

Zone Centre: Tarbert, Route 2

Owner: Mrs H I Blakeney

The address is the Isle of Seil (by Easdale), but you wouldn't notice. No boat or ferry is required to reach this gem of a garden overlooking the Atlantic. It was designed and laid out between 1930 and 1940 by Faith Celli, the actress, and her husband, Col Arthur Murray. Between them they transformed a Highland croft and its three acres of grazing land into a garden of lawns with trees and shrubs, winding borders following the contours of the land, and a rock garden using the natural outcrop, all set against a background of woodland high above, sweet with the music of a small burn and waterfall. Behind are rocky hills. At the top of the path, mostly steps, is a seat counselling 'Rest'. It is a good place for that and from which to view the scene spread below – the Atlantic scattered with magical isles: Scarba, Beulnahua, Fladda and the long thin strip of Luing; with Eilean an Naoimh, the Heavenly Island, and the Garbhelliachs. The whole comprise, most appropriately, the 'Isles of the Sea'. What distinguishes this garden is the clever choice of trees and shrubs. Rarely have I seen trees better chosen for 'garden size'. Some are of the weeping variety, like the charming cotoneasters by the rock garden, and the cherries on the lawn. Their lilliputian dimensions make the garden seem much larger than it is (and they will never hide the view). The rock garden is a delight with its stone seat half-circling the old apple tree there, steps of the local slate leading up and down and a little Narcissus-like figure looking at her image in the pool which is garlanded with azaleas, a colourful corner that merges into great natural boulders planted with flowering shrubs. One needs colour in this sometimes grey climate. Here one can rejoice in it. Beyond the lawn is a series of protected terraces where roses grow well, especially the pinky-red floribunda Betty Prior which flowers the whole season. There is a bank of purple vincas, clumps of blue agapanthus lilies, and among the shrubs the Chilean Holly, *Desfontainea spinosa*, and the pale pink oak-leaved azalea. The retaining walls are bright with such colourful rock plants as *Erinus alpinus* (whose pinkish-purple little flowers cover the arches of the famous 'Only Bridge over the Atlantic' which you will see on your way here). The house, once a glorified but-and-ben, has been extended with a small wing, and a second wing of overlap timber incorporating a loggia. It is a charming and homely dwelling whose creeper- and shrub-clad walls add their colour: the South American *Drimys winteri*, roses and clematis. Over the loggia is the Dutchman's Pipe vine whose leaves in the autumn are ambers, golds and peridot green. An Cala means The Haven – and what better name could it have?

Benmore, The Younger Botanic Garden

Zone Centre: Glasgow, Route 3

Owner: Controlled by The Royal Botanic
Garden, Edinburgh

You could call it a paradise of trees. Rare, tender and
native, most of them are conifers; and the famous avenue of
giant sequoias, 130 to 145 feet high, is a novel introduction
to the glades of rhododendrons for which Benmore is also
famed, more than three hundred species ones and over four
hundred named hybrids. They are arranged in their different
series, the dark-leaved Fulvums (with trusses of smaller
flowers) leading to the Campanulatums which are all from
the Himalayas and whose colours range from white through
pale and deeper rose to lavender-purple. And so on, series
after series, the tree-tall Barbatums, and the Cinnabarinums
which are almost the most beautiful of all, blue-leaved with
long bell-like flowers of rich plum-purple, mauve-pink, buff
and orange to apricot. From May to June they are a wonderful sight. Specimen trees grow among them, the fascinating
Brewer's Spruce whose down-swept feathery foliage is so
beautiful on a misty morning, a 156-foot-high *Tsuga
heterophylla* (the Western Hemlock) which is probably the
tallest specimen in Britain, the handsome oriental spruce
(*Picea orientalis*), Chinese firs, and many more. Some of the
best are the great Douglas Firs from California, introduced

by the plant-hunter David Douglas who seemed to find a new conifer every week! These are easily recognisable by their bare straight boles, the egg-shaped cones which hang downwards, and if the tree is a mature specimen its deeply fissured bark which is greyish, whereas the bark of a Scots Pine is strikingly reddish. Besides the underplanting of rhododendrons there are earlier-flowering shrubs such as the fragrant Chinese *Osmanthus delavayi*, doubly so after a shower of rain, and ones that flower after the rhododendrons are over, like the holly-leaved desfontainea with its yellow-lipped red flowers in August. There are one hundred acres at Benmore and wide pleasant paths to take you round each part of the garden. Seats are provided for you to pause and admire its many different features, not only the woodland glades but the 'vertical garden', a wall in the Water Garden clothed with fuchsias, veronicas, cotoneasters, bergenias, ferns, and bright yellow Welsh poppies; and the pond where golden carp swim. In May and June azaleas scent the whole place and their reflections in the water with those of thousands of primulas is something you will not want to miss. You will also wish to visit the Rock Face, a natural setting for dwarf conifers and dwarf rhododendrons, at their best in May. The path to the View Point can be reached in easy stages, with seats along the way. The climb is worth it, a superb view of Sandbank and the Holy Loch. Benmore is worth visiting at any time of the year: if you miss the great show of rhododendrons the summer eucryphias with their glistening white flowers will be one compensation among many. In September the maples, birches, fothergillas, stranvaesias and skimmias make the dullest day bright with their berries and coloured leaves.

Brodick Castle Garden

Zone Centre: Glasgow, Route 1

Owner: The National Trust for Scotland

Here is another rhododendron garden, this time on the Island of Arran, and as the steamer turns in for Brodick Pier you will see the red sandstone castle snug among its trees on a foothill of the mountains rising up to the peak of Goat Fell. The planting of the wild garden was begun after the First World War when Farrer, Forrest, Kingdon-Ward and other famous plant-hunters were collecting new rhododendron species in China, Yunnan, Burma and Tibet. Many came back to Brodick, and the later expeditions of Ludlow and Sherriff contributed some of the sweet-scented ones which usually have to be grown under glass. Brodick's seventy-inch rainfall and mild climate makes it possible to grow them out of doors, as witness the one called *giganteum*, known in the wilds to reach ninety feet. Brodick is one of the few places in Britain where it comes into flower, and show-blooms are cut from it every year. Another contribution was from the rhododendron fancier, the late Sir John Ramsden, who sent a puffer-load of them from his own garden, and now another collection is joining them – from Sir James Horlick's famous garden on Gigha: he has left his plants to the National Trust and a special home is being made for them in the hills above the garden. There are plenty of flowers and flowering shrubs to be seen out of rhododendron time. If you are there in August you should find among them the tricuspidaria from Chile with its beautiful little lantern flowers, the fascinating Bottle-Brush bushes, scarlet and yellow, and the lily-like clethras. Earlier in the summer find your way to the rose garden which you see from the terrace as you come in, where there is a glorious view of the Firth of Clyde. In fact there is plenty of bloom from early spring to late autumn in eighty acres of gardens that include a rock garden and pond garden, in a setting of trees and spacious lawns.

Crarae Lodge

Zone Centre: Tarbert, Route 2

Owner: Sir Ilay Campbell, Bt

The late Sir George Campbell was over-modest about his garden. He did not, he once told members of the Royal Horticultural Society, consider it among the first rank of Scottish gardens. Strange then that, the year before, Crarae had come out top of the list in the takings for charity! It is certainly much-loved as well as much-visited, and no wonder. The glen in which it is laid out (if you can call it that, for it is all as natural-looking as the Crarae Burn which chuckles down through it) is filled with a sequence of colour from daffodil time when its glades and slopes are 'out of this world', till autumn paints the disanthus bushes first

golden-red and then, in October, a real rich port-wine ruby –
'Vintage', emphasises Sir Ilay Campbell who continues the
work of beautifying Crarae with the same devotion as his
father. There are plenty more autumn things: the azaleas
which, after they have flowered, start to concentrate on
producing bronze in their leaves, scarlets and ambers;
sorbus trees, with their Scottish cousin the rowan hanging
with berries yellow and red; brilliant acers; larches that fade
to a misty gold. And before the frost comes in February the
first rhododendron is in bloom, the gorgeous *barbatum* with
its beautiful smooth brown bark and burning blood-red
flowers. For this is one of Scotland's finest rhododendron
gardens. Sir Ilay's grandmother did the first important plantings, and she was lucky in having the famous plant collector
Reginald Farrer for a nephew; but most of the rhododendrons
came from Sir John Stirling Maxwell's garden at Pollok,
now one of the Glasgow parks. Sir George Campbell carried
on his mother's congenial task with the greatest assembly of
them, many coming as gifts from other gardens. In fact it was
the gift of a tree, *Cunninghamia lanceolata*, which set him off
as a gardener. The late Colonel R F S Balfour gave it to him
in a pot, saying that he couldn't grow it at Dawyck and that
he had better try it at Crarae. The tree is now well over fifty
feet tall. You know immediately you have arrived at Crarae.
Looking from the road you see a house and beside it a mound
covered with a blaze of azaleas, which are the deciduous
rhododendrons. There can't, you feel, be another garden on
the shores of Loch Fyne as lovely as this one promises to be.
And there isn't.

Culzean Castle Gardens

Zone Centre: Newton Stewart, Route 2

Owner: The National Trust for Scotland

It is pronounced Cul-*ain* and it is a show place with one
hundred thousand visitors a year. They come to see its romantic castle (one of Robert Adam's 'jewels') and to wander
round its gardens and policies (as they are called in Scotland,
'grounds' in England, 'demesne' in Ireland), a walk that
takes forty-five minutes, with another hour and a half for the
Woodlands and Outer Policies. A great deal of new planting
has been done recently in the gardens. In 1961 the Trust's
Gardens Committee allocated one thousand pounds to
improve them. The results are now evident in colourful new
shrubs, flowering trees and, in the walled garden, a big
herbaceous border running down the centre, with twenty-
three different kinds of Crab Apple in grass plots. Part of
the project was the restoration of the second walled garden,
the old Pleasure Garden. It was choked with ponticums (the
common pale mauve rhododendrons you see in woods, first
introduced at Culzean around 1760 and since become a
horticultural cannibal), and great was the excitement as they
hacked and sawed away when there was gradually revealed
a grove of Chinese Chusan palm trees! There are plenty of
pleasant places to reach by the many woodland paths. The
seven-acre Fountain Court you will see as you come in: it is
in front of the castle. Behind it, through the trees, is the

Camellia House; and if you want a view of the sea, take the Cliff Walk for the sight of distant Arran and its magical mountains. I think I liked best the walk I took on a May afternoon to Swan Lake. The Happy Valley was full of doronicums, an escape years ago from the garden. Their tall golden daisies were splashing the woodland with sunshine. Nature had more successfully landscaped here than in the Pleasure Garden. American visitors will be particularly interested in Culzean for its association with General Eisenhower who at the end of the Second World War was given the top flat for his lifetime's use.

Glenapp Castle

Zone Centre: Newton Stewart, Route 2

Owners: Lord and Lady Inchcape

This is a happy garden, which is to say that its owners really care about it and, sharing a vision of what it could be, have fired the enthusiasm of everyone around them, as witness the eighty rose bushes they received as a wedding present in 1965, and the attractive tearoom run by the gardener's wife who in this way is drawing more people to see it. So the old walled vegetable garden is turning from a blank space into a secret garden, a nook-and-cranny garden either side of the July and August herbaceous borders that divide it. The ditch that crosses them at right angles ran under a mound of ivy, now removed to reveal a bridge. The enclosing walls grow forty different clematis. An enchanting little rose garden has been created outside the hothouse. Vistas have been made in the undulating woodland to see the views of stream and waterfall and the sea view over the Atlantic. The always dramatic *Gunnera manicata* with its huge rhubarb leaves has been planted by the old fish ponds. It is a gradual but exciting transformation. A formal rose garden looks over the woodland from the back of the house. Below this a heather garden is coming into being, labour-saving and just the right thing to merge into the glades which have been cleared for rhododendrons and azaleas.

Glenarn

Zone Centre: Glasgow, Route 2

Owners: A C Gibson, Esq, and J F A Gibson, Esq

It is known affectionately as 'the Gibsons' garden' because they all own and help to look after it. It is also known as a fine rhododendron garden. The house was built in the 1830s by one of the Macgeorge family who was a friend of Sir William Hooker, then regius professor of botany at Glasgow University, ten years later to leave Glasgow for Kew where he created the Gardens we know today. In the late 1840s his son Joseph was in India discovering the great Himalayan rhododendrons such as *falconeri* (named after his

302

friend Hugh Falconer) and the silver-stemmed *thomsonii* (named after his friend Dr Thomas Thomson). When the seeds came home Sir William distributed them among the West Highland gardens and others where a wet mild climate and peaty soil would be right for them. Some came to Glenarn where a big *falconeri* still remains from those days. When the Gibsons took over about forty years ago the garden was a jungle, but the *falconeri* was there and two other Hooker plants – a *Picea smithiana* and a *Pinus wallichiana* (*excelsis*), named after Dr Nathaniel Wallich, the botanical explorer and friend of both Hookers. This was inspiration enough, if inspiration were needed. Out of the woodland glen the Gibsons have created the outstanding rhododendron garden where they now breed their own hybrids, named after their animals and members of their family – 'Pook', a cat, and 'Pook's Child', 'Ronald', a brother. It is an enchanting walk up the glen to see them all, especially in the company of Mrs A C Gibson who has a great sense of fun. She pointed out the plateau which was a colourful carpet of candelabra primulas. 'Known as "Granny's Hens",' she explained, 'because she kept them there.' We walked on and up, always pausing to admire another rhododendron. ' "Mother's Meat Jelly",' she identified one. It was not its official name, but the description was apt of its orange-tawny bells. In all there are six hundred species rhododendrons to admire, and many other plants. I loved the asteranthera growing up an oak tree, turning its mossy trunk into a cloud of carmine flowers. A climbing hydrangea used another tree as support. The glen is something you should see. It looks down to the Gareloch in its setting of magnificent hills.

Lochinch and Castle Kennedy

Zone Centre: Newton Stewart, Route 1

Owner: Col the Earl of Stair

It is an immense place: you can hardly call it just a garden. It was conceived in the eighteenth century and landscaped on spacious lines, as, for instance, the vista along a couple or more miles between Lochinch Castle, the modern residence built in 1867, and ancient Castle Kennedy which it replaced. The latter is now a roofless ivied ruin, the haunt of rooks and loud with pigeon wings when you enter it. From it stretch acres of lawn to the interesting grassed-over earthworks which are like a giant's stairway. They are known as The Guardsman's Bonnet. The Second Earl of Stair was a military man, a Field Marshal who became Ambassador to France. Inspired by the gardens of the French King at Versailles he commandeered the Royal Scots Greys and the Inniskilling Fusiliers and got them working at a Versailles of his own. But he was a military man and no Versailles emerged, instead a series of campaigns translated into plants. The avenues converging on the circular lily pond like the spokes of a giant wheel are named after the battles he fought. There is Dettingen Avenue, and a mount is named Marlborough. Tree-wise the avenues are unique, one of Monkey Puzzles, now seventy feet tall and the finest in Britain; Dettingen of holm oak, unusual in Scotland. Others are of conifers, each of a different kind. Then there are the

Review Order rhododendrons in the Circular Garden, Castle Kennedy's own hybrid. With many rare shrubs and lilies they all form a huge botanical collection. But even if you know nothing about botany, these grounds are a joy to wander. There are so many delightful things: the view of the round pond through a mass of flowering rhododendrons, the way down to it banked with azaleas, which circle the pond too; the magnolias, the nyssa trees which turn such a wonderful gold in autumn, with two sheets of water, the Black Loch and the White Loch, between which lie the gardens.

Logan

Zone Centre: Newton Stewart, Route 1

Owner: Ministry of Public Buildings and Works

The Logan Garden is a phenomenon, made possible by the mild climate of the Mull of Galloway. It is surrounded on three sides by the sea. A hard frost seldom visits it; hence the tropical plants for which Logan is famous. As you enter the garden gate you see why, for your introduction is an avenue of Chusan Palms with their fuzzy trunks like no British tree, and almost immediately the brilliant red flowers of the New Zealand Parrot's Bill arrest your attention – if, that is, you come in June or July when it is in bloom. But whether you do or not, exotics are in flower here the year round. The very air seems tropical, for Logan is a tight set of gardens, eleven in all, enclosed by sheltering trees. It is hard to believe you are in Scotland: in fact you don't think of it. There are three and a half acres of gardens, each with interesting plants from the hot places of the world (you will see their countries of origin written on their labels), like the *Fuchsia excorticata* whose pollen is used by the Maori women as a cosmetic. Other fuchsias seed themselves all over the place. They are almost a pest here! The Water Garden is a delight, where Tree Ferns grow like inside-out umbrellas, though much more beautiful. Here, too, is the attractive Chilian myrtle with its cinnamon stems, white flowers and black sweet fruits. The next garden is dominated by the Cabbage Palm which is really a member of the lily family: Captain Cook found it in New Zealand in 1772, and in part of the Walled Garden there is a whole avenue of it. In July you can see their great heads of bloom, up to four feet long, creamy white and fragrant. Cabbage Palms are usually called Cordylines, their Latin name; and just as in the tropics trees are covered with creepers, climbing the stems of the cordylines are two attractive ones – the Australian Blue-bell with its little clusters of nodding flowers in July, and the white-flowered *Decumaria barbara* flowering in June and July. You must not miss the drifts of Himalayan Poppies. The single blue one, of an unbelievable blue, was the first to come to this country, sent home by Sir Joseph Hooker. There are others with scarlet and yellow flowers. But I cannot list all the many fascinating plants: I can only say – in any tour of Scottish gardens Logan should not be left out.

Pollok Park

Zone Centre: Glasgow, Route 3

Owner: The Glasgow Corporation

It is not the purpose of this guide-book to write up the many public parks, beautiful as some of them are, in Glasgow as elsewhere – **Bellahouston** with its 176 undulating acres, sunk garden and masses of bulbs in the spring; the **Botanic Garden** with the much-loved Kibble Palace, one of the largest glass structures of its kind in the world; the **Victoria Park** with its Fossil Grove which attracts visitors from all over the world. But I must mention **Pollok Park** because of its association with Sir John Stirling Maxwell who died in 1956. Here over a great number of years he established a magnificent garden full of valuable trees and shrubs. He gave plants to many gardens since become famous. In turn his garden was given to Glasgow by the Maxwell Macdonald family in 1967. Rhododendrons were Sir John's particular interest and he was responsible for many new hybrids. Here his large collection is completely at home in natural woodlands. Although most of the garden is informal there is a charming terrace garden full of roses in knot beds, with a sloping alpine garden, again formal, and on a terrace walk more box-edged beds with pansies and roses.

Strone

Zone Centre: Glasgow, Route 2

Owner: The Rt Hon Michael Noble, MP

What you see from the road (at the bottom of a very steep hill) is pleasant sloping grass attractively planted with shrubs ending in showers of cherry blossom. But this is only the 'front garden'. The rest of the twelve acres is woodland where rhododendrons grow, species ones and a lot of Mr Noble's own hybrids and other people's. He started growing them thirty-five years ago, raising them as small plants and then putting them out in the woods. These are below his house and in them, all among the rhododendrons, is the biggest conifer in Europe, an *Abies alba*, which is probably two hundred years old. It is fantastic, breaking from ground level in four enormous limbs, before which you stand disbelieving. The tree is one hundred and seventy feet tall and each limb weighs a hundred tons. To reach the woods you walk by the River Kinglas. Kingly trees surround you. *Abies alba* is certainly king of them all.

The Threave School of Gardening

Zone Centre: Newton Stewart, Route 2

Owner: The National Trust for Scotland

It may not sound exciting, a school of gardening, but Threave when you see it banishes any such thought. It is not only exciting in its attractive lay-out but in its purpose as a training ground for young gardeners. (Would there were more of them; for after this generation of gardeners has gone, where shall we find the next, except at such places as Threave?) Wisley and Kew cater for much older students. Threave takes them at seventeen and eighteen after only one year of practical gardening. It teaches them every kind of gardening, and here there are gardens of every kind: rock, peat, woodland, heath, rose garden, with the popular water garden and its pool. The students even learn how to shift trees for 'instant gardens'. Threave's heath garden was made only in 1966 but from its first days it looked established with its grove of birches twenty-five feet tall, at which height they had been transplanted. I saw some newly transplanted trees in another part of the garden. From a distance they looked like large woolly mummies. Closer, I found they were conifers wound round with protective sack-cloth. With this and with guy-ropes to keep them steady, they were starting life in their new homes. They tell me it is easy to shift trees from one place to another (and some gardeners I have met positively delight in regrouping great shrubs, just as a woman now and again likes to move around the furniture). So if you are making a new garden on the instant method, come here for a few wrinkles. The fifty acres of Threave are worth visiting, and students come not only from Scotland and England but from many other parts of the world. It is in a perfect setting, looking to the hills.

The following are open only occasionally:

ARMADALE, RHU **(Zone Centre: Glasgow, Route 2. Owner: Lt-Col Kenneth Barge,** DSO, MC**)** is a charming garden of six and a half acres. Orchard thick with crocuses, daffodils and fritillaries followed by moon daisies. Good azalea groups and rhododendrons, and a rock garden with a stream.

CORSOCK, CASTLE DOUGLAS **(Zone Centre: Newton Stewart, Route 2. Owner: F L Ingall, Esq).** Informal woodland and water with interesting follies and bridge. There are good Douglas Firs and a collection of rhododendrons including a *lacteum* which has won many annual awards of the RHS.

ECKFORD, DUNOON **(Zone Centre: Glasgow, Route 3. Owner: J W Younger, Esq).** This is a small rhododendron and shrub glen garden on the shores of Loch Eck, among trees, mostly conifers.

KILORAN, ISLE OF COLONSAY **(Zone Centre: Tarbert, Route 3. Owner: Lord Strathcona and Mount Royal).** It is difficult to get there because of the infrequency of steamers; but if you are holidaying in Colonsay in June, here is a rhododendron garden with special features. One is Sino Valley where you can see the big-leaved ones growing at their best (leaves sometimes two feet long and the flower trusses ten inches in diameter). *Sinogrande* is the finest yellow-flowered rhododendron of them all. Also, Loder was the maiden name of Lord Strathcona's wife: a whole series of rhododendrons was named in her honour, of which Loder's White is acknowledged the best of any white rhododendron. See, too, the scarlet Embothrium Alley. Kiloran is a port of call for the yacht which makes an annual tour of gardens in the Highlands and Islands.

STONEFIELD CASTLE HOTEL GARDENS **(Zone Centre: Tarbert, Route 1. Owners: The Proprietors).** The garden was famous in the 1850s and onwards as the chief repository of Sir Joseph Hooker's rhododendron seeds from the Himalayas. It was then owned by a friend of Joseph's father. Many of the original Hooker plants still grow there, tree-sized *barbatums* with their startling red blooms, and *falconeris*. Stonefield Castle looks over Loch Fyne.

ZONE 11 Edinburgh and The Borders.

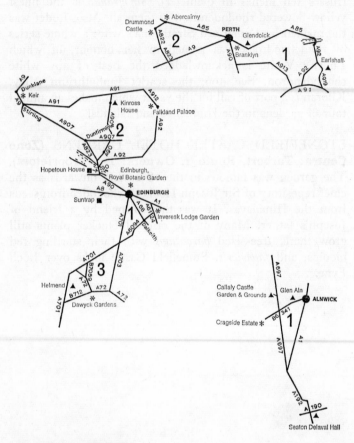

* OPEN FREQUENTLY

■ OPEN LESS FREQUENTLY

▲ OPEN OCCASIONALLY

ZONE 11

Edinburgh and the Borders

THE GARDENS ROUND about Edinburgh are interesting ones, some attached to historic houses and castles having been restored and replanted, and it is surprising what grows on the reputedly cold East Coast with no cosseting in the winter months. Spring is later but it comes with a burst of blossom.

In the capital itself the Edinburgh Royal Botanic Garden is more than its name suggests, beautifully laid out and with a famous collection of rhododendrons. If you have never seen these shrubs in all their splendour of varied colours and habit, this is the place to make their acquaintance.

Driving to and from some of the gardens you will cross the new Forth Road Bridge, spectacular by day and night. You can hardly lose your way: the conical green hill called Arthur's Seat is a landmark for miles around Edinburgh. The capital itself is renowned for its beauty, its one-thousand-year-old Castle perched on the famous Rock high above Princes Street. From this eminence every day at one o'clock a gun booms out the hour. Traffic is kept moving wonderfully: I have never yet known a jam in Princes Street – where, by the way, you can see the celebrated Floral Clock.

You will be surprised how quickly you can lose Edinburgh's

houses. In only minutes, it seems, you are up among the peace of the Braid Hills. Picturesque villages like Cramond hide in coves along the wide River Forth, and there are plenty of holiday places with good bathing.

The other great river you will meet, going for instance to Earlshall, is the Tay, famed for its salmon, as Loch Leven – which you will see when you visit the gardens at Kinross House – is famous for its pink-fleshed trout.

The Lowlands scenery around Dawyck is very lovely, with trees and hills and delightful country roads. History is everywhere, dating back to Roman times. If you visit the garden at Helmend you can see up among the hills and silhouetted against the sky the native forts built against the Roman invasion.

Abercairny

Zone Centre: Perth, Route 2

Owner: Major J S H Drummond Moray

This is the story of a garden that got moved around a bit. There was a complicated Italianate garden involving too much labour for modern times. It was remodelled and Alexander Paton, the head gardener, simplified the borders and sowed much of it down to grass. Behind were forty rhododendrons and Portugal Laurels. The rhododendrons were twenty feet tall. He dug them up three feet from the base and now these lovely old hose-in-hose rhododendrons make a bank of mauve splendour on one side of what is now a dignified lawn with a circular rose garden in the middle. At the back of the lawn was a bank. He dug it up and planted it with five hundred brilliant azaleas. There was a place known as The Dump. It is now a woodland garden gay with the pink and yellow forms of *Meconopsis nepalensis* and the deep blue of *M grandis* – over six feet tall. *Sikkimensis* primulas make clusters of yellow balls to fringe the tiny stream that was just a ditch. The tiny red-hot-poker flowers of *Primula viallii* are at home there too among a host of others – *burmanica* and *pulverulenta, secondiflora, rosea* and *microdonta,* a carpet of brightness in what used to be a bit of dull old woodland. Which all goes to show how you can put a new face on an old garden. The vast herbaceous borders are a special pride, as are the lilacs – the pink Bellicent hybrid and the dark pink Elinor, with the pink laburnum *adamii*. There are some fine old trees, one silver spruce over two hundred years old. The ten acres of Abercairny are worth visiting at almost any time of the year for their flowering shrubs, and for such little plants as the *Astrantia carniolica major*, its small quaint green flower holding a cupful of stamens.

Branklyn

Zone Centre: Perth, Route 1

Owner: The National Trust for Scotland

If you mention that you are going to see Scotland's gardens, anyone who knows it will say at once: 'I hope you're going to Branklyn?' They will say it urgently, lest you miss it. For this you must not do. Branklyn is a jewel of a garden that has been called 'the best two acres in the country'. It could answer that challenge any day, for there is not a wrong note; not a bush, tree or other plant that does not flower or with beauty of leaf or outline add colour and form to its perfect pattern. Branklyn was the creation of the late Mr and Mrs J P Renton. Mrs Renton was a plantswoman, which means that the whole garden is a collection of good things. It is more than that. Each bed was drawn to scale and she knew how high the plants would grow over a period of years: with this in mind she planted each as a foil to the other. So you get a drift of blue meconopsis against the bronze haze of a *Rhus cotinus*, and behind them pink meconopsis against the gold of an *Acer japonicum aureum,* with the satin stem of a Chinese birch striking through the green background of trees – which is one picture, and wherever you look there is another as lovely, a series of changing pictures through the seasons with never two colours together but are complementary. It is a garden of surprises too. You walk along a path and turn a corner to meet the flaming boughs of a Chilean

316

Fire Bush. Another path takes you almost into the arms of a *Rhododendron fictolacteum*. You are brought here to admire it; and what if its white trusses of flowers are over, here is its aftergrowth to wonder at, dusty yellow in wine-coloured sheaths. A scree garden is filled with Mrs Renton's treasures. A *Tsuga canadensis,* the Hemlock Spruce, is the best of its kind in Britain, a beautiful form. A *Daphne retusa* is yards round. It is all laid out in a series of grass paths broadening and narrowing to lead you in and out among the bewildering beauty of it all. There are steps up and steps down to bring you to a fresh viewpoint. Here you must pause to look at the tiny yellow stars of *Corokia japonica,* there to see the white shell-like petals and spiky thorns of *Aegle sepiaria*, the Holy Thorn from the Mediterranean, called, too, the Crown of Thorns Bush. It seemed to me a garden come to perfection.

Cragside Estate

Zone Centre: Alnwick, Route 1

Owner: The Lord Armstrong

The faithful old purple rhododendron we all know is usually dismissed scornfully as 'that Ponticum'. In old gardens they dig it out, bulldoze it, blow it up or set fire to it, to get rid of the stuff. Cragside is literally square miles of it, and it is breathtaking: millions of ponticums growing so closely together that they are an unending sheet of colour pouring

over rock faces and down hillsides, and not only purples
from pale to deepest mauve but pinks and reds infused among
them, with patches of yellow azaleas to add their honey
scent. You can drive all the way, and the stopping places
are smooth tables of rock where you can stand and see it all
reflected in the mirror of a lake – there are four lakes,
man-made but nothing could look more natural. For
Cragside was a millionaire's contrivance. It was the 'Highland home' of Lord Armstrong, the engineer-genius who in
1863 when he was President of the British Association
revisited the Rothbury cottage where he was born and,
looking up at the hill, thought what a pretty site it would
be for a house. The idea haunted him and when he became
rich he transformed 'a bleak Northumbrian moor into an
earthly paradise', making Cragside almost as famous as his
breech-loading guns. He constructed the thirty-two miles of
carriage drives and walks, made the four lakes with their
seventy-seven acres of water and planted over seven million
trees. You must drive your car at a leisurely 15 mph, but who
would want to go faster among this riot of bloom lining the
roadway, covering hillsides, dipping down to the lakes and
fringing their shores, lakes blue as the neck of a peacock?
For mile after mile it goes on till you enter a woodland.
There big trees take over the spectacle. You can see a
White Fir unrivalled in height: it is twelve feet in girth and
one hundred and fifty feet tall to the tip, soaring above the
trees around it, a sort of exclamation mark at the end of your
enchanted journey.

Dawyck Gardens

Zone Centre: Edinburgh, Route 3

Owner: Lt-Col A N Balfour

In the great gale that swept across the waist of Scotland on the night of 15th January 1968 Dawyck lost fifty thousand trees representing half a million cubic feet of timber. It snapped them off as if they were matchsticks, sent acres of them crashing like a pack of cards, twisted even great beeches out of the ground and sometimes dropped them back into their root holes. So much for the tragedy of Dawyck's timber trees. Fortunately for those who love Dawyck's ornamental woodlands the loss was not great, at least by comparison. You still wander by paths and grassy ways up into the sheltered glen through which chuckles the Scrape Burn, to see such wonders as three generations of a *Tsuga heterophylla* – father, son and grandson, two of which are self-sown, a rare occurrence – and of course to see Dawyck's own beech tree (*Fagus sylvatica dawyckii*) which is fastigiate in form, reaching its branches skywards like a Lombardy Poplar. The oldest tree is an *Abies pectinata* planted about 1680. The largest is a Douglas Fir which in 1966 was 144 feet tall. A Sitka Spruce is 137 feet high and there are great Douglas Firs, Noble Firs and others one hundred and thirty years old and older. The glen is made beautiful in spring with more than two hundred and fifty kinds of rhododendrons, azaleas and other flowering shrubs, manyof them

Chinese species rhododendrons like *R davidsonianum* of bright pink buds and single bell flowers, rare and very difficult to grow. Earlier, little American ferns make a fairyland of Dawyck's glen, fringing the lakes of daffodils. The graceful old Scottish house is long and low with crow-stepped gables and a pepper-pot tower. Behind it is a formal garden constructed in 1820 by an Italian landscapist. Round it grow masses of species daffodils. In the old walled garden are yellow and pink Scottish shrub roses from cottage gardens; vegetables and herbaceous borders, honeysuckle and rose arches – flowers grown for delight after the flourish of spring is over.

Drummond Castle

Zone Centre: Perth, Route 2

Owner: The Rt Hon the Earl of Ancaster

The vast parterre for which Drummond Castle is famous spreads like a great carpet below the terraces – six acres of it in the form of a St Andrew's cross 'done' in white anaphalis against the blue background of Maggie Mott and Avril Lawson violas. It is not just as simple as that: the box beds are framed in an intricate design and the whole space of lawn and gravel outside the Cross is dotted with umbrella-clipped Portugal laurels, junipers, green and gold fastigiate yews and cypress trees and Golden and Silver Queen hollies.

They too form a pattern, as do the four flower beds in the central angles of the Cross guarded by four soldier-like purple plums. Right in the centre stands a tall pinnacled sundial with forty-eight faces. Flanking this great design are open rose gardens presided over – on the distaff side – by a figure of Eve, and opposite her (two acres away!) Adam. Each stands in a box-walled circle and beyond them are beds in which twelve hundred roses make a blaze of colour. Through the centre runs a wide path lined with bright blue Hidcote lavender edged with box. It leads past the sundial and on through a Roman archway to a grass ride climbing up to a hill and falling over the top. The trees left and right are great banks of green edged with copper beeches. Surrounding the whole parterre area are immense beech hedges twelve feet high. You look down on it all from the castle terraces which step down in grandeur in banks of azaleas, fuchsias, prostrate cotoneasters and junipers in a loose pattern of solid colour either side of a magnificent twin stairway arching over a grotto fountain. There are sixty-five steps down. Behind towers the castle, one portion a towering bastion with high crenellated gables and slit windows, the other in the romantic Scottish baronial style with pepper-pot turrets. The castle was built in 1491 and the gardens laid out in 1630 by John Drummond, Second Earl of Perth, who was 'a nobleman of learning, probity and integrity'. He it was who turned the grim approaches to the fortress into smiling terraces and laid out the great parterre. It would have been impossible to retain completely the original plan which was much more elaborate, and it is thanks to Lord and Lady Ancaster who rescued it from abandonment that we still have the amazing cross of flowers.

Edinburgh Royal Botanic Garden

Zone Centre: Edinburgh, Route 1

Owner: The Ministry of Public Buildings
and Works

The sixty acres of Edinburgh's Royal Botanic Garden are
famous for many things – for the beauty of its undulating
lay-out of green lakes of grassland scattered with trees and
shrub islands, the work of successive keepers and curators;
for its rock garden covering the two and a half acres of an
irregular mound, for its almost unrivalled collection of
rhododendrons and, just recently, for its new range of
exhibition plant-houses – a glass palace which 'floats'
unsupported by interior pillars. Edinburgh is the second
oldest botanic garden in Britain, following Oxford in 1670.
It has occupied its present site since 1820. Great names have
always been associated with it, men like John Hutton
Balfour and Alexander Dickson who made the Garden great
as a living laboratory for the study of plants; men made
great by it, who went out to found other gardens, like Robert
Fortune to collect unknown plants; doctors, professors,
gardeners: to be an 'Edinburgh man' in even the humblest
category was, and still is, to be a thorough professional.
It was under the keepership of Sir Isaac Bayley Balfour that
Edinburgh won fame as a pioneer in gardening. Hundreds
of new plants were coming in from China – alpines including
gentians, primulas, lilies and a galaxy of rhododendrons. To

accommodate the alpines Sir Isaac built one of the world's most remarkable rock gardens, and there you will find among the wonderful collection of mountain plants some of the dwarf rhododendrons, like the pink-belled *menziesii* named after its discoverer Alexander Menzies (an 'Edinburgh' gardener), Joseph Hooker's sweet-scented *edgeworthii* of white and pale pink flowers (he nearly became Edinburgh's professor of botany and for a time was deputy), the creeping round-leaved *forrestii* discovered by George Forrest (an 'Edinburgh' herbarium worker turned plant-hunter), and many more. Then there are the big rhododendrons with trusses of flowers up to the size of a football, whose after-growth of new leaves are like silver or bronze or gold torches. So many hundreds came pouring in that someone had to start classifying them. Edinburgh did this task. You can see them in April and May, and of course there are all the other plants: the great herbaceous border aglow in summer from end to end against the background of a twenty-foot beech hedge, spring bulbs, summer lilies, the heath garden, the little flowering plants in the scree garden, the marsh garden. Any day will reward you.

Falkland Palace

Zone Centre: Edinburgh, Route 2

Owner: The National Trust for Scotland

In 1947 the gardens were re-created to the old royal plans, though good modern plants are used and new ones constantly being added. It is at Falkland that you can see King James V's tennis court dating back to 1539. It is kept marked and shelters under a roof. The outer half-wall is clustered with clematis and wistaria and beyond it are two large rectangular ponds where tall irises yellow and purple blazon the royal colours. The rest of the garden is a beautiful stretch of lawn islanded with shrubs interplanted with lilies, hostas and ornamental grasses. Surrounding it are stone walls covered with roses including the butter-yellow Frühlingsgold which is one of the finest specimens in Scotland, and the pink Frühlingsmorgen like a big dog-rose. North to south under the wall runs a long border full of summer flowers, blue lupins and mecanopsis, all sorts of irises. It is a surprise to find such a good collection of shrubs on the Scottish east coast, yet neither they nor any other plant here gets any protection in the winter. The gardeners are proud of the beautiful specimen of the tree dogwood *Cornus nuttallii*, good for May when it is covered with flower-like bracts of creamy-white, good for autumn when its foliage turns yellow and scarlet. Falkland is looked upon as a garden that encourages relaxation. Once the hunting palace of the Stuart kings, this was where they relaxed from the cares of State. The National Trust for Scotland owns it now, and as one visiting schoolchild explained to another: 'Y'see, they're trustit to look after it.'

Hopetoun House

Zone Centre: Edinburgh, Route 2

Owners: The Trustees of the Marquess of Linlithgow

Attached to Scotland's greatest Adam mansion are fifty acres of spacious lawns, gardens and wooded grounds with deer parks where you can see fallow and red deer and St Kilda sheep. A delightful river walk takes you alongside the low-walled perimeter where the Forth (an impressive sight) flows by, and there you can see the famous Forth road and railway bridges. There are some fine cedars and two of the original specimens in Britain of the West Himalayan Spruce (*Picea smithiana*). The height of the taller is now eighty-five feet with a girth of ten feet six inches at five feet from the ground. It was first raised at Hopetoun in 1818 from cones sent to the Earl of Hopetoun by Dr Govan of Cupar who had them from his son in the East Indies, under the name khutrow. Rhododendrons and azaleas make the woodland very beautiful in May. The gardens were begun in 1760 and have been developed by successive generations of the family. The most recent addition is a rose terrace with a fountain.

Inveresk Lodge Garden

Zone Centre: Edinburgh, Route 1

Owner: The National Trust for Scotland

This is excitingly a garden in the making, being re-created round the seventeenth-century house which you reach from the main street of beautiful Inveresk village which has one of the oldest preservation societies and is itself a fine example of preservation. The work of reclaiming the garden started in 1962: seven acres including a field and pond, most of it the old walled kitchen garden. All was a tangle of undergrowth, but there were some good rhododendrons and azaleas. Will White, the gardener, rescued them to decorate a woodland walk high above the field. You enter the garden by a wrought iron gate. Through it is a courtyard and terrace, and from then on flowers are everywhere. What is interesting is that in a handful of years it all looks established: the 'Wedding Day' rose cascading over a wall, the border of species and shrub roses, the flowering shrubs and lawns: they might have been there for a lifetime. You will be interested in the choice of plants and by the colour-groupings. In front of the conservatory is an effective flower and 'foliage' border in blues and yellows – the deep yellow of Potentilla 'Longacre', the yellow-leaved mock orange and the small *Rudbeckia newmanii*, all interwoven with blue penstemons and carpeted with silvery-leaved *Antennaria dioica*. Part of the planting policy is to make the garden labour-saving, and ground-

326

cover plants are sometimes unorthodox, such as the use of 'Wedding Day' to cover the ground in one border, a spread of lovely gold blooms turning pink and then white. I look to a garden to include something indigenous, so I liked the collection of pinks at Inveresk, the dark-centred Highland hybrids which are native to Scotland. None the less attractive, though, was the early Dutch honeysuckle, the hybrid foxgloves in lovely new colours, and the *Acer cappadocicum aureum* from the Caucasus with golden leaves on long red stalks, turning scarlet in August and becoming golden again in autumn. A peat garden is now being made, and the meadow where the cows are grazing is to be planted. Fittingly for a Scottish garden, there will be a good collection of heathers.

Keir

Zone Centre: Edinburgh, Route 2

Owner: Lt-Col W J Stirling of Keir

This is a very large garden indeed (sixty acres) and everything is planted on a generous scale: seas of daffodils, an upper glen filled with azaleas, an avenue of Japanese maples, and all through the woodlands sheets of rhododendrons. It is an old garden which in its heydey must have kept an army of gardeners busy. It followed a very definite design of woodland walks ending in such set-pieces as the Ladies'

Pool with its cascade flowing from a baroque shell, and its bathing temple with ornate pillared front. Another path led to a Yew Cottage whose roof and green walls are still kept clipped. The woodland trees have been thinned, to let sunlight stream into the glades where the rhododendrons grow in their splendour. Azaleas too. The head gardener who is a 'rhododendron man' planted a great bank of them as an approach. Their colours are every shade of orange, gold, apricot, peach and flame, a dazzling sight. Magnolias and flowering trees add their colour. There is a *Eucryphia nymansensis* thirty-five feet high, white to the top in October with its lovely scented flowers. And this is only the woodland. At the back of the large lawn is a wall glorious with climbing plants: masses of *Clematis spooneri* with its big white flowers, actinidia of white, green and pink leaves (beloved by cats), and such wonderful roses as Frühlingsgold, with its semi-double rich golden blooms. There are dark green Irish yews, a battlemented holly hedge, twin herbaceous borders full of colour, and on a fine day a view to the Ochil Hills and Stirling Castle. Above the lawn is the house, buttressed with pencil junipers, and on higher ground yet a collection of flowering shrubs and conifers among the broad-leaved trees, with new ones being added, such as the fascinating purple-coned *Picea likiangensis* from China. What a place this is for views: a Victorian brick balustraded look-out commands the Field of Bannockburn. Garden-wise the picture is completed by clouds of species and shrub roses scenting the long summer into autumn.

Suntrap

Zone Centre: Edinburgh, Route 1

Owner: The National Trust for Scotland

This is a good idea, a centre where enthusiastic amateurs can learn how to make a small garden. They can learn indeed almost every aspect of gardening by attending the lectures here. Suntrap is a demonstration garden of two acres showing the varied ways in which a small garden can be made attractive, useful and labour-saving. The meeting hall has seating for fifty and there is a greenhouse at one end for indoor demonstrations. For garden work there is a series of half a dozen small greenhouses and frames, and the lay-out has been designed to show every type of garden, while in itself being most attractive.

Also open are:

CALLALY CASTLE GARDENS AND GROUNDS (Zone Centre: Alnwick, Route 1. Owner: Major A S C Browne, DL) loved by Newcastle people who come at weekends to enjoy the peace of its spreading lawns in front of the seventeenth-century mansion, the shade of the truly immense copper beech there and the brown stream that cuts the garden in two and then wanders off into woodland, widening in a chain of ponds along a wooded mile. There is a beautiful Russell lupin bed, an iris bed, shrub roses and some seventy years old. The borders are a joy.

SEATON DELAVAL HALL (Zone Centre: Alnwick, Route 1. Owner: Lord Hastings) has a parterre garden re-created in 1950, with a pair of statues at the far end by Gian Bologna and Baccio Bandinelli. Beside the enclosed lawn is a rose garden. In the woodlands are rhododendrons, azaleas and other flowering shrubs.

Open occasionally are :

EARLSHALL (Zone Centre: Perth, Route 1. Owner: Mrs Arthur Purvis, OBE). One of the few topiary gardens in Scotland, its thirty-two yew trees representing the pieces on a chessboard. The whole garden is utterly charming and planted with a rich variety of flowers. Specialities are irises, species roses, dahlias, and flowering trees.

GLEN ALN (Zone Centre: Alnwick, Route 1. Owner: Col G A Barnett) is an enchanting little garden in a wood with a stream bordered by moisture-loving plants, among them the rare *Mimulus radicans*. There is an interesting scree garden and glimpses of the Cheviots and the hills to Callaly.

GLENDOICK (Zone Centre: Perth, Route 1. Owners: Messrs E H M Cox and P A Cox) is a semi-wild woodland glen with a stream, where from the middle of April to the end of May you will see some of the best rhododendrons in Scotland, over six hundred different species and cultivars. The garden was made between 1750 and 1920 when the

Farrer rhododendrons came in. Azaleas are also a speciality, and by the house is a border full of interesting plants.

HELMEND **(Zone Centre: Edinburgh, Route 3. Owners: Mr and Mrs Hendrie)** is the owners' 'attempt to make a garden at seven hundred feet high blown by south-west gales'. They have succeeded. Fourteen years ago it was a bare field. It is now well planted, with a terrace view of Broadlaw and the Tweedsmuir Hills. There are collections of willows and cotoneasters, and a fernery in the making.

KINROSS HOUSE **(Zone Centre: Edinburgh, Route 2. Owner: Mrs H K Purvis-Russell-Montgomery)** is one of the most beautiful gardens in Scotland, indeed in Britain, with a magnificent formal garden, two rose gardens, a long border with clipped yew buttresses against a grey stone wall hung with clematis, and a breathtaking view over Loch Leven to the island where Mary Queen of Scots was imprisoned. Two beautiful 'colour' borders in a sequence of white-yellow-blue-red-pink look up to the house from the Loch gate. A topiary hedge represents three pheasants on plates. There is statuary, exquisite spiral topiary, and brilliant rhododendrons on the lawn. The gardens were the work of Sir William Bruce in the seventeenth century and were restored in 1902–28 by Sir Basil Templer Graham Montgomery.

ZONE 12 Inverewe and round to Royal Deeside

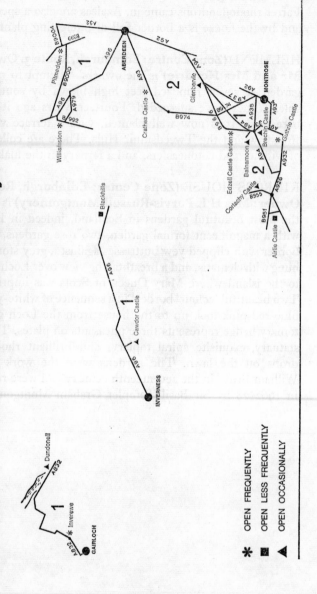

* OPEN FREQUENTLY

▣ OPEN LESS FREQUENTLY

▲ OPEN OCCASIONALLY

ZONE 12

Inverewe and round to Royal Deeside

INVEREWE IS THE farthest garden of our tour, and whichever way you approach it – east from Inverness or up the West Coast – the road from the junction at Achnasheen is one of spectacular grandeur. You will find yourself stopping along the way to gaze at the unbelievable beauty of distant Loch Maree where blue hills piled upon blue hills line the silver length of its waters. The roads are good, with passing places where they are single-track. You are now in Wester Ross, a strange and barren land softened by groves of birch trees. Long glens and big lochs lie among the wild hills of the Torridon range which rise to the volcanic peaks of Suilven, Stac Polly and An Teallach.

Inverness, the Capital of the Highlands, has a kinder beauty, though there are still wild tracts of country, called deer forests, a term meaning large waste places. South are the great shoulders of the Cairngorms, Scotland's most alpine mass, with peaks rising over four thousand feet. They lie east of the Great North Road and west of Aberdeenshire's beautiful Deeside where Balmoral can be visited when the Royal Family are not in residence.

Aberdeenshire is like a great green garden, a countryside

of splendid salmon rivers whose names make music: the Dee, the Don and the Deveron. Overseas visitors wishing to refresh their eyes will find balm here in the grazing lands of the Aberdeen Angus cattle.

The seaport of Angus is Montrose at the mouth of the River Esk, a royal burgh which received its charter from David I in 1352. The coastline is broken by beautiful red sandstone crags and cliffs.

Airlie Castle

Zone Centre: Montrose, Route 2

Owner: The Dowager Countess of Airlie

They call it the Bonnie House of Airlie, and what bonnie views it commands – across deep gorges tumbling with the waters of the Isla and Melgum. High-walled and turreted it rises above the valley trees, and round it a bonnie garden. When Lord and Lady Airlie celebrated their Golden Wedding in 1967 wellwishers said it with golden flowers: a Laburnum Walk was planted, curving round a lawn, with golden azaleas lining it and yellow American honeysuckles climbing up its pergola. The laburnums, by the way, are *vossii* hybrids of the 'Scotch' *alpinum* which has extra long racemes. Already the avenue is an enchanting sight. Beyond it are rose beds which the members of the local Women's Rural Institute filled with golden roses. Airlie is unique for its antique plants. In the beautiful Yew Garden is a double white narcissus not to be found in catalogues, and the deep blue 'Avril Lawson' viola from Glen Esk, which Lady Airlie grows in a picot edging under the yew pyramids of the central walk interplanted with loops of white *Antennaria dioica*. She is re-creating the old garden, using always unusual plants: in her island borders that wander across a lawn are such beautiful shrubs as the white *Viburnum calophyllum,* among primulas 'Garryarde Guinevere' of reddish-bronze leaves and pink heads, and *P ioessa* with its violet bell-shaped flowers.

Blackhills

Zone Centre: Inverness, Route 1

Owner: Sylvester Christie, Esq

There is something very exciting about this garden. Mr Christie calls it 'an irregular garden', meaning that it does not conform to a pattern. It is in fact a most lovely woodland – created, nevertheless, by the hand of man, first by Mr Christie's uncle Thomas North Christie, who in 1911 retired from a tea planting career in Ceylon and took to gardening. He constructed a rock garden and a new flower garden (where there is a fine collection of species roses), and after the Great War he became interested in rhododendrons. Blackhills is now first and foremost a place where these

335

gorgeous shrubs find a natural home, the hillsides of its two glens simulating the untouched mountain ravines where they grow in their natural state. On the south-facing bank of a grove of century-old Scots pines is the Himalayan Patch where you will find the tree-sized *arboreum* and the Hooker discoveries *griffithianum*, the blood-red *thomsonii,* the cinnamon-stemmed *falconeri* and others, most of them over twenty feet tall. At Blackhills even the tender *delavayi* is eighteen feet high. When Forrest's rhododendrons came pouring into the country and later Kingdon-Ward's, the plantings had to extend throughout the woodland, and Thomas North Christie made contour paths shelving up and up, as he had done on his tea estate. The way is marked by vivid patches of colour – the intense blue of *R augustinii,* the flame of *R venator*, the waxy flowers of *cinnabarinum*, the yellows of *wardii* and *campylocarpum*. The pools mirror their colours in a frame of primulas and miniature maples. On the woodland floor are drifts of the blue Himalayan poppy and the star-like wildflower *Trientalis europaea*. Davidia trees flutter their white handkerchiefs (one is known by the Christies as the *Lady's* Handkerchief Tree because its bracts are much smaller!) The rock garden by the house is full of dwarf rhododendrons, and above an old cottage doorway used as a decorative arch is a Marriage Stone spelling out the words: 'The Glory of Man is as the Flower in the Forest', a motto singularly appropriate to the making of this garden.

Crathes Castle

Zone Centre: Aberdeen, Route 2

Owner: The National Trust for Scotland

The beautiful formal gardens of Crathes have as their background the romantic stone castle with its corbelled turrets and crow-stepped gables. There are seven gardens divided by magnificent walls and twelve-foot-high yew hedges planted in 1702, separating the yew borders, the fountain garden and the rose garden, the aviary border, what is called the Four Squares, the camel garden (because of the hump in its lawn!), the trough garden and the Doocot and herbaceous borders. What distinguishes the Crathes borders are the exquisite weavings of colour, in, for instance, the upper pool garden with its purple foliage and red and yellow flowers, a scheme devised by the late Lady Burnett. The fountain garden is a delight, its parterre planted entirely with blues. The trefoil beds in the rose garden are filled with floribundas in melting shades. The west herbaceous border is pink, blue and mauve, and everywhere under the walls are shrubs for colour throughout the year. Crathes has one of the best shrub collections in Britain, many of them rare, like the white-flowered *Peraphyllum ramosissimum* from Colorado in the camel garden, and two halesias – *monticola* and *vestita* with its creamy-white buds opening to pink bells, both species of the Snowdrop Tree. Among the delphiniums is the unusual orange-belled *nudicaule*. The whole picture is one of flowery loveliness as you wander from one garden to the next. There are wonderful Persian lilacs, among them the uncommon *Syringa pinnatifolia,* the early flowering Chinese lilac with white flowers and small rowan-like leaves which has been called a 'shrubby conundrum', and the elegant *sweginzowii,* also from China, with its sweetly fragrant trusses of flesh pink. Among the unusual variegated plants are a hybrid symphytum and a hoheria so delicate that it can die after the slightest scratch. A picture I shall never forget is the view up to the castle between the June borders, a gorgeous mixture of plants where there is a *Rosa rubrifolia* 'photographed every five minutes of the day!' as the gardeners will tell you. The walls are gardens in themselves, covered with climbers – the spectacular Souvenir de Louis Späth lilac, *Actinidia kolomikta,* the Chinese Vine, honeysuckles like the uncommon *Lonicera tragophylla* from China with its coral buds opening to yellow trumpets four inches long, and *splendida* from Spain, of grey foliage and champagne flowers. No wonder Crathes is one of Scotland's best loved gardens.

Edzell Castle Garden

Zone Centre: Montrose, Route 1

Owner: Ministry of Public Buildings
and Works

Surrounded by fine old sycamore trees but open to the sunshine is Edzell's flowery jewel, a Renaissance parterre laid out in 1610 by Sir David Lindsey, Lord Edzell, who was the eldest son of the Ninth Earl of Crawford. He was a Knight of the Order of the Thistle and the parterre follows the original design in the Thistle Chapel. The Lindsey family motto *Dum spiro spero endure forte* – While I breathe I hope – is spelled out in exquisitely clipped box forming the edging to the seven-sided knot beds. The whole pattern is set in a velvet lawn surrounded by a red sandstone wall unique in Britain. In it are the chequered squares of the Lindsey coat-of-arms made as niches for holding pans of flowers, white and blue lobelia carrying out the family colours argent and azure, completed by the *or* of yellow tagetes in bigger pans in the bee boles at ground level. There is a frieze of six-pointed stars, and in the centre of each a hole to let the bees in and out. The wall also displays a series of sculptured panels portraying the cardinal virtues, the liberal arts and the planetary deities. Part of the ruined castle forms the fourth wall, and there is an old summer house with carved oak panels, once in the castle, dating back to the sixteenth century.

M

Guthrie Castle

Zone Centre: Montrose, Route 2

Owner: The National Trust for Scotland

The castle was built in 1468, and what more romantic picture than this ancient home of the Guthrie family mirrored in its loch on a still evening, with long shadows casting across the lawn to the walled garden whose date is proclaimed on its wrought iron gate, 1614. Entering, you see that the garden is in the shape of a horseshoe. Its walls are covered with roses and straight ahead is a wide grass path between thick wavy yew hedges. Stone steps climb up a series of terraces whose background wall is hung with clematis. There is a pool. Lavender riots and aubrietias cascade in a profusion of purple, and from here you have another view of the pink stone castle and its sturdy battle-mented keep, mounds of rhododendrons on the left of the lawn, round the islanded loch battalions of wild lupins. Outside the walled garden a broad avenue of birches takes you to the wild garden where groves of meconopsis stand blue and tall under the trees, in spring a carpet of bulbs. All through the woodland are bright splashes of coloured azaleas, with mounds of the yellow azalea whose honey-scent fills the air.

Inverewe

Zone Centre: Gairloch, Route 1

Owner: The National Trust for Scotland

It could be described as a wilderness of flowers. Its beauty is breathtaking from the moment you enter the gates. Sky and earth are filled with colours. You wonder how it all came about, for all around are the stony and barren Torridon Hills, and you sense that these blue stretches of the Atlantic can be storm-tossed: you can almost taste the salt in the air. It happened in 1862 when Osgood Mackenzie began his task of transforming a bare headland into a sheltered and fertile place where garden plants, even the tenderest, could flourish. When he died in 1922 his daughter, Mrs Mairi Sawyer, went on with the work, and the year before her own death in 1952 she handed the garden over to the National Trust for Scotland. The great horticulturalist Dr J M Cowan was appointed to look after it. To reach Inverewe is a long and difficult journey, yet one hundred thousand people come here every year, as on a pilgrimage. The drive is ribboned with flowering shrubs and trees, great cascades of 'Warminster' brooms, long-tasselled laburnums and brilliant azaleas, with a satin-stemmed *Eucalyptus gunnii* holding its silvery blue head a hundred feet above them, vivid blue lithospermums carpeting their feet, plantain lilies and the rust-red crests of euphorbias, silver senecios, veronicas, variegated sage and a thousand other colourful plants. There

341

are golden clouds of azaleas, grown for their scent, and against the sky huge conifers beckoning you into the woodland where new floods of colour startle you, a rhododendron bowed down by the weight of its blossoms – clusters of rich pink-red silhouetted against the rich blue of the Atlantic. As you walk the woodland paths there is always a sudden glimpse of this incredible blue, and always there is the ceaseless singing of the pines towering above. Here a path is bordered by Inverewe's own primula in a carpet of gleaming brick-red, and the yellow *helodoxa* from Burma is interplanted with blue meconopsis. Periwinkles wreath banks of heathers. On the West Bank a sea of azaleas breaks upon the view. 'You would hardly credit it,' as a Scot remarked after dumbfounded gazing. In the Wet Valley is a botanical joke, two members of the same genus planted one in front of the other, *Gunnera manicata* with its enormous rhubarb leaves and the lilliputian *Gunnera magellanica*. At the bottom of the valley is a pond jewelled with the stars of water lilies. There is hardly room to reflect the white plumes of pampas grasses. In the Giant Rhododendron Walk you will find the football-size blooms of *sino-grande* and will recognise the rhododendron *hodgsonii* with its drooping leaves and silvery bark (one here is the biggest specimen in the country). Calamities happen at Inverewe as in any other garden, but here a broken birch tree is garlanded with a pink clematis. When the garden was being made shelter belts had to be created. Griselinia with its beautiful shiny leaves was used as a wind-break and hedges of escallonia which in August are covered with red flowers, while pernettyas became snow-white acres and almost a weed. So in July the giant cardiocrinum lilies are a dramatic feature with their great clustering heads of white flowers. Even palm trees grow here, and in the part of the garden known as Bambooselem are all sorts of bamboos and tender plants, with trees tropical in appearance: a tall larch is almost entirely covered by the Japanese climbing hydrangea *petiolaris,* and the normally difficult plant *Mitraria coccinea* has spread from the bank where it was planted and is now climbing up all the nearby trees in an effort to mantle them with its scarlet mitre-shaped flowers. In the centre of this garden is a forty-foot-high forty-year-old *Magnolia campbellii* which at the end of March is a pyramid of hundreds of huge pink blooms, each about eight inches across. This is the sort of garden Inverewe is, a luxuriance of every kind of flower and beautiful tree, from the lowliest little plants in the rock garden to the lofting heights of the great conifers, a garden cradled in the blue bosom of the Atlantic stirring at the feet of seal-haunted rocks.

Pitmedden

Zone Centre: Aberdeen, Route 1

Owner: The National Trust for Scotland

They call it the Great Garden. It was made by the son of 'Bonnie John Seton' who was knighted by Charles II in 1664 as Sir Alexander of that ilk and later created baron. With his brother James he had visited the great houses of their kinsmen – Winton, Pinkie, the Tower of Elphinstone, all with great gardens. Falling heir to Pitmedden, Alexander made his own Great Garden. Alas, with the years its pavilions decayed, its parterres were engulfed by weeds. The Garden you see today is a work of magnificent restoration.

Even the garden ornaments have been put together from fragments found lying around when the National Trust for Scotland took it over. The parterre itself is composed of four designs covering four acres of ground, three modelled on the King's Garden at Holyroodhouse, the fourth – on the north-west – laid out as a tribute to Lord Pitmedden himself. It shows the four shields of the Seton coat of arms in all its true colours. Surrounding it is the family motto: *Sustento sanguine signa* – 'I bear the standard with blood' – which refers to the incident at the Brig of Dee when Bonnie John was shot through the heart defending the King's standard. *Merces haec certa laborum* – 'This sure reward of our labours' – completes the fantastic pattern, the letters of the mottoes laid down in box. In two of the corners are broderie thistles; in the other two St Andrew's crosses. The colours of the four parterres are made with thirty-five thousand plants, varied each year. They take a fortnight to plant, and it takes four gardeners three weeks to clip the miles of box edging and scrollwork. There is not a leaf or, it seems, a single petal out of place. Surrounding the whole are four great herbaceous borders, all in exquisite order. An amazing feat, an entrancing spectacle.

Williamston

Zone Centre: Aberdeen, Route 1

Owner: W T H Haughton, Esq

In severe winters here you cannot get a spade into the ground till March. This must rob the garden of weeks of labour, but you would not think so to see its beautifully kept borders and perfectly trimmed yews. You will find Williamston an enchanting place full of charming corners: the fountain garden over which a gentle St Francis presides, with stone birds at his feet and flowers surrounding him, beds of polyanthus roses, tulips and bedding-out plants which make colour all through the season; the little yew-enclosed shrine where St Michael leans on his sword. You pass him on the way to a long walk between clipped yews with a vista of the Fouland Hills, and come to the Poplar Pass where a path takes you to St Michael's Well, a pre-Christian sacred well afterwards dedicated to the warrior saint. For centuries it was the scene of pilgrimages on the first Sunday in May, when 'St Michael' dispensed water to the poor. You go up semi-circular steps to a half-circle of lawn commanding a vista back through the garden, and you will notice the use made of red-foliaged plants as eye-catchers – prunus, *Cornus coccinea*, red acers – a planned feature of the garden. There are other colourful magnets, a willow that glows golden in the autumn, seen through an archway. It is all surprises, kept from you by a yew hedge or a rose pergola till you

345

suddenly come upon them. Yet everywhere you can look down long green aisles framing a hill. A flowery garden of quiet and charm.

Open occasionally are :

BALNAMOON (Zone Centre: Montrose, Route 1. Owner: Mrs W B Carnegy-Arbuthnot) is pronounced Bonnie Moon, a glorious feature being the Balnamoon lupins, as spectacularly different from the Russell lupins as the Russells were from the old blues and pinks, columnar in form with an upstanding standard, and immense and prolific. A single bloom can measure thirty-six inches, and there may be thirty-six heads on one plant. Mr Carnegy-Arbuthnot has raised ten thousand of them, and to reach perfection threw out ninety-five per cent. He knows the pedigree of each seed back twenty-six years. Other attractive features are the fernery in the Burn Garden, long herbaceous borders and sweet old Scottish roses.

BRECHIN CASTLE (Zone Centre: Montrose, Route 1. Owner: The Earl of Dalhousie) has a beautifully planted garden with a heart-shaped wall covered with unusual roses such as the Austrian copper rose. There are sorbus and malus plantations and a collection of white paper birches, a primula garden, an open scree garden, and on the sloping grass below the castle magnificent island beds of flowering shrubs. There is a rock garden, and a collection of species rhododendrons and azaleas.

CAWDOR CASTLE (Zone Centre: Inverness, Route 1. Owners: The Earl and Countess Cawdor) has an exquisite formal garden whose background is the long house-wall of the castle. Behind rises a square tower, corbell-turreted at each corner, and it is from there, from a window right at the top, that Lady Cawdor plans the colour schemes of the large formal beds. The woodland garden outside the curtain wall is full of unusual things such as the dear little Mouse Plant arum (and anything more like a mouse would be hard to find), the pretty *Oxalis rosea* – pink flowers veined with purple, trilliums, a dark mullein with green petals, and bright blue patches of mecanopsis. The main drive is lined with cherries underplanted with daffodils, and every apple tree has its rose or clematis climbing up it.

CORTACHY CASTLE (Zone Centre: Montrose, Route 2. Owners: The Lord and Lady Ogilvy) has a delightful pond gaily fringed with candelabra primulas and hostas, with banks of azaleas, rhododendrons and forsythias surrounded by tall conifers and beech trees. There are heath borders with dwarf conifers, an American garden full of rhododendrons and trees planted by royalties. The River Esk flows through the grounds.

DUNDONNELL (Zone Centre: Gairloch, Route 1. Owners: Messrs Alan, Neil and Alastair Roger) is an old 'Scotch walled garden' turned into a haven. The Roger brothers decided to buy a house with a bit of land – 'perhaps an acre': they saw Dundonnell and fell in love with it. The acre was some thousands of acres including the mountains behind, the dramatic peaks of An Teallach pocketed with snow and the mecca of ski parties. The garden is a dream, with a laburnum avenue, glorious flower borders round and across, with Britain's second oldest yew tree (thirteen or fourteen hundred years old) in which a baby was once born! There are peacocks, ornamental pheasants and Archangel pigeons among other enchantments such as the collection of bonsai round a rectangular pond in the Japanese manner.

347

GLENBERVIE (Zone Centre: Aberdeen, Route 2. Owner: Mrs P M Badenoch Nicholson) is a lovely summer garden where quantities of annuals make a blaze of colour in wide borders, where roses, carnations and pansies grow along the whole front of the greenhouse which is a feature of the garden, full of interesting plants: an apricot climbing mimulus, a hoya of stiff pink umbrella flowers, cockscombs like yellow and scarlet Victorian braid. A summer house is tangled with jasmine, quince and honeysuckle, and at the bottom of a glen is a bog garden through which runs the Pilkerty Burn.

ZONE 13 Ireland.

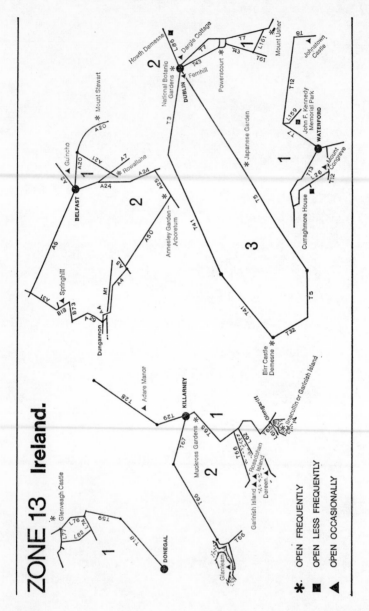

350

OPEN FREQUENTLY   ✻

OPEN LESS FREQUENTLY   ■

OPEN OCCASIONALLY   ▲

Glenveagh Castle ✻

L77
L76
L82
T59
T1
T18

1

DONEGAL

Springhill ■
A31
B18
B73
T29
A4
A5
M1
Dungannon

BELFAST
A2
A20
Guincho
12V
A7
Rowallane ▲
A24
A24
A6
A50
1
2

Mount Stewart ✻
A20

Annesley Garden Arboretum ✻
A25
T41
2
T41
3
T41
T32

Adare Manor ▲
T28
T29
KILLARNEY ✻
T68
T67
1
Muckross Gardens ✻
T66
T66
Rossdohan Island ▲
Garinish Island ▲
Dereen ▲
Glanleam ▲
T66
T66
2
Glengarriff
Ilnacullin or Garinish Island ✻

Birr Castle Demesne ✻
T41
T5

Japanese Garden ✻
T5
T3

National Botanic Gardens ✻
DUBLIN
Howth Demesne ■
Dargle Cottage ■
L8
T7
Fernhill ■
T43
Powerscourt ✻
T43
T7
L161
1
L161
Mount Usher ✻
B1
Johnstown Castle ▲
2

Curraghmore House ■
T12
T7
L159
John F. Kennedy Memorial Park ✻
T7
WATERFORD
T13
L26
Mount Congreve ✻
T12
1

ZONE 13

Ireland

MOST OF THE Irish gardens are lucky in having a scenic background of mountains or loughs or both, and rarely are the gardens themselves entirely flat. There is usually a stream at least, if not a river, and natural outcrop provides a ready-made home for rock plants; all of which goes a long way to making an attractive garden. The climate helps too: parts of southern and western Ireland are almost frost-free, due to the beneficent Gulf Stream which laps these shores. The approaches are sometimes dramatic. Nothing, for instance, could be a more powerful stimulant to enjoyment of the beauties of Killarney than the great purple massif of Macgillicuddy's Reeks striking awe into you as you make the long winding descent.

All these, however, could be regarded as a bonus, for the Irish are good gardeners who love their few acres or larger demesnes passionately. They delight in putting the mild climate to use by planting tender and rare things usually to be seen only in greenhouses or more southerly climes.

It is sad that some of the superb gardens are known only to the few. Ireland is as yet only in its infant days of a Gardens Scheme such as exists for the large majority of English, Scottish and Welsh gardens, though happily many owners, while having no regular opening days, will allow the public in if they write or ask for permission. Hence

351

some regrettable blanks, and hence the reiterated *By appointment* that appears in the index dealing with opening times. There are, however, enough wonderful gardens open regularly to make your tour one of full enjoyment.

The years 1846 and 1847 were responsible for several of Ireland's great gardens coming into being: those at Birr Castle and Powerscourt, to name two. These were the years of the Potato Famine. Kindly landowners thus employed hundreds of men to save them and their families from starvation.

For all the numbers of tourists Ireland attracts to her shores, the roads are marvellously uncrowded. Motoring there is a rare pleasure. You will enjoy 'doing' the Irish gardens on that account alone, even if the scenery were half as enchanting, the gardens themselves half as excitingly varied, a quarter as beautiful.

The Annesley Garden Arboretum

Zone Centre: Belfast, Route 2

Owner: The Ministry of Agriculture for Northern Ireland

This beautiful arboretum is more generally known as Castlewellan. It lies on a foothill of the Mountains of Mourne made famous in song and was laid out in the 1850s by the Fifth Earl of Annesley. You will first see the lovely old walled garden with its borders criss-crossing and lying under the walls, one border a hundred and fifty yards long.

They give colour from May to September. Yew and myrtle hedges are used as backgrounds, their dark green laced with the brilliant scarlet of tropaeolum. Pretty fountains centre the intersections of the paths. Your way to the arboretum is through a brick archway where you glimpse the first of the beautiful conifers, standing free as individual specimens and thus growing to full perfection of form. At the fountain ringed with red Japanese acers and flanked by clipped yews you take leave of the garden and become surrounded by their wonder, feasting your eyes on the golden column of a *Cupressus nootkatensis,* on the towering blue foliage of a *Cedrus atlantica.* Another cedar has fascinating blue cones, and there is a Brewer's Spruce whose feathery weeping branches make a green circular room. The collection of conifers is comprehensive and there are two *Sequoia gigantea,* one hundred feet high, which were planted in 1856. Rhododendrons and azaleas bring flowery colour to the arboretum and you must not miss the eucryphia avenue snow-white with scented flowers. Australian visitors will see how well their Daisy Bush grows in Ireland and the Bottle Brushes with their scarlet and yellow spikes.

Birr Castle Demesne

Zone Centre: Dublin, Route 3

Owners: The Earl and Countess of Rosse

Romantic Birr Castle is a square battlemented edifice whose corners are rounded with turrets. The grounds, or demesne, surrounding it are famous for their beauty and for the Giant Telescope standing midway between the castle and the lake. For thirty years after its completion in 1845 it was the largest in the world and responsible for many important discoveries, some in connection with the Milky Way. Famous, too, is the avenue of box hedging sheltering the kitchen gardens. Over two hundred years old and thirty-five feet tall it is the oldest and tallest in Europe. There is a cherry avenue to the right and nearby a square walled garden full of lovely old shrub roses in box borders. Fuchsias in black tubs surround great stone vases, and crossing the garden are pleached alleys of hornbeam with windows cut to view it. Behind is a border of cherry trees and lilies. The Low Walk takes you along by the river which you can cross by a bridge at the far end by a big-leaved catalpa and a spectacular *Malus sargentii* from Japan. Notice among the flowers that grow here the handsome *Lobelia tupa* with its wine-red lip and green stigma. It has downy white leaves and grows only in sheltered places. You are among trees on the other side of the Camcor, and bordering the walk are groups of flowering shrubs. From here you can see the castle set on flowery terraces against the sky. At the end of the path is St Brendan's Well surrounded by a carpet of Blue-Eyed Mary. The well dates back to the earliest Christian days when St Brendan, a disciple of St Patrick, founded a monastery here. Birr is beautiful at any time, as famous for its autumn colouring as for its spring-flowering magnolias.

Curraghmore

Zone Centre: Waterford, Route 1

Owner: The Marquess of Waterford

In the garden is the unique Shell House. It was made in 1754 by Catherine, Countess of Tyrone, and there is a life-size statue of her there in white marble. The shells came from all parts of the world and under the floodlighting you can see the exquisite patterns she made of them from the floor to the top of the rounded dome. The colours are like a thousand rainbows. It took the Countess 261 days to complete her task and although made so long ago not one shell has ever fallen out of place. It is said that ox blood was mixed with the mortar to make it hard. The garden is a spacious one of broad walks among lawns and ancient oaks, set against the backdrop of the Curragh Mountains, blue hills rising to the peak of Croushaun. A famous Sitka Spruce is over one hundred and seventy feet high: it is mentioned in the *Guinness Book of Records*. Another is not far off this height. Just by the Shell House is a shrub garden with camellias and rhododendrons, and if you are lucky you may see a heron fishing by the lake. In spring the approach alongside the River Clodiagh is carpeted with bluebells.

Glenveagh Castle

Zone Centre: Donegal, Route 1

Owner: H P McIlhenny, Esq

It is impossible to describe Glenveagh's garden without first mentioning its castle – it is so much a setting for the grey stone fantasy of fairy-tale turrets – surrounding it on two sides, with the long sleeve of Lough Veagh below reflecting it in still waters, steeply rising wooded hills protecting it from behind. The stony moorlands of the deer forest which lie around will not prepare you for the lush vegetation that grows in Mr McIlhenny's garden, which seems to have been dropped from a summer dream. Tree ferns grow in the pleasure ground, and tender rhododendrons like Lady Alice Fitzwilliam and *R lindleyi* scent the terrace, growing as they would in a southern clime. You will probably first see the Italian Garden: a lawn with six statues, three aside, in niches of the griseliana hedge surrounding it, a pine tree in the middle, two stone vases flanking a seat. And that is all, but what artistry, what green and silent peace. Beyond, left and right, are groups of eucryphias. In September when they flower you can hardly see a leaf on the trees for the crowd of white blossom. You can see them on the Swiss Walk where mimosas flower, Polar Bear rhododendrons and, down by the Lough, white azaleas. Then you must explore the Walled Garden which is a cloud of flowers its length and breadth – shrub roses and phloxes, Gold Plate solidago (covered with Red Admiral butterflies when I was there), the fiery red of *Lychnis chalcedonica*, blue delphiniums and pink sidalceas, the big yellow pompons of Armenian marigolds. It is hard to say what flowers are not in this garden. But above all there are the lilies. Names like *Lilium speciosum rubra* do not really convey the beauty of these elegant flower creatures with their swooning scent and their proud trumpets gazing at you from tall stems sometimes your own height – no, not even *Lilium gloriosa Rothschildiana*. To appreciate and know them you must gaze into this trumpet and that one, to see how the long folded green and pink buds have opened to speckled and golden-throated loveliness. You will see a little summer house over the wall, with a pine-shingled roof like a coolie hat. The gate there leads to more lilies. Then you must make for The Steps. There are sixty-seven of them rising sheer up the hillside in a glorious woodland where azaleas and rhododendrons make splashes of colour, where Chain Ferns bend across the path and lysosteria grows, its bracts shrimp-pink. At the top is a belvedere looking down on the castle with the Duich Hills to the left. Across the woodland a steep path leads down to the Belgian Walk and the pleasure grounds, a woodland of such surprises as the Red Cone Flower, the rare *Fascicularia pitcairniifolia* with its spiky orange leaves. It grows in crevices of the rocks, brilliant-coloured even in the dense shade. From here you can glimpse the lawn, far below and half hidden among the tops of Corsican pines, a vast lawn surrounded by wandering borders, *Alchemilla mollis* making a golden foam along the edges. Again the variety of plants bewilders you, again the growth is fantastic, auratum lilies seven feet tall, others ten

357

feet tall. Here grow the tree ferns and bronze-leaved cordy-lines, flowering trees of all kinds behind the borders: hoherias with their long pale green heart-shaped leaves and single white flowers, eucalyptus trees that flower, a huge arboreum rhododendron with blood-red flowers, hundreds of shrubs that burst into colour; and, everywhere it can, tropaeolums garland hedges and trees and shrubs with scarlet flowers. It is nothing less than a dreamland, this garden which Henry McIlhenny has created. You must see it.

Howth Demesne

Zone Centre: Dublin, Route 1

Owner: Howth Estate Company

The St Lawrence family have lived at Howth for eight hundred years and in the present castle since 1564, and there you can see the oldest introduced tree in Ireland, an English elm planted in 1565. Nearby is an extraordinary labyrinth of beech hedges reaching tree height. But the great feature is the Rhododendron Walk, a woodland reached by an avenue of cherry trees. Be prepared to walk a mile or more if you would see the full glory of the rhododendrons for which Howth is famous. You are greeted by a mountain of them, and there are seats round a little green where you can sit and feast your eyes on their colours. The path leads past tumbled boulders, and it is all as wild as the Himalayan gorges whence so many of these species rhododendrons came. Pillars of honeysuckle swarm up the trees. There are tree ferns, and ground ferns of every kind. The rhododendrons are spectacular, white, yellow, scarlet, pink and purple and, as if there were not bloom enough, azaleas of blazing colours shine wherever a shaft of sunlight pierces the trees. You can climb the rocky path to the top where a glorious panorama stretches before you, of Ireland's Eye and Dublin Bay. It seems impossible to believe that before all these rhododendrons were planted there was nothing here but a rockslide. Hundreds of thousands of tons of soil had to be brought to it before a single one could find a toehold.

Ilnacullin

Zone Centre: Killarney, Route 1

Owner: The Commissioners of Public Works

Before Mr Annan Bryce had anything to do with it, the thirty-seven-acre island of Garinish, otherwise known as Ilnacullin, was gorse and heather scratching for a living among sphagnum peat and blue shale. But it was sheltered and its winters tempered by the Gulf Stream. There were two interesting features, a Martello tower and a fort erected against the threatened Napoleonic invasion. In 1910 Mr Bryce decided to build a large house adjoining the tower and surround it with a beautiful garden. He employed

359

Harold Peto to design both. The house was never built but until the outbreak of the First World War one hundred men were continuously employed on the garden. You can see the results they achieved, and I know you will love the Italian Garden with its wistaria-hung Casita (all-important in an Italian garden), the Medici House opposite and between them a long lily pool set in the paving. On the terrace surrounding it are dazzling flower borders, and at each corner huge leptospermums forty years old, the Australasian shrub related to the myrtle, which bears its white flowers in May and June. A rock fourteen feet high was quarried out to make this garden, and the view is beautiful – Big Sugar Loaf and Small Sugar Loaf, with the sea between. A most lovely walk leads to a temple where you can sit and listen to the slapping of the Atlantic against the rocks below. Blue shale steps lead up to it, and lining the approach are huge clumps of blue agapanthus lilies. Left and right are graceful conifers. There are winding walks in and out of woodlands, opening into glades of flowering shrubs; and a broad grass walk lined with trees leads to the Tower. There sudden beauties catch the eye – a russet carpet of pine needles, gorgeous lumps of smooth bare rock against the sky, rising out of the trees like the grey backs and shoulders of elephants. A rhododendron wafts its fragrance and there are rare conifers to admire: the Australian Cypress Pine (*Callitris oblonga*), the Huon Pine of Tasmania, its slender arching branches bright with scale-like leaves. There are seventy-five steps up to the Martello Tower, and there you will get a three-hundred-and-sixty-degree view over the Atlantic with Bantry Bay on your left. The herbaceous borders at Ilnacullin are magnificent, beautifully grown and grouped: phloxes and hydrangeas, purple-headed teazels, four-foot-tall campanulas of palest blue, the vermilion spikes of watsonias, blue delphiniums, yellow verbascums and purple erigerons, a flood of colour each side of the path, with buddleias and lilacs behind. To reach this little paradise there is a ferry-boat trip into the bargain.

The Japanese Garden, Tully

Zone Centre: Dublin, Route 3

Owner: The Irish National Stud Company

The garden tells a story, as all Japanese gardens should, and this one is authentic, created by a Japanese water engineer brought in by Colonel Hall Walker to control the natural springs in a swamp. The task completed, Colonel Hall Walker, later Lord Wavertree, asked Eida to make a pathway. Eida made it and found himself making other pathways following the winding course of his ditches, and planting a little tree here and there to lean over the water, and putting down a few stepping stones. . . . This is how it is with the Japanese: they must have a garden. Colonel Hall Walker fell in with his idea, and the result is the exquisite Tully you see today, planned to symbolise the Life of Man. There is not a stone or bend in the way that does not mean something – the difficulties of life, its ups and downs on the Hill of Ambition. Here you are tempted to look too high – and 'ware the hole at your feet into which you may tumble (a few inches) and come to the level of your fellows. I must say I sympathised with Eida's hero when he nearly followed the Path of Temptation, for the glimpses of the Easy Life on the island, where the Geisha House stands, are tantalising: it is a paradise of ferns and little maple trees, of pools of sparkling spring water, of the lights and shades of a thousand blending and contrasting greens (count them if you can!).

361

To the Japanese the greens of pine trees and mosses are far more beautiful than any quantity of flower-colour. They reject roses and lilies as unworthy, their charms too obvious, just as they reject a crowded vase in their houses, preferring to contemplate a single lovely bloom. At Tully, Eida's mastery of the art is perfection. He allows a shower of cherry blossom to symbolise the sweetness of spring and youth, and in autumn the maples burn with colour to symbolise the richness of maturity. The rest is a tapestry of greens. If you are interested in the art of Bonsai, you may like to know that one tree on the Hill of Ambition is reputed to be two thousand years old, and on the smooth green lawn of Peace and Contentment you will see another age-old bonsai tree representing 'Father, Mother, Son and Daughter'. Father is a dried-out twig, Mother has faded away; the Son and Daughter branches are vigorous. The stepping stones that lead away across the lawn are faltering now and placed closer and closer. Eida's hero goes to his grave past the last lantern, past the weeping trees and into the Hall of Mourning, and so his pilgrim soul passes through the Gateway of Eternity. It might be Japan, and indeed it is.

The John F Kennedy Memorial Park

Zone Centre: Waterford, Route 1

Owner: The President Kennedy Memorial Committee

This is a great forest garden and arboretum in the making. It will take a long time to grow, this natural park with plantings planned over five years of six thousand species of trees and shrubs, but already there is much to see. In the simple and dignified memorial hall is a copper map of the world showing where all the plants and trees are coming from – the coniferous forests, broad-leaved forests and meadows, sub-tropical evergreen forests, Mediterranean and semi-desert regions of the twenty-two countries with which Ireland has diplomatic relations. At the Dublin Botanic Garden is a new glasshouse which is the quarantine house for the plants as they are brought in. There are four hundred and sixty acres of parkland. The site chosen was on the lower slopes of Slieve Coillte, a commanding hill rising above the Kennedy ancestral home in Dunganstown, Co Wexford. Already seven hundred species were planted by the winter of 1968–9, one specimen of each species of tree or shrub. Precedence is being given to trees, though shrubs will be planted for amenity purposes. They are being arranged in two circuits for scenic effect, one mainly of conifers, the other mainly of broad-leaved trees. There will be an ericaceous garden with rhododendrons, azaleas and heathers, and a maple collection for rich autumn colouring. The trees will also be arranged in their geographical regions, blocks being allocated to each of the five continents.

Mount Stewart

Zone Centre: Belfast, Route 1

Owner: The National Trust

You might expect to find a shamrock in Ireland. If so, you can see it at Mount Stewart, a paved garden of that shape wherein is a bed planted with the red-leaved *Iresine herbstii* in the shape of a left hand to denote the Red Hand of Ulster. Here too is an Irish harp in exquisitely cut yew, and round about – on top of the twelve-foot-high macrocarpa hedge – is a topiary hunting party depicting the arrival of the family by boat, the shooting of a stag, the snatching of the stag by the Devil, and the sad homecoming of the hunters with only a rabbit! These are only a few of the joys of Mount Stewart's eighty acres. Garden follows garden. There is the Mairi Garden where the baby of the family used to be put to sleep. A pretty and peaceful place it is, shaped this time in the form of a Tudor rose. In the centre is a fountain with a lead statue of the little Viscountess Bury who in the family was 'Mairi, Mairi, quite contrary'. Blue- and white-flowered plants are used for the beds, mostly blue agapanthus and fragrant white lilies. In May every year a tall *Drimys winteri* becomes covered with ivory-white flowers, mingling its scent with the lily perfume of the tender rhododendrons *dalhousiae* and *lindleyi* growing nearby. An interesting tree in this little garden is *Koelreuteria bipinnata*, supposed to be the tree of the Willow-pattern plate. Next comes the Dodo Terrace with two red stone griffins guarding its entrance and four dodos guarding a stone ark. It overlooks the Italian Garden where all round on plinths are other fabled creatures representing members of the 'Ark Association' over which Lady Londonderry used to preside: it was quite a power in politics. The beauty of this garden is achieved by the use of intense colour, flower varieties being specially chosen to produce this effect. The roses are all vivid-coloured ones, the blues of the delphiniums rich and deep. The island borders have pleasingly different edgings: instead of box there are clipped heathers, santolina and the red-leaved *Berberis thunbergii atropurpurea*. Cordylines heavy with their huge bunches of creamy flowers grow by the two ponds full of white water lilies. In the pool of the Spanish Garden next door are pink water lilies, and up the green-tiled summer house grows a climber usually seen only in a greenhouse, *Lapageria rosea,* which hangs with crimson bells. Wherever you go at Mount Stewart, in and out of its gardens or by the lake, there are unusual and rare plants and a wealth of them. Almost entirely the creation of Edith, Lady Londonderry, Mount Stewart is magnificent.

Mount Usher

Zone Centre: Dublin, Route 1

Owner: R B Walpole, Esq

The garden at Mount Usher is a botanist's paradise: hardly a plant or tree grows here that is not an unusual species. But equally it is a place anyone can enjoy. Its most beautiful feature is the wide grass avenue bordered by trees and shrubs, though the walk along the river is equally lovely; and for sheer enchantment there is the little stream with stepping stones the length of its burbling course where you can walk under boughs in a fairyland of ferns; and there is the maple walk that goes into a wood where you can sit at a viewpoint to see a panorama of tree-tops with a silvery-boled eucalyptus thrusting itself one hundred and twenty feet up to show its silvery-blue foliage against the sky. Starting from the house you will meet some charming flowers in the formal part of the garden – Balloon Flowers and Irish Molly pansies and Jackanapes, the blur of tiny white daisies which is *Helichrysum scutellifolium*, with one of the most beautiful trees in the world, *Myrtus luma,* whose bark is like polished mahogany. Across the weir is the Palm Walk, planted in 1927. The first shrub attracting attention is *Mutisia retusa,* its pink daisies poking through a colletia with weird aeroplane-shaped spined leaves, and then comes a handsome eucryphia hybrid raised at Mount Usher. It was explained to me: 'Mum cordifolia and Dad glutinosa are the parents

366

of the Nymans hybrid. Ours is the opposite way. It was all an accident years and years ago.' There is the feathery-foliaged *Cupressus elegantissimus* and a rare *Austrocedrus chilina* with fascinating foliage turned up at the edges. *Stranvaesia nussia* is a delight: its new foliage is silky grey like satin with a pink sheen and its white clusters of flowers are followed by downy orange fruits. Mount Usher boasts the best specimen in Europe of *Pinus montezuma*. It is truly magnificent. Along the azalea walk the *Myrtus bullata* will intrigue you with its scarab foliage and pink-tipped stamens. This is the New Zealand Ramarama tree. The Riviera is the name of the walk alongside the Vartry, the flower border on the right of the path a glorious mixture of everything – bright red Bottle Brushes, hypericums of soft yellow flowers, veronicas, *Stranvaesia undulata* which colours red in the autumn, a Handkerchief Tree, brilliant cerise phloxes, the Rock Lily from Yorkshire and pink-flowered dogwood. The other side of the river is a shrub garden with exciting things such as *Decaisnea fargesii* whose pods turn a bright metallic blue, and *Alangium chinense* whose little white pods become daisies with long bright yellow stamens. Of course you know that the tea we drink comes from the leaf of a Camellia, and here one of them grows, the bronze-leaved *Camellia cuspidata*. This is only a sample of lovely Mount Usher, where you can find hour after hour of such treasures.

Muckross Gardens

Zone Centre: Killarney, Route 1

Owner: The Office of Public Works

These beautiful gardens lie at the foot of the Killarney Mountains, with one of the famous lakes in the demesne. In fact there are three of them: the Upper Lake and Muckross Lake, with Lough Leane beyond. The approach is through a glorious woodland, and as you pass in front of the house the air is sweet with the scent of floppy pink shrub roses. Round the corner to the left is a gay little walled garden of dwarf dahlias and annuals, and behind it a natural rock garden where plants nestle in the crevices of the outcrop. It is all beautifully kept, and if you think of Ireland as the Emerald Isle it is here you will find emerald grass. The sheets of green are islanded with splendid old trees, copper beeches and conifers, with huge mounds of rhododendrons a glorious sight in spring and early summer. The Stream Walk is one of peace in a quiet woodland, and if you turn right you will come on a glade colourful with pink and crimson astilbes shading into the pale mauve of hostas. You can follow the course of the stream by the twin ribbons of colour along its banks: hostas both white and mauve, ornamental grasses, pink astilbes and golden lysimachia ending in dramatic groups of *Yucca filamentosa*, noble white flower-spikes thrown up from sabre-like leaves. The *Arbutus unedo* or Strawberry Tree is native to Ireland, so it is good to find

368

at Muckross an Arbutus Walk. There are miles of woodland walks with rhododendrons, azaleas, camellias and magnolias growing among the trees in this eleven-thousand-acre national park and garden.

The National Botanic Gardens, Glasnevin

Zone Centre: Dublin, Route 2

Owner: The Department of Agriculture

This is a pleasant garden in itself, apart from being a botanic garden: sweeping stretches of grass with trees and groups of shrubs, a walk between glorious herbaceous borders, a good rock garden laid against a slope, a rose garden with an excellent collection of modern hybrids, and the River Liffey running through in a widening course. A wet day can be rewardingly spent in the hothouses. In the Palm House is one of the best collections of cycads anywhere. It was built up by Sir Frederick Moore who was curator from 1879. Soon after, he began forming a collection of orchids and one was named in his honour, *Neomoorea*. He also built up collections of tropical plants, temperate woody plants and tender monocotyledons. Nor did he forget the claims of horticulture: it is due to his energy in this direction that Glasnevin has a traditional display of well grown garden plants. The West Arboretum was planted entirely by him;

he was responsible for the new Palm House and the Aquatic House, a house for tree ferns and a cactus house. You can still see his original plants including a *Philodendron notabile* and the unique *Arachnanthe lowii* whose first two flowers are totally different from the later ones – brown, black and yellow spikes which later come pure yellow, and yards long! You could spend many an interesting hour among Glasnevin's hothouse collections. There is a historical note: the sombre yew walk where Addison the essayist used to pace, and if you are botanically minded there are the Natural Order beds to see. Among the interesting trees is an eighty-year-old *Cedrus atlantica pendula,* a rare weeping form of the Atlas cedar; and if you remember Harry Lauder, why not go and find the funny twisted hazel known as Harry Lauder's Walking Stick?

Powerscourt

Zone Centre: Dublin, Route 1

Owner: The Powerscourt Estate

It is all granite and glory. The glory is of architecture and the grand scale of everything – the statuary, the staircase of the terraces that plunge down a hillside with magnificent lawns either side circling vast and beautiful rose beds and reaching a pool where a fountain one hundred feet high plays against the distant Sugar Loaf Mountain. Here, it seems, even trees do not grow to the accepted size but strive to equal the surrounding magnificence. A group of huge conifers dominates a lawn on the right: you discover it is a single tree, the many-boled *Thuja dolobata*. Some people shy from the vastness of Powerscourt: I found it exciting from start to finish, its very name ringing like a clarion. As a good start you enter by the Eagle Gate and follow a two-hundred-year-old avenue of beeches. The first garden is gained by the Bamberg Gate which opens on to a lawn with clipped Portugal laurels and gay flower beds. Through the exquisite Venetian wrought ironwork of another gate, incorporating the curling tendrils of a vine, you catch a glimpse of the next garden and of the first fountain with its eighteenth-century lead merman. This is really the kitchen garden, but broad herbaceous borders hide the utilitarian part with a sea of bloom: phloxes and shrub roses, scabious and paeonies, red-hot-pokers and purple geraniums, penstemons, and at the front campanulas as blue as Irish eyes. Another gate beckons, the English Gate depicting the rose, the thistle and the shamrock, and another cooling splash of water greets you, four dolphins supporting the three-tiered fountain with their tails. It is called the Green Pond because of its green reflections, for here there are only trees, no flowers but the white water lilies. Two stone urns point the way onward. A *Eucalyptus globulus* planted in 1898 is 112 feet high. The end of the path frames a glimpse of the lovely Sugar Loaf, that graceful Fuji-like summit which makes the Dublin horizon so enchanting. You pass a vast *Cupressus macrocarpa* which is only seventy years old, but, it was explained to me: 'The man who planted it pinched out the leader.' There is a Japanese garden, not so authentic perhaps as the one at Tully, but it leads to an incomparable view where you are up as high as the tops of the tall conifers and looking through a gap between two great groups of them to that magic blue hill.

Rowallane

Zone Centre: Belfast, Route 1

Owner: The National Trust

This is a garden utterly different. No bulldozers or gangs of workmen came here to shift tons of rocks or delve away a hillside. It was all left entirely as its owner found it, and in planting his garden Hugh Armytage-Moore followed the natural contours that were there. He left the dry-stone walls boxing in the little fields and made them into gardens. When it came to making a rock garden, the existing outcrop could not be bettered. If you knew nothing of all this you would instinctively recognise that an artist had gone hand in hand with nature. You come down to the series of little gardens by way of a rounded plateau stretching down in a long irregular slope of uneven levels. It is mounded with rhododendrons on the right, and in spring daffodils make golden carpets in front of them. Here and there the bare rock shows through the grass, and when you walk down you feel somehow as if you were treading on history. The rock garden is right at the bottom and as you open the small gate a *Rhus cotinus*, russet red, greets you from a rocky summit. It is not, strictly speaking, an Alpine Garden, but everything grows together, large and small, just as it would do in a real alpine pass. There are cistus in profusion, shedding their daily quota of petals over rocks scarred by the action of ancient glaciers. Celmisia grows here with its woolly silvery-white leaves, heathers, a sprawl of yellow alchemilla, shrubby little *Drimys colorata* with pink-veined and pink-tipped leaves, roses, and the miniature Robert Chapman spruce, its foliage reddish gold as if tipped with the setting sun – a host of them as if they had all grown up in this one spot from the seeds of a single cone. The gardens climb up grassy slopes – the Old Wood, the Hospital (where ailing calves were brought on the one-time farm), and the Stream Ground, full of heathers and flowering shrubs, wonderful rhododendrons, magnolias, fothergillas, kalmias. You will notice the remarkable *Cornus kousa chinensis* whose clematis-shaped bracts dusted with pink lie piled along its branches like snow, and the beautiful *Acer osakazuki* with lime-green leaves, the Dove Tree, and, unexpectedly in the Paddock, a *Rosa moschata* var. *grandiflora* smothering a holly tree in a mound of white. In complete contrast is the formal walled garden by the entrance, with borders in the shape of a Celtic cross. In the centre is a magnificent specimen of *Viburnum tomentosum* bred at Rowallane, with round flower heads of snowy white. The famous and vastly superior 'Rowallane' variety of hypericum also of course originated here, and there is the beautiful Rowallane Rose primula, growing here with 'Old Gold' and the dark-stemmed *aurantiaca*. The borders are full of roses, hydrangeas, mecanopsis, lilies, tall blue delphiniums, backed by shrubs and flowering trees, and the walls draped with climbers, among them the fascinating Spanish honeysuckle *Lonicera splendida* with blue-green leaves and cream flowers stained purple outside. Two unusual plants are the blue-stemmed *Kirengeshoma palmata* from Japan with tubular waxy canary-yellow flowers (it doesn't need staking), and the quaint *Arisaema candidissima* whose white spathes are like little ship's ventilators!

Also open are:

ADARE MANOR (Zone Centre: Killarney, Route 3. Owner: The Earl of Dunraven) in whose park are two ruins, one a Franciscan priory erected in 1464 and destroyed when Henry VIII suppressed the monasteries; the second Desmond Castle dating back to 1226. On the south side of the house is a Geometric Garden with box scrollwork, a shrub garden and a rose border. A broad flight of steps leads down to the river where there is a very fine Cedar of Lebanon.

JOHNSTOWN CASTLE (Zone Centre: Waterford, Route 2. Owner: The Agricultural Institute) which is the headquarters of the Soils Division of the Department of Agriculture. Here soil is tested for the whole of Ireland. There is a formal walled garden with double herbaceous borders, otherwise mature woodland and three lakes, with very good collections of azaleas, fuchsias, acers, camellias and hybrid rhododendrons.

SPRINGHILL (Zone Centre: Belfast, Route 2. Owner: The National Trust) is a 'Plantation' house of James I's time with a charming garden in which you can see the first Macartney roses ever grown. There is a collection of shrub roses and old French roses and a camomile lawn in a herb garden. In the woodland are yews which are relics of the ancient Forest.

Open occasionally are:

DARGLE COTTAGE (Zone Centre: Dublin, Route 1. Owners: Sir Basil and Lady Goulding) has a superb garden occupying the steep slopes of a valley through which flows the Dargle River. It is richly planted with trees and shrubs for colour and contrast effects, and a feature are the roses grown amongst them and in the rose garden and on a delightful pergola. Camellias, magnolias, rhododendrons and azaleas are a sight in spring, with splendid autumn colouring of maples and shrubs.

DEREEN (Zone Centre: Killarney, Route 2. Owners: The Viscount and Viscountess Mersey) has a fine collection of rhododendrons, Loderi and many grown from the seeds of Kingdon-Ward and Cox expeditions. The trees are magnificent: two *Eucalyptus globulus* with gigantic trunks, one of a hundred and seventy feet and one of a hundred and eighty. A *Cryptomeria japonica* is nearly ninety feet and there is a grove of tree ferns (*Dicksonia antarctica*) which are immense. The lake at the bottom of the garden is really the Atlantic, and there are wonderful views. On the lawn is a two-hundred-year-old macrocarpa claimed to be the biggest in the country. Luxuriant growth is not confined to trees: a Japanese *Vitis coignetiae* has leaves almost a foot across, *Fuchsia excorticata* grows fifteen feet tall and *Senecio elaeagnifolius* is at least ten feet tall. An exciting experience to see them all.

FERNHILL (Zone Centre: Dublin, Route 2. Owner: Ralph J Walker, Esq) is a garden and woodland on the side of the Three Rock Mountain overlooking Dublin Bay and Ireland's Eye. Some of the trees are over two hundred years old and a specimen of the beautiful *Picea smithiana* is one hundred feet high and over a century old. The woodland is full of rhododendrons, among them a superb specimen of *R arboreum* raised here over a hundred years ago. There are good eucalyptus trees and a noble sweet chestnut.

GARINISH ISLAND (Zone Centre: Killarney, Route 2. Owner: G R Browne, Esq) is a sub-tropical island in the Kenmare River which opens into the Atlantic. Imagine a garden where you can pick vasefuls of flowers all the year round. It is a wonderland of avenues of New Zealand tree ferns and palm trees, nine miles of walks round the island's fifty-six acres, with a camellia garden and shrubs that grow to tree size, like the *capitata* dogwood from the Himalaya which is nearly thirty feet by thirty feet with a trunk fifty-two inches in girth. The Australasian *Mühlenbeckia axillaris* is usually a creeping and matted shrub. Here it is grown as a hedge. Among all the colourful treasures, familiar rhododendrons and azaleas adding their beauty, the rare Kerry Lily strikes a vibrant note with its scarlet flowers.

GLANLEAM, VALENTIA ISLAND (Zone Centre: Killarney, Route 3. Owner: Lt-Col R J Uniacke, DSO) has a woodland planted ninety years ago where many tender trees have reached great size. The lovely Chilean myrtle (*Myrtus luma*) seeds almost too freely, and the Lily of the Valley tree is equally at home. A beautiful scarlet-flowered embothrium has reached thirty-five feet. Tender rhododendrons, tree ferns and shrubs like *Olearia semidentata* of lilac flower make a walk through this twenty-acre woodland a 'must' for the plantsman. The bulbs are a wonderful sight in March, and the house itself you can hardly see for climbers – passion-flowers, clematis and climbing double geraniums.

GUINCHO (Zone Centre: Belfast, Route 2. Owners: Mr and Mrs Frazer Mackie) is a labour-saving garden where not a single plant needs staking. It is all very beautiful, sixteen acres of mass plantings and spacious circular lawn, with a unique collection of kniphofias, among them an un-known brilliant yellow 'Red Hot Poker'. The variety of plants is bewildering and almost every species an unusual one. The curving borders brim with colour. Ericas and shrub roses are special favourites in this very personal garden that was not 'laid out' but grew as more and more plants were added. There are rare things like pink dandelions and the enchanting Elizabethan rose plantain. A woodland full of rhododendrons completes the picture, in spring carpeted with dog's-tooth violets.

MOUNT CONGREVE (**Zone Centre: Waterford, Route 1. Owner: Ambrose Congreve, Esq**) is going to be one of the world's great gardens – five hundred of one species of azalea in one place, one thousand in another. But then Mr Congreve has nearly one hundred acres, mostly intensely cultivated. He has just finished restoring the beautiful family home, and now the garden is being brought to the same pitch of perfection. Imagine half a mile of herbaceous borders in one walled garden alone, thousands of plants in hundreds of varieties. Conjure up the beauty of eight hundred groups of white, soft pink, dark pink and red *Camellia japonica*, a corner filled with a sheet of five hundred hydrangeas, a hillside covered with shrub roses. Five years ago the whole place was a sea of laurel twenty-five feet high. Vistas are still being created and views of the Suir River which curves in a great U below. Completion of the planting is planned for 1970, but already the place is gorgeous with colour, and exciting for its many tender and unusual plants growing in the woodlands and in the series of gardens.

ROSSDOHAN ISLAND (**Zone Centre: Killarney, Route 2. Owners: Messrs P and R J Walker**) was a windswept place with a solitary hawthorn bush when Samuel Thomas Heard took it over in 1870. It is now much as he left it, a sub-tropical woodland where immense tree ferns grow, among them the beautiful Silver Tree Fern with stems up to six feet long and great fronds over ten feet, bluish green above and silver below, unique even for southern Ireland. There are fantastic acacias seventy and eighty feet tall crowded with yellow bloom, and a *Eucalyptus globulus* that has grown forty feet in six years. A Pepper Bush is at least fifty-two feet high. But mere statistics do not convey the atmosphere of this beautiful and exotic woodland described as 'a chunk of Australia', scented with musk when the Australian *Olearia argyrophylla* is in flower, with tree-trunks clothed in bright green ferns or scarlet with the Mitre Flower.

Appendix I

Zone Centres with Suggested Hotels

Aberdeen, Scotland	Caledonian
Alnwick, Northumberland	Schooner, Alnmouth
Bath, Somerset	Francis*
Battle, Sussex	George*
Bedford, Beds	Lion*
Belfast, N Ireland	Conway*
Betws-y-Coed, N Wales	Gwydyr
Cambridge, Cambs	Blue Boar*
Canterbury, Kent	Chaucer*
Chester, Cheshire	Queen*
Cirencester, Glos	Fleece*
Coventry, Warwicks	*several*
Crawley, Sussex	George*
Donegal, Ireland	*several*
Dublin, Ireland	Shelbourne*
Edinburgh, Scotland	Carlton*
Exeter, Devon	Great Western*
	or White Hart*, Moretonhampstead
Gairloch, Ross and Cromarty	The Gairloch
Glasgow, Scotland	*several*
Guildford, Surrey	Angel*
Harrogate, Yorks	Cairn*
Hereford, Herefordshire	Green Dragon* or City Arms*
Inverness, Scotland	Royal*
Killarney, Ireland	International*
King's Lynn, Norfolk	Duke's Head*
Leicester, Leics	Bell*
London	Brown's*, Cavendish*, Grosvenor House*, Hertford*,
	Hyde Park*, Meurice*, St George's*

Matlock Bath, Derbyshire	New Bath*
Montrose, Scotland	Central
Newton Stewart, Scotland	*several*
Norwich, Norfolk	Bell*
Oxford, Oxon	Randolph*
Perth, Scotland	Royal George*
Richmond, Yorks	Black Lion
Salisbury, Wilts	White Hart*
Shrewsbury, Salop	Lion*
Stratford-upon-Avon, Warwicks	Shakespeare* or White Swan*
Tarbert, Argyll, Scotland	Kilmory Castle, Lochgilphead
Tavistock, Devon	Bedford*
Truro, Cornwall	Brookdale
Tunbridge Wells, Kent	Wellington* or Rose & Crown*, Tonbridge
Waterford, Ireland	Tower
Weymouth, Dorset	*several*
Windermere, Westmorland	Old England

* *Trust House Hotel*

Appendix II

The Gardens – County by County

Aberdeenshire: Pitmedden; Williamston

Angus: Airlie Castle; Balnamoon; Brechin Castle; Cortachy Castle; Edzell Castle; Guthrie Castle

Argyll: Achamore, Isle of Gigha; An Cala; Benmore (Younger Botanic Garden); Crarae Lodge; Eckford; Kiloran; Stonefield Castle; Strone

Ayrshire: Culzean Castle; Glenapp Castle

Bedfordshire: The Lodge, Sandy; Luton Hoo; Woburn Abbey; Wrest Park

Berkshire: Cliveden; Folly Farm; Kingston House; Quarry Wood; Savill Garden and the Valley Gardens

Buckinghamshire: Stowe

Bute: Brodick Castle, Isle of Arran

Caernarvonshire: Gilfach; Penrhyn Castle

Cambridgeshire: Anglesey Abbey; Cambridge Botanic Garden and College Gardens; Peckover House

Cheshire: Arley Hall; Capesthorne; Liverpool University Botanic Gardens, Ness; Raby Vale; Tatton Park Gardens

Co Cork: Ilnacullin (Garinish Island)

Cornwall: Cotehele House; Glendurgan; Lanhydrock; Penjerrick; Trelissick Gardens; Trengwainton Gardens; Tresco Abbey Gardens, Isles of Scilly; Trewithen

Cumberland: Muncaster Castle

Denbighshire: Bodnant; Chirk Castle; Gwydir Castle

Derbyshire: Chatsworth; Haddon Hall; Kedleston Hall; Lea Rhododendron Gardens; Melbourne Hall

Co Derry: Springhill

Devon: Bicton Gardens; Casa di Sole; Chambercombe Manor; Dartington Hall Gardens; The Garden House, Buckland Monachorum; Killerton Garden; Knightshayes Court; Lee Ford; Moyclare; Old Rectory; Saltram House; Sharpitor; Stonelands; Tapeley Park Gardens

Co Donegal: Glenveagh Castle

Dorset: Abbotsbury Sub-tropical Gardens; Athelhampton; Cerne Abbey; Compton Acres; Cranborne Manor; Creech Grange; Forde Abbey; Hyde Crook; Minterne; Priory of Lady St Mary; Yaffle Hill

Co Down: Annesley Garden and Arboretum; Guincho; Mount Stewart; Rowallane

Co Dublin: Fernhill; Howth Demesne; The National Botanic Gardens

Dunbartonshire: Armadale; Glenarn

Durham: Raby Castle

Essex: Audley End; Gun Hill Place; Hill Pasture; Kelvedon Hall; St Osyth's Priory; Tewes

Fife: Earlshall; Falkland Palace

Gloucestershire: Batsford Park; Chastleton House; Court House; Daneway House; Dodington House; Dyrham Park; Hidcote Manor; Hodges; Kiftsgate Court; Malcolm House; Sezincote; Snowshill Manor; Sudeley Castle; Vine House; Westonbirt Arboretum

Hampshire: Bramdean House; Exbury Gardens; Headbourne Worthy Grange; Hinton Ampner House; House in the Wood; Jermyns House; Longstock Park Water Garden; Monks Rest; Pylewell Park

Herefordshire: Berrington Hall; Croft Castle; Dinmore Manor; Eastnor Castle; Hergest Croft Gardens and Park Wood

Hertfordshire: Hatfield House; St Paul's Walden Bury

Kent: Bedgebury National Pinetum; Chartwell; Chilham Castle Gardens; Crittenden House; Emmetts; Godinton Park; The Grange, Benenden; Hall Place Gardens; Hever Castle; Hole Park; Northbourne Court; Oakenwood; Owl House Gardens; Penshurst Place; St John's Jerusalem; Scotney Castle; Sissinghurst Castle; Sissinghurst Place Gardens

Co Kerry: Dereen; Garinish Island; Glanleam; Muckross Estate; Rossdohan

Co Kildare: Japanese Garden, Tully

Kincardineshire: Crathes Castle; Glenbervie

Kinross-shire: Kinross House

Kirkcudbrightshire: Corsock House; Threave School of Practical Gardening

Lanarkshire: Pollok House, Glasgow

Lancashire: Cranford; Holker Hall

Leicestershire: Beaumont Hall Botanic Gardens; Belgrave Hall

Co Limerick: Adare Manor

Lincolnshire: Gunby Hall; Well Vale

London: Chiswick House; Derry and Toms Roof Garden; Hampton Court Palace Gardens; Kew, The Royal Botanic Gardens; Syon Park Gardening Centre; Walpole House

Merioneth: Glan-y-Mawddach; Plas Brondanw; Portmeirion

Midlothian: Edinburgh, The Royal Botanic Garden; Inveresk Lodge Garden; Suntrap

Montgomeryshire: Powis Castle

Morayshire: Blackhills

Nairnshire: Cawdor Castle

Norfolk: Blickling Hall; Bressingham; Holkham Hall; Oxburgh Hall; Sandringham; Sheringham Hall; Talbot Manor

Northamptonshire: Castle Ashby; Rockingham Castle; Sulgrave Manor

Northumberland: Callaly Castle; Cragside Estate; Glen Aln; Seaton Delaval Hall

Nottinghamshire: Hardwick Hall; Newstead Abbey; Thoresby Hall

Co Offaly: Birr Castle

Oxfordshire: Blenheim Palace; Oxford Botanic Garden; Rousham; Waterperry Horticultural School

384

Peebles-shire: Dawyck Gardens; Helmend

Perthshire: Abercairny; Branklyn; Drummond Castle; Glendoick; Keir

Ross and Cromarty: Dundonnell; Inverewe

Shropshire: Burford House Gardens; Hodnet Hall; The Magnolias; Weston Park

Somerset: Ammerdown Park; Barrington Court; Bath Botanic Garden; Claverton Manor; Clevedon Court; Cothay Manor; Dunster Castle; East Lambrook Manor; Montacute House; Tintinhull House

Staffordshire: Alton Towers; Blithfield Hall; Sandon Hall

Suffolk: Heveningham Hall; Ickworth; Melford Hall; Somerleyton Hall

Surrey: Coverwood; Dunsborough Park; Grayswood Hill; Hascombe Court; Isabella Plantation Woodland Garden, Richmond Park; Polesden Lacey; Pyrford Court; Winkworth Arboretum; Wisley (RHS garden); Yew Cottage

Sussex: Batemans; Beeches Farm; Borde Hill Gardens; Charleston Manor; Great Dixter; Heaselands; Highdown; Leonardslee; Michelham Priory; Nymans; Parham Park; Sheffield Park Gardens; Sutton End; Wakehurst Place

Warwickshire: Admington Hall; Arbury Hall; Birmingham Botanic Garden; Compton Wynyates; Packwood House; Shakespearian Gardens, Stratford-upon-Avon; Upton House

Co Waterford: Curraghmore; Mount Congreve

West Lothian: Hopetoun House

Westmorland: Briery Close; Levens Hall; White Craggs

Co Wexford: Johnstown Castle; Kennedy Memorial Park

Co Wicklow: Dargle Cottage; Mount Usher; Powerscourt

Wigtownshire: Lochinch and Castle Kennedy; Logan

Wiltshire: Avebury Manor; Corsham Court; The Courts; Great Chalfield Manor; Hungerdown House; Little Cheverell House; Littlecote; Longleat; Seales Farm; Stourhead; Wilton House

Worcestershire: Spetchley Park

Yorkshire: Bramham Park; Burnby Hall Gardens; Castle Howard; Harewood House; Harlow Car Gardens; Newby Hall; Parcevall Hall; Rudding Park; St Nicholas

Appendix III

Gardens of Special Interest

Bracketed numbers = Zone reference number

▲ *Open only occasionally*

Abbotsbury Sub-tropical Gardens (3)
Achamore, Isle of Gigha (10)
Airlie Castle (12)
Alton Towers (7)
Ammerdown Park (3)
An Cala, Easdale (10)
Anglesey Abbey (6)
Annesley Garden and Arboretum (13)
Arley Hall (7)
Athelhampton (3)
Avebury Manor (3)

Barrington Court (3)
Bedgebury National Pinetum (2)
Benmore (Younger Botanic Garden) (10)
Bicton Gardens (4)
Birr Castle (13)
Blackhills (12)
Blenheim Palace (5)
Bodnant Gardens, Tal-y-Cafn (9)
Borde Hill Gardens (2)
▲ Bramdean House (3)
Bramham Park (8)
Branklyn (11)
Bressingham (6)

Brodick Castle (10)
Burford House Gardens (9)
Burnby Hall Gardens (8)

Castle Ashby (5)
▲ Cawdor Castle (12)
Charleston Manor (2)
Chartwell (2)
Chatsworth (7)
Chiswick House Grounds (1)
Claverton Manor (3)
Cliveden (1)
Compton Acres Gardens (3)
Compton Wynyates (5)
Cotehele House (4)
Courts, The, Holt (3)
▲ Coverwood (2)
Cragside Estate (11)
Cranford (7)
Crarae Lodge (10)
Crathes Castle (12)
Crittenden House (2)

▲ Dargle Cottage (13)
Dartington Hall Garden (4)
Dawyck Gardens (11)
Dinmore Manor (9)
Drummond Castle (11)

▲ Earlshall (11)
East Lambrook Manor (3)
Edinburgh, Royal Botanic Garden (11)
Exbury Gardens (3)

Forde Abbey (3)

Glan-y-Mawddach (9)
Glenarn (10)

Glendurgan (4)
Glenveagh Castle (13)
Godinton Park (2)
▲ Grange, The, Benenden (2)
Grayswood Hill (2)
Great Dixter (2)
▲ Guincho (13)
Gunby Hall (6)

Haddon Hall (7)
Hall Place Gardens (2)
Hampton Court Palace Gardens (1)
Harewood House (8)
Harlow Car Gardens (9)
▲ Headbourne Worthy Grange (3)
Heaselands (2)
Hergest Croft Garden and Park Wood (9)
Hever Castle (2)
Hidcote Manor Gardens (5)
Highdown (2)
▲ Hill Pasture (6)
▲ Hinton Ampner (3)
Hodnet Hall (9)
Hole Park (2)
Hungerdown House (3)

Ilnacullin (13)
Inveresk Lodge Garden (11)
Inverewe (12)

Japanese Garden, Tully (13)
▲ Jermyns House Garden and Arboretum (3)
▲ Kelvedon Hall (1)
Kew, The Royal Botanic Gardens (1)
▲ Kiftsgate Court (5)
Killerton Garden (4)
▲ Kinross House (11)
Knightshayes Court (4)

Lea Rhododendron Gardens (7)
Leonardslee (2)
Levens Hall (8)
Liverpool University Botanic Gardens, Ness (7)
Lochinch and Castle Kennedy (10)
Logan (10)
Longstock Park Water Gardens (3)
Luton Hoo (1)

Melbourne Hall (7)
Minterne (3)
Montacute (3)
▲ Mount Congreve (13)
Mount Stewart (13)
Mount Usher (13)
Muncaster Castle (8)

Newby Hall (8)
Newstead Abbey (7)
Nymans (2)

Packwood House (5)
Penjerrick (4)
Penshurst Place (2)
Pitmedden (12)
Powerscourt (13)
Powis Castle (9)
Priory of Lady St Mary (3)
Pylewell Park (3)
Pyrford Court (1)

Quarry Wood (1)

▲ Raby Vale (7)
▲ Rossdohan (13)
Rousham (5)
Rowallane (13)
Rudding Park (8)

St Paul's Walden Bury Gardens (1)
Savill Garden, The, and The Valley Gardens (1)
Scotney Castle (2)
▲ Sezincote (5)
Shakespearian Gardens, The (5)
Sharpitor (4)
Sheffield Park Gardens (2)
Sissinghurst Castle (2)
Snowshill Manor (5)
Spetchley Park (5)
Stourhead (3)
Stowe (5)
Syon Park Gardening Centre (1)

▲ Talbot Manor (6)
Tatton Park Gardens (7)
Tintinhull House (3)
Trengwainton Gardens (4)
Tresco Abbey Gardens (4)
Trewithen (4)

Upton House (5)

Wakehurst Place (2)
Westonbirt Arboretum (5)
White Craggs (8)
Wisley (The RHS garden) (1)
Wrest Park (5)

Yaffle Hill (3)

Appendix IV

Maps

Appendix V

National Trust Gardens

(Open free to Members)

Anglesey Abbey
Batemans
Berrington Hall
Blickling Hall
Bodnant
Chartwell
Clevedon Court
Cliveden
Cotehele House
Courts, The
Croft Castle
Dyrham Park
Emmetts
Glendurgan
Great Chalfield Manor
Gunby Hall
Hardwick Hall
Hidcote Manor
Ickworth
Killerton Garden
Lanhydrock
Melford Hall
Montacute

Mount Stewart
Nymans
Oxburgh Hall
Packwood House
Peckover House
Penrhyn Castle
Polesden Lacey
Powis Castle
Rowallane
Saltram House
Sharpitor
Sheffield Park Gardens
Sissinghurst Castle
Snowshill Manor
Springhill
Stourhead
Tatton Park
Tintinhull House
Trelissick Garden
Trengwainton Gardens
Upton House
Wakehurst Place
Winkworth Arboretum

For membership apply: The National Trust Membership Department, Blewcoat School, 23 Caxton Street, London SW1

National Trust for Scotland Gardens

Branklyn
Brodick Castle
Crathes Castle
Culzean Castle
Falkland Palace

Inveresk Lodge
Inverewe
Pitmedden
Suntrap
Threave School of Practical
    Gardening

For membership apply: The National Trust for Scotland, 5 Charlotte Square, Edinburgh 2

Appendix VI

Visiting Days and Hours of Opening

Garden	Location	Opening Times	Refreshments (R) Transport (T)
Abbotsbury Sub-tropical Gardens	Weymouth, Dorset	April to mid-Sept., weekdays 10–4.30, Suns. 2–6	T
Abercairny	Crieff, Perthshire	April to Sept., Weds. dawn to dusk	T
Achamore	Isle of Gigha, Argyll	April to Sept., daily dawn to dusk	T (Ferry on request: Gigha 217)
Admington Hall	Shipston-on-Stour, Warwickshire	April and June, Sats. and Suns. 2–7; and by appt.	

Garden	Location	Opening Times	Refreshment (R) Transport (T)
Airlie Castle	Kirriemuir, Angus	By appt.	R and T on days of special openings
Alton Towers	Alton, Staffordshire	Good Fri. to 1st weekend Oct., daily 9.30 to dusk	R T
Ammerdown Park	Radstock, Somerset	April, June and July, one Sat. each month, summer Bank Hol. 11–7; and by appt.	T
An Cala	Easdale, Argyll	April to Sept., Thurs. 2–6; and by appt.	T
Anglesey Abbey Gardens	Lode, Cambridgeshire	Easter Sat. to end Oct., Weds., Thurs., Sats., Suns., and Bank Hol. Mons. 2–6; Oct. 2–5; and by appt.	T
Annesley Garden and Arboretum	Castlewellan, Co. Down	All year daily, sunrise to sunset	R
Arbury Hall	Astley, Nuneaton, Warwickshire	All Suns. from Easter to 1st in Oct., and Bank Hol. Mons. and Tues. 2.30–6; and by appt.	R T 1 m.
Arley Hall	Northwich, Cheshire	May to Sept., Sats., Suns. and Bank Hols. 2.30–7. Parties by appt.	R T 2 m.

	Location	Opening times		
Athelhampton	Dorchester, Dorset	Easter to Sept., Weds. and Thurs; June to August, Suns. 2–6; and by appt.	R	T
Audley End	Saffron Walden, Essex	April to Sept, daily except Mons. 11.30–6.30	R	T 1½ m.
Avebury Manor	Nr. Marlborough, Wiltshire	May, July, Aug, daily except Tues; Mid- to end April, June and Sept., Sats. and Suns. 2–6; Bank Hols. 10–6; and by appt.	T	
Barrington Court	Ilminster, Somerset	All year, Weds. 10–6; winter 10–4	T	
Batemans	Burwash, Etchingham, Sussex	March to Oct., Mons. to Thurs. 11–12.30, 2–6; Good Fri, Sat. and Sun. 2–6; and by appt.	R	T
Bath Botanic Garden	Bath, Somerset	All year, 10 to 1 hr. before sunset	R	T
Beaumont Hall Botanic Garden	Leicester, Leics.	All year, Mon. to Fri. 10 to dusk	T	
Bedgebury National Pinetum	Nr. Goudhurst, Cranbrook, Kent	All year, 10–8 or dusk	T 1 m.	
Beeches Farm	Buckham Hill, nr. Uckfield, Sussex	Easter to Oct, daily 10–5	T	

Garden	Location	Opening Times	Refreshment (R) Transport (T)
Belgrave Hall Gardens	Leicester, Leics.	All year, Mons. to Sats.: Nov. to Feb. 10–5; March, April, Sept. and Oct. 10–6; May to Aug. 10–7; Suns. 2–5 all year	T
Benmore (Younger Botanic Garden)	Nr. Dunoon, Argyll	April to Sept., daily 10–6; and by appt.	R & T July & Aug.
Bicton Gardens	East Budleigh, Budleigh Salterton, Devon	Easter to Sept., daily: Easter to June 2–6; July to Sept. 11–6	T
Birmingham Botanical Gardens	Westbourne Rd., Edgbaston, Birmingham 15, Warwickshire	Daily 9 till dusk	R T
Birr Castle	Birr, Co. Offaly	All year: May to Sept. 2–6; Oct. to April 2–5 'Any time to those interested.'	T
Blackhills	By Elgin, Morayshire		
Blenheim Palace	Woodstock, Oxford, Oxon.	April to last Thurs. July and 4th Mon. Sept. to end Oct., Mons., Tues., Weds., Thurs.: last Sat. July to 3rd Thurs. Sept., every day except Fri.: Easter Sat, Sun. and	R T

Blickling Hall	Nr. Aylsham, Norfolk	Mon. but not spring Bank Hol. weekend. 1–6 Easter Sat. to 1st Sun. Oct., Weds., Thurs., Sats., Suns. and Bank Hols. 2–6	R	T
Blithfield Hall	Rugeley, Staffordshire	Easter to end Sept., Sats., Suns., Weds., Thurs. 2.30–6: Bank Hols. and Tues. following 12–7; and by appt.	R	T
Bodnant	Tal-y-Cafn, Colwyn Bay, Denbighshire	April to Oct., Tues., Weds., Thurs., Sats. and Bank Hol. Mons. 1.30–4.45	T	
Borde Hill	Haywards Heath, Sussex	April to Aug., Suns. and Weds., 2–7: Sept., Suns. 2–5; and by appt.	R	T
Bramham Park	Boston Spa, Yorkshire	Easter to Sept., Suns. 2–6; and by appt.	R	T
Branklyn	Perth, Perthshire	May to Sept., Mon. to Sat. 2–5; Suns. 2–6	T	
Bressingham Hall	Diss, Norfolk	Last Sun. May to 1st Sun. Oct.: last Thurs. May to Thurs. mid-Sept. 1.30–6.30; and by appt. for	R	

Garden	Location	Opening Times	Refreshment (R) Transport (T)
Briery Close	Windermere, Westmorland	parties, Tues. and Thurs. evenings Some Suns, April, May, June, and spring Bank Hol. 11–7	T
Brodick Castle	Isle of Arran, Bute	Easter to Sept., daily, 10–5	R May–Sept.　T
Burford House Garden	Tenbury Wells, Worcs.	May to Sept., daily 2–5	R
Burnby Hall Gardens	Pocklington, Yorkshire	April to Sept., daily 2–6; and by appt.	R at weekends and on prior notice　T
Cambridge University Botanic Garden	Trumpington Rd., Cambridge	All year, weekdays winter 8 till dusk, summer 8–8	T
Capesthorne	Macclesfield, Cheshire	April to Sept, Suns, and from 2nd Wed. in May also Weds.; Good Fri. and Bank Hol. Sats. and Mons.; 2.15–5.45; and by appt.	R　T
Castle Ashby	Northampton, Northants.	April to Sept., Suns., Thurs., Sats., Bank Hols. 2–6	R　T (20 mins. walk)
Castle Howard	York, Yorkshire	Easter Sun. to 1st Sun. Oct., daily except Mons. and Fris. 12.30–6.30; Bank	R　T

		Hol. Mons.	
Charleston Manor	Westdean, Seaford, Sussex	11.30–5.30 Mid-May to Sept., Mon. to Fri.; Sats. and Suns. by appt. 11–5.30	T ¾ m.
Chartwell	Westerham, Kent	April to mid-Oct., Weds., Thurs. 2–6 or dusk; Sats. Suns. and Bank Hol. Mons. 11–6 or dusk. Parties by arrangement	T
Chastleton House	Moreton-in-Marsh, Glos.	All year, daily except Weds. 2–6 or dusk; Suns. 2–5	R by previous arrangement
Chatsworth	Bakewell, Derbyshire	1st Wed. April to 1st Sun. Oct., Mon to Fri. 11.30–4.30; Sats. and Suns. 2–6; Bank Hol. Mons. and Tues. 11.30–6	T ½ m. and 1 m.
Chilham Castle	Chilham, Kent	May 1st to Oct. 30th, Weds., Thurs., Suns. and Bank Hols. 2–6; and by appt.	R T
Chirk Castle	Wrexham, Denbighshire	Easter Sat, Sun. and Mon. and Suns. in April; May to Sept.,	R T 2 m.

Garden	Location	Opening Times	Refreshments (R) Transport (T)	
		Tues., Thurs., Sats. and Suns. 2–5. Bank Hols. 11–5. Parties by appt.		
Chiswick House	Burlington Lane, London W4	All year, daily 7.30 till ½ hr. after sunset	R	T
Claverton Manor	Bath, Somerset	Good Fri. till mid-Oct., daily except Mons.; Bank Hol. Mons. 2–5; and by appt.	R	T
Clevedon Court	Clevedon, Somerset	April to Sept, Weds., Thurs., Suns. and Bank Hols. 2.30–5.30; and by appt.	R	T 1 m.
Cliveden	Taplow, nr. Maidenhead, Berks.	April to Oct, daily except Mons. and Tues., and Bank Hols. 11–6.30	R	T
Compton Acres Gardens	Canford Cliffs, Poole, Dorset	April to Oct, daily 10.30–6.30	T	
Compton Wynyates	Tysoe, Warwick, Warwickshire	April to Sept, Weds., Sats, Suns. and Bank Hols. 2–6		
Corsham Court	Chippenham, Wiltshire	April to mid-July and	T	

		mid-Sept. to Oct., Weds., Thurs., Suns.; mid-July to mid-Sept., daily except Mons. and Fris.; Nov. to March, Suns.; Bank Hol. Mons. and during Bath Festival; 11–12.30 and 2–6.		
Cotehele House	Calstock, Cornwall	Closes 4.30 mid-Oct. April to Sept., daily except Mons. 10–6; Oct. to March, Weds., Sats., Suns. and Bank Hols. 2–6 or dusk	R	T 1 m.
Cothay Manor	Greenham, Wellington, Somerset	June to mid-Sept., Thurs.; also Weds. in Aug., and 1st Suns. Spring and summer Bank Hols. Suns. and Mons. 2–6; and by appt.	R	T 2½ m.
Court House Courts, The	Shipton Moyne, Glos. Holt, Wiltshire	By appt. at any time. April to Oct., Tues., Weds., Thurs. 2–5; and by appt.		T
Cragside Estate	Rothbury, Northumberland	March to Sept., daily 10–6		T

o

Garden	Location	Opening Times	Refreshments (R) Transport (T)
Cranborne Manor	Wimborne, Dorset	April to Oct., 1st Sats. and Suns. Garden Centre daily, Suns. 2–6	R T
Cranford	Formby Lane, Aughton, Lancashire	April to Oct., 10 to dusk	T
Crarae Lodge	Inveraray, Argyll	March to Oct., dawn to dusk	T
Crathes Castle	Banchory, Kincardineshire	All year, daily 9.30 to dusk	R Suns. in May, daily June–Sept. T ½ m.
Creech Grange	Wareham, Dorset	Mid-July to mid-Sept., Weds., Thurs., Suns. and summer Bank Hol.	T 2 m.
Crittenden House	Matfield, Tonbridge, Kent	2.30–5.30 1 Sun., April to Aug. and spring Bank Hol. 2–7. 1 Sat. May, July, Aug. 9–midnight.	T 1 m.
Culzean Castle	Maybole, Ayrshire	All year, daily 10–8 or dusk in winter	R Easter to Sept. T
Curraghmore	Waterford, Co. Waterford	Thurs. afternoons during summer	
Dartington Hall	Totnes, Devon	All year, daily, all day. Parties by appt.	T

Dawyck Gardens	Stobo, Peebles-shire	End April to Aug., Weds., Sats. and Suns. 2–5; and by appt.	R Sats and Suns. and parties by arrangement T R
Derry and Toms Roof Garden	Kensington High Street, London W8	Mid-April to mid-Oct., Mon. to Wed. and Fri. 9–5; Thurs. 9–6.30; Sat. 9–12.30	T
Dinmore Manor	Nr. Hereford, Herefordshire	April to Sept., daily 2–6	T 1 m.
Drummond Castle	Crieff, Perthshire	April to mid-Aug., Weds. and Sats. 2–6	T 1½ m.
Dunster Castle	Minehead, Somerset	Oct. to May, Weds. 2.15–3.30: June, Weds. and Thurs.; July to Sept., Tues., Weds., Thurs. and Bank Hol. Mons. 10.15–12.40 and 2.15–4.40	T ½ m.
Dyrham Park	Nr. Chipping Sodbury, Glos.	Easter to Sept., daily except Mons. and Tues.; Bank Hols.; 12–6. March to Easter, Oct. and Nov., Weds., Sats. and Suns. 2–6 or dusk; and by appt.	R Easter to Sept. T
East Lambrook Manor	South Petherton, Somerset	May to July and Sept., Thurs. 2–5; some Suns. June and July 2–7; and by appt.	T 2 m.

405

Garden	Location	Opening Times	Refreshments (R) Transport (T)
Edinburgh Royal Botanic Garden	Inverleith Row, Edinburgh 3	Feb. to Oct., weekdays 9 till 1 hr. before sunset, Suns. 11 till 1 hr. before sunset; Nov. to Jan., weekdays 9.30–5, Suns. 11–5	R T
Edzell Castle Garden	Edzell, Angus	April to Sept., weekdays 10–7, Suns. 2–7; Oct. to March, weekdays 10–4; Suns. 2–4	
Emmetts	Nr. Brasted, Kent	April to Oct., Weds. and Sats. 2–6	T
Exbury Gardens	Nr. Southampton, Hampshire	Mid-April to early June, daily except Sats. 2–7	
Falkland Palace	Falkland, Fife	April to Oct., weekdays 10–6, Suns. 2–6; and by appt.	T
Forde Abbey,	Chard, Somerset	May to Sept., Weds.; also certain Suns. 2–6	R T 1 m.
Garden House	Buckland, Monachorum, Yelverton, Devon	Mid-April to mid-Sept., Weds. 3–7; and by appt.; parties by arrangement	T
Gilfach	Tyn-y-Groes, Conway, Caernarvonshire	April to Sept, daily except Suns. 10–10	T

Glan-y-Mawddach	Barmouth, Merioneth	12 times in summer; and by appt.	R T
Glenapp Castle	Ballantrae, Girvan, Ayrshire	April to Oct, daily, dawn to dusk	R T
Glenarn	Rhu, Dunbartonshire	March to Aug, daily 2 to dark; and by appt.	T
Glendurgan	Helford River, Cornwall	April to Sept: April and May, Mons, Weds., Fris.; June to Sept. Mons. and Weds.; 10.30–4.30	T
Glenveagh Castle	Church Hill, Letterkenny Co. Donegal	June to Aug, Weds. 2–5	
Godinton Park	Ashford, Kent	June to Sept, Suns. 2–5	T $\frac{3}{4}$ m.
Grayswood Hill	Haslemere, Surrey	May to Oct, Suns. 2–7; and by appt.	T
Great Chalfield Manor	Melksham, Wiltshire	Mid-April to mid-Oct., Weds. 12–1, 2–5	T $1\frac{1}{4}$ m.
Great Dixter	Northiam, Sussex	Easter and May to Sept, daily except Mons.; Bank Hol. Mons.; 2–6; and by appt.; parties by arrangement	T
Gunby Hall	Burgh-le-Marsh, Lincolnshire	April to Oct, Weds. 2–6; Thurs., Fris. and Bank Hol. Mons. 2.30–5.30	T

408

Garden	Location	Opening Times	Refreshments (R) Transport (T)
Guthrie Castle	By Forfar, Angus	Mid-May to Aug., Suns. 2–6; parties by appt.	R T
Haddon Hall	Bakewell, Derbyshire	1st April or Easter to Sept., Tues. to Sats. 11–6	R T
Hall Place Gardens	Leigh, nr. Tonbridge, Kent	May to 3rd week Sept., Suns. and spring and summer Bank Hols. 2.30–6.30	R T
Hampton Court Palace Gardens	Greater London	May to Sept., weekdays 9.30–6, Suns. 11–6; Nov. to Feb., weekdays 9.30–4, Suns. 2–4; March, April and Oct., weekdays 9.30–5, Suns. 2–5; closed Good Fri., Xmas Day and Boxing Day	T
Hardwick Hall	Nr. Chesterfield, Derbyshire	Easter Sat. to end Oct., Weds., Thurs., Sats., Suns., Bank Hol. Mons. 2–6 or dusk; and by appt.	R T 1 m.
Harewood House	Nr. Leeds, Yorkshire	Easter Sat. to Sept., daily; Oct, Suns.; 11–6	R T 1 m.
Harlow Car Gardens	Harrogate, Yorkshire	Daily 9 to sunset	T ½ m.

Hatfield House	Hertfordshire	East and West Gardens – May to Sept., Mons. 2–5, excluding Bank Hols. West Gardens only – mid-April to end April, weekdays and Bank Hol. Suns. and Mons. 12–5; May 1st to Oct. 6th, daily except Mons. 12–5, Suns. 2.30–5.30	R	T
Heaselands	Haywards Heath, Sussex	Certain Weds. and Suns. in May and July, and by appt. 2–7	R	T 1 m.
Hergest Croft Garden and Park Wood	Ridgebourne, Kington, Herefordshire	Mid-May to mid-June, daily 11–7; and by appt.	T 1 m.	
Heveningham Hall	Nr. Halesworth, Suffolk	April, May and Oct., Thurs. and Suns.; June, July and Sept., Weds., Thurs., Sats. and Suns.; Aug., Tues., Weds., Thurs., Sats. and Suns.; 2–5.30	R	
Hever Castle	Nr. Edenbridge, Kent	Easter Sun. to Sept., Weds., Suns. and Bank Hols.; Aug. and Sept., Sats.; 1–7; and by appt.	R	T

Garden	Location	Opening Times	Refreshments (R) Transport (T)
Hidcote Manor Gardens	Nr. Chipping Campden, Glos.	Easter Sat. to Oct., daily except Tues. and Fris. 11–8	R T ½ m.
Highdown	Goring-by-Sea, Worthing, Sussex	All year, Mon. to Fri., 9–4.30; 1st Sun. July, Aug., Sept., Good Fri. and Bank Hols. 2.30 to sunset. Some extra Suns.	
Hodnet Hall	Market Drayton, Shropshire	April to Sept, daily, weekdays 2–5, Suns. and Bank Hols. 12–6.30; and by appt.	R T
Hole Park	Rolvenden, Cranbrook, Kent	April, May, June, Oct., certain Weds. and Suns. 2–7	R Suns. only T
Holker Hall	Cark-in-Cartmel, Lancs.	Easter Sat. to Sept., daily except Fris. and 1 weekend Aug. 10.30–6	R T
Holkham Hall	Wells-next-the-Sea, Norfolk	July and Aug., Mons. and Thurs.; June and Sept., Thurs.; 2–5	R T 10 mins
Hopetoun House	South Queensferry, West Lothian	May to Sept, daily except Thurs. and Fris. 1.30–5.45; and by appt.	R T

House in the Wood	Bartley, Hampshire	April to Oct., Mons. and Weds. except Bank Hols. (only if fine) 9–9	T
Howth Demesne	Dublin	April to mid-Sept., daily; April 2.30–6, May and June 11–9, July-Sept. 11–6	T
Hungerdown House	Seagry, Chippenham, Wilts.	3 or 4 times in summer, and by appt.	
Hyde Crook	Frampton, nr. Dorchester, Dorset	Last Sun. March, all Suns. April, 1st Sun. May 2–7; any time by appt.	
Ickworth	Nr. Bury St Edmunds, Suffolk	Easter Sat. to 1st week Oct., Weds., Thurs., Sats., Suns. and Bank Hols. 2–6	T 1 m.
Ilnacullin (Garinish Island)	Glengariff, Co. Cork	All year, daily 2.30–6	T
Inveresk Lodge Gardens	Musselburgh, Midlothian	All year, Mon. to Fri. 10–4.30; Suns. May-Sept. 2–5; and by appt.	T
Inverewe	Poolewe, Ross and Cromarty	All year, daily 10 to dusk	R T
Isabella Plantation Woodland Garden	Richmond Park, Surrey	All year, daily, daylight to dusk	T ½ m.

Garden	Location	Opening Times	Refreshments (R) Transport (T)
Japanese Garden	Tully, Co. Kildare	Easter to Oct. daily, weekdays 10–6, Suns. 2–6; and by appt.	T 1 m.
Jermyns House Garden	Ampfield, nr. Romsey, Hampshire	by appt.	T ½ m.
Kedleston Hall	Derby	Easter to Sept, Suns. and Bank Hols. 2–7	R T
Keir	Dunblane, Perthshire	April to Oct., Weds. 2–6	T
John F Kennedy Memorial Park	Nr. Dunganstown, Co. Wexford	Daily till dusk	
Kew, The Royal Botanic Gardens	Kew, Richmond, Surrey	All year, daily 10–8 summer, 10 to sunset winter	R T
Killerton Garden	Nr. Exeter, Devon	All year, daily, dawn to dusk	T ¾ m.
Knightshayes Court	Tiverton, Devon	April to June, Thurs. and 2 Suns. 2–8; and by appt.	T 1 m.
Lanhydrock	Nr. Bodmin, Cornwall	April to Sept., most days of week, 2–6	T
Lea Rhododendron Gardens	Matlock, Derbyshire	April to June, Sats. and Suns. 2 to dusk; and by appt.	R T ½ m.
Lee Ford	Budleigh Salterton,	March to Sept., certain	T

	Devon	Suns. and Easter Mon. 2–6; and by appt.		T
Leonardslee	Lower Beeding, Horsham, Sussex	May, Weds., Thurs., Sats., Suns. 10–6	R	T
Levens Hall	Kendal, Westmorland	May to mid-Sept., daily, 10–5.30; and by appt.	R	T
Littlecote	Nr. Hungerford, Berkshire	April to mid-Oct. Mons. and Sats. 2–5, Tues., Weds. and Bank Hols. 10–1 and 2–5, Suns. 2–6	R	T 1 m.
Liverpool University Botanic Gardens	Ness, Neston, Wirral, Cheshire	All year, daily 9 to sunset	T	
Lochinch and Castle Kennedy	Stranraer, Wigtownshire	April to Sept., daily 9–5	T	
Lodge, The	Sandy, Bedfordshire	April to Sept., daily 9–5		
Logan	Ardwell, nr. Stranraer, Wigtownshire	April to Sept., daily except Sats. 10–6; and by appt.	R	T
Longleat	Nr. Warminster, Wiltshire	All year, Easter to Sept. 10–6, Oct. to Easter 10–4	R	T
Longstock Park Water Gardens	Stockbridge, Hampshire	April to Sept., 3rd Sun. each month 2–4.30	T	
Luton Hoo	Luton, Bedfordshire	Easter to July, Weds., certain Suns., and spring Bank Hol, Aug. and Sept., Mons., Weds.,	R	T

Garden	Location	Opening Times	Refreshments (R) Transport (T)
Malcolm House	Batsford, Moreton-in-Marsh, Glos.	Thurs., Sats., Suns.: weekdays 11–6, Suns. 2–6 April to Oct., daily 10–7	T 1½ m.
Melbourne Hall	Melbourne, Derbyshire	Easter weekend to Tues. and all Suns. Easter to end June; 1st Sat July to end Sept. daily except Mons. and Fris.; 1st 2 Suns Oct.; 2–6: Bank Hol. Mons. 11–6	R T
Minterne	Cerne Abbas, Dorset	April to June, Suns. and Bank Hols. 2–7	
Montacute House	Yeovil, Somerset	March to Easter, Oct. and Nov., Weds., Sats., Suns., 2–6; Easter to Sept., daily except Tues. 11–6	R T
Mount Stewart	Newtownards, nr. Belfast, Co. Down	April to Sept., Weds., Sats., Suns., Bank Hol. Mons. 2–6; and by appt.	T
Mount Usher	Ashford, Co. Wicklow	Daily except Suns., summer 10–6, winter 10–5	R T

Moyclare	Liskeard, Cornwall	1 weekend monthly Easter to end Sept., most Bank Hol. Mons., and by appt.	T
Muckross Gardens	Killarney, Co. Kerry	All year, daily	R
Muncaster Castle	Ravenglass, Cumberland	Easter to June, daily; July to mid-Sept., Sats., Suns., Weds., late Bank Hol.; 1–6; and by appt.	R
National Botanic Gardens	Glasnevin, Dublin	All year, daily. March to Sept., weekdays 9–6; Suns. 11–6; Oct. to Feb., weekdays 10–4.30; Suns. 11–4.30	T
Newby Hall	Skelton-on-Ure, Ripon, Yorkshire	Easter to Oct, daily 10.30–7 or dusk	T R Weds., Thurs., Sats., Suns., and Bank Hols. Mons. and Tues. following
Newstead Abbey	Linby, Nottinghamshire	All year, daily 10 to sunset	R T
Nymans	Handcross, Haywards Heath, Sussex	April to Oct., Tues., Weds., Thurs., Sats., Suns. 2–7; and by appt.	T
Owl House Gardens	Lamberhurst, Kent	All year, Mons., Weds., Fris., Suns. and Bank	T 1½ m.

Garden	Location	Opening Times	Refreshments (R) Transport (T)
Oxburgh Hall	Swaffham, Norfolk	Hols. 11–9; Suns. 3–5; and by appt. Easter Sat. to 1st Sun. Oct., Weds., Thurs., Sats., Suns., and Bank Hol. Mons. 2–6	
Oxford Botanic Garden	Rose Lane, Oxford	All year, weekdays 7.30–5, Suns. 10–12, 2–6; closed 4.30 in winter	T
Packwood House	Hockley Heath, Solihull, Warwickshire	April to Sept, Tues., Weds., Thurs., and Sats. and Bank Hols. 2–7, Suns. 3–7; Oct. to March, Weds., Sats., and Bank Hols. 2–5, Suns. 3–5; closed Good Fri.	T 2 m.
Parcevall Hall Gardens	Appletreewick, Skipton, Yorkshire	May to Sept, Tues. and Weds.	T 2 m.
Parham Park	Pulborough, Sussex	Easter Sun. to 1st Sun. Oct., Suns., Weds., Thurs. and Bank Hols.: Suns. and Bank Hols. 2–5; Weds. and Thurs. 1–4.30	T 1 m.

Peckover House	Wisbech, Cambridgeshire	Easter Sat. to Oct., Weds., Thurs., Sats., Suns. and Bank Hols. 2–6; Oct. 2–5	T
Penjerrick	Falmouth, Cornwall	All year, Suns. and Weds. 1.30–4.30; and by appt.	T
Penrhyn Castle	Bangor, Caernarvonshire	June to Sept., weekdays inc. Bank Hols. 10–12, 2–4.30; July and Aug. 2–4.30; April, May, Oct., Mons. inc. Bank Hols., Weds. and Thurs. 2–4.30	R during hol. period. / T
Penshurst Place	Tonbridge, Kent	Easter to mid-Sept.: April to June, Weds., Thurs., Sats. and Suns. 2–5.30; July to Sept., Tues., Weds., Thurs., Sats. and Suns. 12–5.30	R T
Pitmedden	Udny, Aberdeenshire	All year, daylight hours	R
Polesden Lacey	Dorking, Surrey	All year, daily 11 to dusk	R April to Oct. / T 1½ m.
Pollok House	97 Haggs Rd., Glasgow, S.1, and 2060 Pollokshaws Rd, S.3	All year, Mon. to Sat. 10–5, Suns. 2–5; and by appt.	R T
Portmeirion	Penrhyndeudraeth, Merioneth	Easter to early Oct., daily 10–6.30	R T

Garden	Location	Opening Times	Refreshments (R) Transport (T)	
Powerscourt	Enniskerry, Co. Wicklow	Easter to Oct., daily 10–5.30	R	T 1¾ m.
Powis Castle Gardens	Welshpool, Montgomeryshire	May to Sept., daily except Suns. and Mons. 2–6; Spring and late summer Bank Hol Mons. 10.30–5.30	R	T 1 m.
Priory of Lady St Mary	Wareham, Dorset	June to Sept., Weds. 2–7; and by appt.	R	T
Pylewell Park	Lymington, Hampshire	Certain Suns. in May and June, 2–7; and by appt.	T	
Pyrford Court	Woking, Surrey	Certain Suns. in May and June	T	
Quarry Wood	Burghclere, Berkshire	2 Suns. in May, 1 Sun. in Oct. 2–6; and by appt.	T	
Raby Castle	Staindrop, Darlington, Durham	Easter to Oct., Sats. and Weds. 2–5; 2 Suns. in July, 2–6; and by appt.	T	
Rockingham Castle	Market Harborough, Leicestershire	Easter to Sept., Thurs., Bank Hol. Suns. and Mons. 2–6; and by appt.	T	
Rousham	Steeple Aston, Oxfordshire	June to Aug., Weds., Suns. and Bank Hols. 2–6		T 1 m.

418

Rowallane	Saintfield, Belfast, Co. Down	April to June, daily 9–6; July to Oct, Weds., Sats. and Suns. 2–6; and by appt.	R	T
Rudding Park	Harrogate, Yorkshire	Easter to Oct, daily except Fris. 2–6; Bank Hols. 11–7	R	T
St Nicholas	Richmond, Yorkshire	Every weekend 11–8; and by appt.	T	
St Osyth's Priory	Nr. Clacton, Essex	Easter weekend, and May to Sept, daily 10–7	T	
St Paul's Walden Bury Gardens	Hitchin, Hertfordshire	Certain Suns. in May, June and Aug, 2–7; and by appt.	R	
Saltram	Plympton, Plymouth	April to Sept, daily except Tues. and Good Fri.	R	T
Sandon Hall	Sandon, Staffordshire	Certain Suns. in April to July, 2–7	R	T
Sandringham	Norfolk	May, June, Sept., Weds. and Thurs.; July and Aug., Tues., Weds., Thurs., Fris., spring and summer Bank Hols.; 11–5 (except when the Royal Family are in residence)	T	

P

Garden	Location	Opening Times	Refreshments (R) Transport (T)
Savill Garden and the Valley Gardens	The Great Park, Windsor, Berkshire	March to Oct., daily 10–6 and till 7 on long summer days	R T 1½ m.
Scotney Castle	Lamberhurst, Kent	Easter Sat. to Oct., Weds., Sats. and Bank Hols., also Suns. in Oct. 2–6	T
Shakespearian Gardens	Stratford-upon-Avon, Warwickshire	*Birthplace and Anne Hathaway's Cottage*: April, May and Oct., Mons., Tues., Weds. and Fris. 9–6, Thurs. and Sats. and June to Sept. weekdays 9–7. Nov. to March (*Birthplace*), weekdays 9–4, Suns. 2–4. Nov. to March (*Anne Hathaway's Cottage*), weekdays 9–12.45, 2–4, Suns. 2–4. *Hall's Croft, Mary Arden's House and New Place*: April to Oct., weekdays 9–6, Suns. 2–6; Nov. to March, weekdays 9–12.45, 2–4	T

Name	Location	Opening times	Transport
Sharpitor	Salcombe, Devon	All year, daily 9–6	T 1½ m.
Sheffield Park Gardens	Fletching, nr. Uckfield, Sussex	April to Oct.: April, Weds., Sats. and Suns. 2–7; May to Sept., daily 11–7; Oct., daily 12–5; Bank Hol. Mons. 12–7; Nov., by appt.; closed Good Fri.	R T 20 mins. walk
Sissinghurst Castle	Kent	April to Oct., daily 10–7; and by appt.	R T 1½ m.
Sissinghurst Place Gardens	Cranbrook, Kent	April to Oct., daily 10–7	T
Snowshill Manor	Broadway, Worcestershire	April to Oct., Weds., Thurs., Sats. and Suns. 11–1, 2–6; and by appt.	T
Somerleyton Hall	Nr. Lowestoft, Suffolk	May to Sept., Suns., Thurs., and Bank Hol. Suns. and Mons. 2–6	T
Spetchley Park	Worcester, Worcs.	April to Sept., Suns. 2 till sunset, and by appt.	R T
Stourhead	Stourton, nr. Mere, Wiltshire	All year, daily 11–7 or dusk	T 1½ m.
Stowe	Buckingham, Bucks.	4 days at Easter, 16 days in Aug., 2–6.30; and by appt.	
Strone	Cairndow, Argyll	Mid-April to end June, daily dawn to dusk; and by appt.	T

Garden	Location	Opening Times	Refreshments (R) Transport (T)	
Sudeley Castle	Winchcombe, Glos.	May to Sept., Tues., Weds., Thurs., Sats. and Suns.; Bank Hol. Mons.; weekdays 2–5.30, Suns. 2–5; parties by appt.	R	T
Suntrap	Gogarbank, Edinburgh	Mons. to Fris., 9–5; Sats. 9–12		
Sutton End	Nr. Petworth, Sussex	May to Aug., 1 week each month 11–7		
Syon Park Gardening Centre	Brentford, Middlesex	All year, daily March to May 10.30–5.30; June and July 10.30–9; Aug. 10.30–7.30; Sept. 10.30–5.30; Oct. 10.30–4; Nov. to Feb. weekends only 10.30–4	R	T
Tatton Park Gardens	Knutsford, Cheshire	April to mid-Oct., daily except Mons. but inc. Bank Hols. 2–6	R	T Weds., Sats., Suns. and Bank Hols.
Thoresby Hall	Nr. Ollerton, Newark, Notts.	April to Sept., Suns. 12.30–5.15; June to Aug., Weds., Thurs. and Sats. 2.30–5.15; Sept., Weds.	R	T some days

		and Thurs. 2.30–5.15; Good Fri, Easter Sat., spring hol. and autumn hol. Tues. 2.30–5.15; Easter Sun. and hol. Mons. 12.30–5.15	
Threave School of Gardening	Castle Douglas, Kirkcudbrightshire	All year, 9 to sunset	T 1½ m.
Tintinhull House	Nr. Martock, Somerset	April to Oct., Weds., Thurs., Sats., and Bank Hol. Mons. 2–6	T
Trelissick	Feock, nr. Truro, Cornwall	March to Oct., Weds., Thurs., Fris. and Bank Hols. 10–5; and by appt.	T 1¼ m.
Trengwainton Gardens	Madron, nr. Penzance, Cornwall	March to Sept., Weds., Fris., Sats. and Bank Hol. Mons. 11–5	T
Tresco Abbey Gardens	Isles of Scilly	All year, weekdays only, 10–4	T (island ferry boats)
Trewithen	Grampound Rd., Probus, nr. Truro, Cornwall	March to June and Sept., Tues. and Thurs. 2–4.30	T
Upton House	Edgehill, Warwickshire	All year: Weds. 2–6 or dusk; July to Sept. also Sats. 2–6; and by appt.	T

Garden	Location	Opening Times	Refreshments (R) Transport (T)
Vine House	Henbury, Bristol, Glos.	3 weekends during May and June 2–7; and by appt.	R T
Wakehurst Place	Ardingly, nr. Haywards Heath, Sussex	All year, daily except Xmas Day: Nov. to Jan. 12–4; Oct. and Feb. 1–5; March to Sept. 2–6	T
Weston Park	Shifnal, Shropshire	May to early Sept., Weds., Thurs., Sats. and Suns. and Easter 2–7, Suns. and Bank Hols. 11–7; parties by appt.	R T 2 m.
Westonbirt Arboretum	Nr. Tetbury, Glos.	All year, daily 10–8 or sunset	R T
White Craggs	Clappersgate, Ambleside, Westmorland	All year, daylight hours	T
Williamston	Insch, Aberdeenshire	June to Oct. 1st, daily 10–6; and by appt.	
Wilton House	Salisbury, Wiltshire	April to Sept, Tues. to Sats. and Bank Hols. 11–6; Aug and Sept. most Suns. 2–6	R T
Winkworth Arboretum	Nr. Godalming, Surrey	All year, daily.	T weekdays
Wisley (RHS garden)	Nr. Ripley, Surrey	All year, weekdays	R summer months T

Name	Address	Opening times	Notes
Wrest Park	Silsoe, Bedfordshire	10–7.30 or sunset; closed Good Fri. and Xmas Day; April to Sept, Sats., Suns. and Bank Hols.: April 2–5.30, May to Sept. 2–7	R Suns. and Bank Hols. T
Yaffle Hill	Broadstone, Dorset	Suns. in April and May; 3 Suns. Oct. 2–7; and by appt.	T
Yew Cottage	Fairmile Lane, Cobham, Surrey	5 Sats. and Suns. during June and July, 2–7; and by appt.	R Suns. T

Appendix VII

Garden Centres – Zone by Zone

The following Garden Centres are ones approved by the Horticultural Trades Association.

ZONE I

Barralet's Garden Centre, Western Avenue, Perivale Lane, Perivale, Greenford, Middx.

Bygrave's Garden Centre, North Orbital Road, London Colney, St Albans, Herts.

Coolings Nurseries, Willow Grove, Chislehurst, Kent.

Cramphorn Ltd, 17 Bridge Street, Writtle, Essex.

Croydon Garden Centre, (James Relf & Sons Ltd), Sanderstead, South Croydon, Surrey.

Orchard Garden Centre, Chadwell Road, Grays, Essex.

L R Russell's Garden Centre and Nurseries, London Road, Windlesham, Surrey.

St Clare Nurseries, Uxbridge Road, Hampton Hill, Middx.

F J Seymour & Sons, The By-Pass, Ewell, Epsom, Surrey.

Squire's Garden Centre, Blackmoor Nurseries, Twickenham, Middx.

Sutton & Sons Ltd, London Road, Earley, Reading, Berks.

Warley Rose Gardens, Great Warley, Brentwood, Essex.

John Waterer Sons & Crisp Ltd, The Floral Mile, Twyford, Berks.

John Waterer Sons & Crisp Ltd, Bagshot, Surrey.

William Wood & Son Ltd, Bath Road, Taplow, Maidenhead, Berks.

ZONE 2

Barnham Nurseries Ltd, Barnham, Nr Bognor Regis, Sussex.

Brook Garden Centre Ltd, Marstrand Farm, Brook, Nr Godalming, Surrey.

Arthur Charlton & Sons Ltd, Summervale Nurseries, Eridge Road, Tunbridge Wells, Kent.

Flowerland Garden Centre, Upperton Road, Eastbourne, Sussex.

Oakover Garden Centre, Cranbrook Road, Hawkhurst, Kent.

The Complete Garden Service, North End Road, Yapton, Sussex.

Tillhill Forestry Nursery, Greenhills, Tilford, Farnham, Surrey.

ZONE 3

George Bailey, College Street, Petersfield, Hants.

Burrington Combe Garden Centre, Burrington, Bristol, Somerset.

Cross Elms Nurseries Ltd, (K H Smith & Co Ltd), 47 Coombe Lane, Bristol 9, Somerset.

Christopher Fairweather Ltd, Beaulieu Garden Centre, High Street, Beaulieu, Hants.

I Hammond, The Nurseries, Stubbington Lane, Stubbington, Nr Fareham, Hants.

Harraways' Cash & Carry Garden Centre, Sambourne Road Nurseries, Warminster, Wilts.

Hillier's Garden Centre, West Hill Nursery, Romsey Road, Winchester, Hants.

Hillier's Garden Centre, Winchester Road, Chandler's Ford, Hants.

Roger Morland, Church Street, Westbury, Wilts.

Row Farm Garden Centre, (Roger Morland), Chapmanslade, Westbury, Wilts.

John Scott & Co of Merriott, The Royal Nursery, Merriott, Somerset.

Stewart's Gardenlands, Wimborne Road, Ferndown, Dorset.

Stewart's Gardenlands, Lyndhurst Road, Nr Somerford Roundabout, Christchurch, Hants.

ZONE 4

St Bridget's Nurseries, Old Rydon Lane, Exeter, Devon.

ZONE 5

Baker's Nurseries, Codsall, Wolverhampton, Staffs.

Blakedown Nurseries Ltd, Roseacre Garden Centre, West Hagley, Stourbridge, Worcs.

Forest Products Ltd, Ross Road, Huntley, Glos.

Frost's Garden Centre, Woburn Sands, Bletchley, Bucks.

Gardenland (H Mills), Bridgnorth Road, Shipley, Nr Wolverhampton, Staffs.

Grasmere Gardens, Lichfield Road, Brownhills, Staffs.

Hurran's Nursery Gardens, Cheltenham Road East, Churchdown, Gloucester, Glos.

Ingram's Garden Centre, Flowerland, Newton Road, Great Barr, Birmingham, Warwicks.

Peet's Garden Centre, Alcester Road, Mappleborough Green, Studley, Warwicks.

Roses & Shrubs Ltd, Albrighton By-Pass, Albrighton, Wolverhampton, Staffs.

Rugby Garden Centre, Jeffrey Bernhard & Sons Ltd, Bilton Road, Rugby, Warwicks.

Severnvale Garden Centre, Milbury Heath, Falfield, Glos.

Snitterfield Garden Centre, Snitterfield, Stratford-upon-Avon, Warwicks.

Stretton's Nurseries, Garden Centre & Nursery, Bewdley Road, Kidderminster, Worcs.

Sydenham-Notcutt Ltd, Garden Centre, Stratford Road, Shirley, Solihull, Birmingham, Warwicks.

Twyford Garden Centres Ltd, London Road, Wheatley, Oxford, Oxon.

Watkins' Garden Centre, Kenilworth Road, Hampton-in-Arden, Solihull, Warwicks.

Webb's Garden Centre, Wychbold, Nr Droitwich, Worcs.

ZONE 6

By-Pass Nurseries Ltd, Ipswich Road, Colchester, Essex.

By-Pass Nurseries Ltd, Chevalier St, Ipswich, Suffolk.

Cramphorn Ltd, Newton Road, Chilton, Sudbury, Suffolk.

W Crowder & Sons, Thimbleby Nurseries, Horncastle, Lincs.

Notcutt's Garden Centre, Woodbridge, Suffolk.

ZONE 7

Barton Grange Garden Centre, Barton, Preston, Lancs.

Brookside Garden Centre, Macclesfield Road, Poynton, Cheshire.

Caldwell & Sons Ltd, The Nurseries, Knutsford, Cheshire.

Fowkes Garden Centre, Fosseway, Syston, Leicester, Leics.

Godley Gardens Ltd, Abbeydale Road, South Dore, Sheffield, Yorks.

Merryweather's Garden Centre, Halom Road, Southwell, Notts.

Ned Yates Esq, Walk Round Nurseries & Garden Store, Moor Lane House, Wilmslow, Cheshire.

ZONE 8

T R Hayes & Sons, Lake District Nurseries, Ambleside, Westmorland.

Stephen H Smith, Pool Road, Otley, Yorks.

Ward's Garden Centre, Homestead, Menston, Nr Ilkley, Yorks.

C Webb & Co Ltd, Stricklandgate, Highgate, Kendal, Westmorland.

ZONE 9

Horton Nurseries, Horton, Nr Port Fynon, Swansea, Glam.

Wyevale Garden Centre, H Williamson (Hereford) Ltd, Kings Acre, Hereford, Herefordshire.

ZONE 10

Falconer & Co Ltd, Glasgow Nurseries, Muirend, Glasgow S4, Lanarks.

Samson's Ltd, 91 King Street, Kilmarnock, Ayrshire.

ZONE 11

Dobbie's, Melville Nursery, Eskbank, Midlothian.

O'Hare & Bowman, Whitley Road, Benton, Newcastle-upon-Tyne, Northumberland.

ZONE 12

W Smith & Son Ltd, Hazlehead Garden Centre, Aberdeen, Aberdeenshire.

ZONE 13

Samuel McGredy & Sons Ltd, Royal Nurseries, Portadown, Belfast, N Ireland.

431

Index

Bracketed numbers=Zone reference number
Bold type numbers=Map page number

432

435

439